GRAPHING CALCULATOR MANUAL

DARRYL NESTER

Bluffton College

to accompany

COLLEGE ALGEBRA AND TRIGONOMETRY

THIRD EDITION

AND

PRECALCULUS

THIRD EDITION

Margaret L. Lial
American River College

John Hornsby
University of New Orleans

David I. Schneider
University of Maryland

PEARSON

Addison
Wesley

Boston   San Francisco   New York
London   Toronto   Sydney   Tokyo   Singapore   Madrid
Mexico City   Munich   Paris   Cape Town   Hong Kong   Montreal

Reproduced by Pearson Addison-Wesley from electronic files supplied by the author.

Copyright © 2005 Pearson Education, Inc.
Publishing as Pearson Addison-Wesley, 75 Arlington Street, Boston, MA 02116

ISBN   0-321-22771-9

1 2 3 4 5 6 QEP 07 06 05 04

TABLE OF CONTENTS

This manual contains four chapters, each devoted to one calculator. The table below lists, for each calculator, the topics covered in the introductory section (which contains a brief introduction to using the calculator), followed by the examples from *College Algebra and Trigonometry/Precalculus* which are discussed in this manual. The page numbers in parentheses in the first column—e.g., "Section R.1 Example 2 (page 4)"—refer to *College Algebra and Trigonometry/Precalculus*, while the page numbers in the other four columns (under "83/83+/84+," etc.) refer to this manual. For example, information about the TI-86 begins on page 79.

— continued —

— continued —

— continued —

— continued —

Introduction

The information in this section is essentially a summary of material that can be found in the TI-83 manual. Consult that manual for more details. **All references in this chapter to the TI-83 also apply to the TI-83+ and the TI-84+.**

While the TI-82 and TI-83 differ in some details, in most cases the instructions given in this chapter can be applied (perhaps with slight alteration) to a TI-82. The icon [82] is used to identify significant differences between the two, but some differences (e.g., a slight difference in keystrokes between the two calculators) are not noted. TI-82 users should watch for these comments. Also, see page 39 for information on computing with complex numbers on the TI-82.

1   Power

To power up the calculator, simply press the [ON] key. This should bring up the "home screen"—a flashing block cursor, and possibly the results of any previous computations that might have been done.

If the home screen does not appear, one may need to adjust the contrast (see the next section).

To turn the calculator off, press [2nd][ON] (note that the "second function" of [ON]—written in yellow type above the key—is "OFF"). The calculator will automatically shut off if no keys are pressed for several minutes.

2   Adjusting screen contrast

If the screen is too dark (all black), decrease the contrast by pressing [2nd] then pressing and holding [▼]. If the screen is too light, increase the contrast by pressing [2nd] and then press and hold [▲].

As one adjusts the contrast, the numbers 1 through 9 will appear in the upper right corner of the screen. If the contrast setting reaches 8 or 9, or if the screen never becomes dark enough to see, the batteries should be replaced.

3   Replacing batteries

To replace the four AAA batteries, first turn the calculator off ([2nd][ON]), then remove the back cover, remove and replace each battery, replace the back cover, then turn the calculator on again. (After replacing batteries, one may need to adjust the contrast down as described above.)

PREFACE

This graphing calculator manual was written to help owners of Texas Instruments graphing calculators (TI-83 through TI-89) use them to solve problems from *College Algebra and Trigonometry/Precalculus* by Lial, Hornsby, and Schneider. Owners of other TI calculators, like the TI-80, -81, -82, and -92, as well as owners of other brands of graphers, may find the information useful as well, but certainly some of the specific details will not translate directly. In particular, TI-82 users should find many comments in the TI-83/83+/84+ chapter that apply to their calculator, while TI-92 users should read the chapter on the TI-89.

Please contact me with any questions or corrections concerning this material. My web site also contains additional resources for using graphing calculators; I welcome suggestions as to what else would be useful.

This manual was created with TI calculators (of course), the TI-Graph Link and TI-Connect software, Adobe Photoshop, and TEX (Textures from Blue Sky Research).

Darryl Nester
Bluffton College
Bluffton, Ohio
nesterd@bluffton.edu
http://www.bluffton.edu/~nesterd
February 2004

4   Basic operations

Simple computations are entered in essentially the same way they would be written. For example, to compute $2 + 17 \times 5$, press [2][+][1][7][×][5][ENTER] (the [ENTER] key tells the calculator to act on what has been typed). Standard order of operations (including parentheses) is followed.

```
2+17*5
             87
■
```

The result of the most recently entered expression is stored in Ans, which is typed by pressing [2nd][(-)] (the word "ANS" appears in yellow above this key). For example, [5][+][2nd][(-)][ENTER] will add 5 to the result of the previous computation.

```
2+17*5
             87
5+Ans
             92
■
```

After pressing [ENTER], the TI-83 automatically produces Ans if the first key pressed is one which requires a number before it; the most common of these are [+], [−], [×], [÷], [^], [x⁻¹], [x²], and [STO▶]. For example, [+][5][ENTER] would accomplish the same thing as the keystrokes above (that is, it adds 5 to the previous result).

```
2+17*5
             87
5+Ans
             92
Ans+5
             97
■
```

Pressing [ENTER] by itself evaluates the previously typed expression again. This can be especially useful in conjunction with Ans. The screen on the right shows the result of pressing [ENTER] a second time.

```
2+17*5
             87
5+Ans
             92
Ans+5
             97
            102
■
```

Several expressions can be evaluated together by separating them with colons ([ALPHA][.]). When [ENTER] is pressed, the result of the *last* computation is displayed. The screen shown illustrates the computation $2(5 + 1)^2$.

```
3+2
              5
Ans+1:Ans²:2Ans
             72
■
```

5   Cursors

When typing, the appearance of the cursor indicates the behavior of the next keypress. When the standard cursor (a flashing solid block, ■) is visible, the next keypress will produce its standard action—that is, the command or character printed on the key itself.

If [2nd][DEL] is pressed, the TI-83 is placed in INSERT mode and the standard cursor will appear as a flashing underscore. If the arrow keys ([▲], [▼], [▶], [◀]) are used to move the cursor around within the expression, and the TI-83 is placed in INSERT mode, subsequent characters and commands will be inserted in the line at the cursor's position. When the cursor appears as a block, the TI-83 is in DELETE (or OVERWRITE) mode, and subsequent keypresses will replace the character or command at the cursor's position. (When the cursor is at the end of the expression, this is irrelevant.)

The TI-83 will return to DELETE mode when any arrow key is pressed. It can also be returned to DELETE mode by pressing [2nd][DEL] a second time.

Pressing [2nd] causes an arrow to appear in the cursor: ▯ (or an underscored arrow). The next keypress will produce its "second function"—the command or character printed in yellow above the key. (The cursor will then return to "standard.") If [2nd] is pressed by mistake, pressing it a second time will return the cursor to standard.

Pressing ALPHA places the letter "A" in the cursor: ▣ (or an underscored "A"). The next keypress will produce the letter or other character printed in green above that key (if any), and the cursor will then return to standard. Pressing ALPHA a second time cancels ALPHA mode. Pressing 2nd ALPHA "locks" the TI-83 in ALPHA mode, so that all of the following keypresses will produce characters until ALPHA is pressed again, or until some menu or second function is accessed.

6   Accessing previous entries ("deep recall")

By repeatedly pressing 2nd ENTER ("ENTRY"), previously typed expressions can be retrieved for editing and re-evaluation. Pressing 2nd ENTER once recalls the most recent entry; pressing 2nd ENTER again brings up the second most recent, etc. The number of previous entries thus displayed varies with the length of each expression (the TI-83 allocates 128 bytes to store previous expressions).

7   Menus

Keys such as WINDOW, MATH and VARS bring up a menu screen with a variety of options. The top line of the menu screen gives a collection of submenus (if any), which can be selected with the ◄ and ► keys. The lower lines list the available commands; these can be selected using the ▲ and ▼ keys and ENTER, or by pressing the number (or letter) preceding the desired option. Shown is the menu produced by pressing MATH; the arrow next to the 7 in the bottom row indicates that there are more options available below.

The various commands in these menus are too numerous to be listed here. They will be mentioned as needed in the examples.

8   Variables

The letters A through Z can be used as variables (or "memory") to store numerical values. To store a value, type the number (or an expression) followed by STO►, then a letter (preceded by ALPHA if necessary), then ENTER. That letter can then be used in the same way as a number, as demonstrated at right.

Note: The TI-83 interprets 2A as "2 times A"—the "∗" symbol is not required (this is consistent with how we interpret mathematical notation). As for order of operations, this kind of multiplication is treated the same as "∗" multiplication.

[82] *This latter comment is **not** true of the TI-82; on the TI-82, implied multiplication (such as 2A) is done before other multiplication and division, and even before some other operations, like the square root function ∫. Therefore, for example, the expression 1/2A is evaluated as 1/4 on the TI-82 (assuming that A is 2).*

9   Setting the modes

By pressing the MODE key, one can change many aspects of how the calculator behaves. For most of the examples in this manual, the "default" settings should be used; that is, the MODE screen should be as shown on the right. Each of the options is described below; consult the TI-83 manual for more details. Changes in the settings are made using the arrows keys and ENTER.

The Normal Sci Eng setting specifies how numbers should be displayed. The screen on the right shows the number 12345 displayed in Normal mode (which displays numbers in the range $\pm 9,999,999,999$ with no exponents), Sci mode (which displays all numbers in scientific notation), and Eng mode (which uses only exponents that are multiples of 3). Note: "E" is short for "times 10 to the power," so $1.2345\text{E}4 = 1.2345 \times 10^4 = 1.2345 \times 10000 = 12345$.

The Float 0123456789 setting specifies how many places after the decimal should be displayed. The default, Float, means that the TI-83 should display all non-zero digits (up to a maximum of 10).

Radian Degree indicates whether angle measurements should be assumed to be in radians or degrees. (A right angle measures $\frac{\pi}{2}$ radians, which is equivalent to $90°$.) Most of the examples in the text include reminders to set the calculator in the appropriate mode, in cases where this is important.

Func Par Pol Seq specifies whether formulas entered into the Y= screen are functions (specifically, y as a function of x), parametric equations (x and y as functions of t), polar equations (r as a function of θ), or sequences (u, v and w as functions of n). All four are used in this text.

When plotting a graph, the Connected Dot setting tells the TI-83 whether or not to connect the individually plotted points. Sequential Simul specifies whether individual expressions should be graphed one at a time (sequentially), or all at once (simultaneously).

Real a+bi re^θi specifies how to deal with complex numbers. Real means that only real results will be allowed (unless i is entered as part of a computation)—so that, for example, taking the square root of a negative number produces an error ("NONREAL ANS"). Selecting one of the other two options means that square roots of negative numbers are allowed, and will be displayed in "rectangular" ($a+bi$) or polar ($re^{i\theta}$) format. This text uses the $a+bi$ format for complex numbers (beginning in Section 1.3); polar format is not discussed in this text, but is closely related to trigonometric format (see page 28 of this manual).

82 *The TI-82 does not support complex numbers, so it does not include this setting. However, some complex computations can be done with a TI-82; see the appendix at the end of this chapter, page 39.*

Finally, the Full Horiz G-T setting allows the option of, for example, showing both the graph and the home screen, as in the screen on the right (this shows a "horizontal split").

The third option, G-T, has no effect on the home screen display, but will show
graphs and tables side by side when GRAPH is pressed.
82 *The TI-82 supports only the horizontal split.*

A related group of settings are found in the FORMAT menu (2nd ZOOM). The default
settings are shown in the screen on the right, and are generally the best choices for
most examples in this book (although the last two settings could go either way).
82 *The TI-82 does not include the* ExprOn ExprOff *option.*

RectGC PolarGC specifies whether graph coordinates should be displayed in rectangular (x, y) or
polar (r, θ) format.   Note that this choice is independent of the Func Par Pol Seq mode setting.   The CoordOn CoordOff setting determines whether or not graph coordinates should be displayed. GridOff GridOn specifies whether or not to display a grid of dots on the graph screen, while
AxesOn AxesOff and LabelOff LabelOn do the same thing for the axes and labels (y and x) on the axes.
ExprOn ExprOff specifies whether or not to display the formula (expression) of the curves on the GRAPH
screen when tracing. (This can be useful when more than one graph is displayed.)

10   Setting the graph window

The exact contents of the WINDOW menu vary depending on whether the calculator is in function, parametric,
polar, or sequence mode; below are four examples showing the WINDOW menu in each of these modes.

Function mode   Parametric mode   Polar mode   Sequence mode

All these menus include the values Xmin, Xmax, Xscl, Ymin, Ymax, and Yscl. When the GRAPH key is
pressed, the TI-83 will show a portion of the Cartesian (x-y) plane determined by these values. In function
mode, this menu also includes Xres, the behavior of which is described in section 12 of this manual
(page 7).   The other settings in the WINDOW screen allow specification of the smallest, largest, and step
values of t (for parametric mode) or θ (for polar mode), or initial conditions for sequence mode.

With settings as in the example screens shown above, the TI-83 would display
the screen at right: x values from -4.7 to 4.7 (that is, from Xmin to Xmax),
and y values between -3.1 to 3.1 (Ymin to Ymax). Since Xscl $=$ Yscl $= 1$,
the TI-83 places tick marks on both axes every 1 unit; thus the x-axis ticks are
at -4, $-3, \ldots, 3$, and 4, and the y-axis ticks fall on the integers from -3 to
3. This window is called the "decimal" window, and is most quickly set by
pressing ZOOM 4.

Below are four more sets of WINDOW settings, and the graph screens they produce. Note that the first graph
on the left has tick marks every 10 units on both axes. The second window is called the "standard" viewing

window, and is most quickly set by pressing ZOOM 6 . The setting Yscl = 0 in the final graph means that no tick marks are placed on the y-axis.

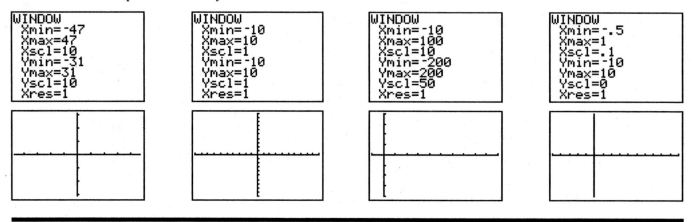

11   The graph screen

The TI-83 screen is made up of an array of square dots (pixels) with 63 rows and 95 columns. All the pixels in the leftmost column have x-coordinate Xmin, while those in the rightmost column have x-coordinate Xmax. The x-coordinate changes steadily across the screen from left to right, which means that the coordinate for the nth column (counting the leftmost column as column 0) must be $\text{Xmin} + n\Delta\text{X}$, where $\Delta\text{X} = (\text{Xmax} - \text{Xmin})/94$. Similarly, the nth row of the screen (counting up from the bottom row, which is row 0) has y-coordinate $\text{Ymin} + n\Delta\text{Y}$, where $\Delta\text{Y} = (\text{Ymax} - \text{Ymin})/62$.

Note: In (horizontal) split screen mode, $\Delta\text{Y} = (\text{Ymax} - \text{Ymin})/30$. In G-T (vertical split screen) mode, $\Delta\text{X} = (\text{Xmax} - \text{Xmin})/46$ and $\Delta\text{Y} = (\text{Ymax} - \text{Ymin})/50$.

It is not necessary to memorize the formulas for ΔX and ΔY. Should they be needed, they can be determined by pressing GRAPH and then the arrow keys. When pressing ▶ or ◀ successively, the displayed x-coordinate changes by ΔX; meanwhile, when pressing ▲ or ▼, the y-coordinate changes by ΔY. Alternatively, the values can be found by pressing VARS 1 8 ENTER (for ΔX) or VARS 1 9 ENTER (for ΔY). This produces results like those shown on the right.

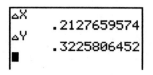

In the decimal window $\text{Xmin} = -4.7$, $\text{Xmax} = 4.7$, $\text{Ymin} = -3.1$, $\text{Ymax} = 3.1$, note that $\Delta\text{X} = 0.1$ and $\Delta\text{Y} = 0.1$. Thus, the individual pixels on the screen represent x-coordinates $-4.7, -4.6, -4.5, \ldots, 4.5, 4.6, 4.7$ and y-coordinates $-3.1, -3, -2.9, \ldots, 2.9, 3, 3.1$. This is where the decimal window gets its name.

Windows for which $\Delta\text{X} = \Delta\text{Y}$, such as the decimal window, are called square windows. Any window can be made square be pressing ZOOM 5 . To see the effect of a square window, observe the two pairs of graphs below. In each pair, the first graph is on the standard window, and the second is on a square window (after pressing ZOOM 5). The first pair shows the lines $y = 2x - 3$ and $y = 3 - \frac{1}{2}x$; note that on the square window, these lines look perpendicular (as they should). The second pair shows a circle centered at the origin with a radius of 8. On the standard window, this looks like an oval since the screen is wider than it is tall. (The reason for the gaps in the circle will be addressed in the next section.)

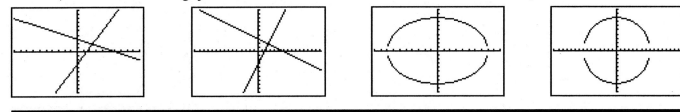

12   Graphing a function

This introductory section only addresses creating graphs in function mode. Procedures for creating parametric and polar graphs are very similar; they are covered beginning on page 29 of this manual, in material related to Chapter 8 of the text. Sequence plotting is covered on page 36 of this manual, in the material related to Section 11.3 from the text.

To see the graph of $y = 2x - 3$, begin by entering the formula into the calculator. This is done on the [Y=] screen of the calculator. Select one of the variables Y₁, Y₂, ..., and enter the formula. If other y variables have formulas, either erase them (by positioning the cursor on that line and pressing [CLEAR]) or position the cursor

on the equals sign "=" for that line and press [ENTER] (this has the effect of "unhighlighting" the equals sign, which tells the TI-83 not to graph that formula). Additionally, if any of Plot1, Plot2 or Plot3 are highlighted, move the cursor up until it is on that plot and press [ENTER]. In the screen on the right, only Y₁ will be graphed.

The next step is to choose a viewing window; see the previous section for more details on this. This example uses the standard window ([ZOOM][6]).

Finally, press [GRAPH], and the line should be drawn. In order to produce this graph, the TI-83 considers 95 values of x, ranging from Xmin to Xmax in steps of ΔX (assuming that Xres = 1; see below for other possibilities). For each value of x, it computes the corresponding value of y, then plots that point (x, y) and (if the calculator is in Connected mode) draws a line between this point and the previous one.

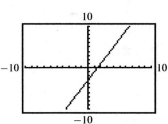

If Xres is set to 2, the TI-83 will only compute y for every other x value; that is, it uses a step size of 2ΔX. Similarly, if Xres is 3, the step size will be 3ΔX, and so on. Setting Xres higher causes graphs to appear faster (since fewer points are plotted), but for some functions, the graph may look "choppy" if Xres is too large, since detail is sacrificed for speed.

Note: If the line does not appear, or the TI-83 reports an error, double-check all the previous steps. Also, check the mode settings (discussed in section 9, page 4).

Once the graph is visible, the window can be changed using [WINDOW] or [ZOOM]. Pressing the [TRACE] key brings up the "trace cursor," and displays the x- and y-coordinates for various points on the line as the [◄] and [►] keys are pressed. Tracing beyond the left or right columns causes the TI-83 to adjust the values of Xmin and Xmax and redraw the graph.

To graph the function

$$y = \frac{1}{x-3},$$

enter that formula into the $\boxed{Y=}$ screen (note the use of parentheses). As before, this example uses the standard viewing window.

When $\boxed{\text{GRAPH}}$ is pressed, the TI-83 produces the graph shown on the right. This illustrates one of the pitfalls of the connect-the-dots method used by the calculator: The nearly-vertical line segment drawn at $x = 3$ *should not be there*, but it is drawn because the calculator connects the points

$x = 2.9787234$, $y = -46.99999$ and $x = 3.1914894$, $y = 5.2222223$.

Calculator users must learn to recognize these flaws in calculator-produced graphs.

The graph of a circle centered at the origin with radius 8 (shown on the square window $\boxed{\text{ZOOM}}\boxed{6}\boxed{\text{ZOOM}}\boxed{5}$) shows another problem that arises from connecting the dots. When $x = -8.064516$, y is undefined, so no point is plotted (that is, there is no point on this circle that has x-coordinate less than -8, or greater than 8). The next point plotted on the upper half of the circle is $x = -7.741935$ and

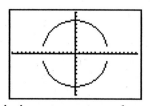

$y = 2.0155483$; since no point had been plotted for the previous x-coordinate, this is not connected to anything, so there appears to be a gap between the circle and the x-axis. The calculator is not "smart" enough to know that the graph should extend from -8 to 8.

One additional feature of graphing with the TI-83 is that each function can have a "style" assigned to its graph. The symbol to the left of Y_1, Y_2, etc. indicates this style, which can be changed by pressing $\boxed{\blacktriangleleft}$ until the cursor is over the symbol, then pressing $\boxed{\text{ENTER}}$ to cycle through the options. These options are shown on the right (with brief descriptive names); complete details are in the TI-83 manual.

13   Adding programs to the TI-83

The TI-83's capabilities can be extended by downloading or entering programs into the calculator's memory. Instructions for writing a program are beyond the scope of this manual, but programs written by others and downloaded from the Internet (or obtained as printouts) can be transferred to the calculator in one of three ways:

1. If one TI-83 already has a program, it can be transferred to another using the calculator-to-calculator link cable. To do this, first make sure the cable is firmly inserted in both calculators. On the sending calculator, press $\boxed{\text{2nd}}\boxed{\text{X,T,}\Theta\text{,}n}$ (LINK), then $\boxed{3}$, and then select (by using the $\boxed{\blacktriangle}$ and $\boxed{\blacktriangledown}$ keys and $\boxed{\text{ENTER}}$) the program(s) to be transferred. Now press the $\boxed{\blacktriangleright}$ to bring up the TRANSMIT submenu. *Before* pressing $\boxed{\text{ENTER}}$ on the sending calculator, prepare the receiving calculator by pressing $\boxed{\text{2nd}}$ $\boxed{\text{X,T,}\Theta\text{,}n}\boxed{\blacktriangleright}\boxed{\text{ENTER}}$, and *then* press $\boxed{\text{ENTER}}$ on the sending calculator.

2. If a computer with the TI-Graph Link is available, and the program file is on that computer (e.g., after having been downloaded from the Internet), the program can be transferred to the calculator using the TI Graph Link software. This transfer is done in a manner similar to the calculator-to-calculator transfer described above; specific instructions can be found in the documentation that accompanies the Graph Link software. (They are not given here because of slight differences between platforms and software versions.)

3. View a listing of the program and type it in manually. (**Note:** Even if the TI-Graph Link cable is not available, the Graph Link software can be used to view program listings on a computer.) While this is the most tedious method, studying programs written by others can be a good way to learn programming. To enter a program, start by choosing [PRGM][◄][1] ("Create New"), then type a name for the new program (like "QUADFORM" or "MIDPOINT")—note that the TI-83 is automatically put into ALPHA mode. Then type each command in the program, and press [2nd][MODE] (QUIT) to return to the home screen when finished.

To run the program, make sure there is nothing on the current line of the home screen, then press [PRGM], select the number or letter of the program (a sample screen is shown), and press [ENTER]. If the program was entered manually (option 3 above), errors may be reported; in that case, choose GOTO, correct the mistake and try again.

```
EXEC EDIT NEW
1:AAA
2:AASTAT1
3:ANNUITY
4:ASTAT
5:BB9697
6:COIN
7↓CONVOLVE
```

Programs can be found at many places on the Internet, including:

- http://www.awl.com/lhs—the Web site for the text;

- http://www.bluffton.edu/~nesterd—the Web site of the author of this manual;

- http://tifaq.calc.org—A "Frequently Asked Questions" page maintained by Ray Kremer; and

- http://www.ticalc.org.

Examples

Here are the details for using the TI-83 for several of the examples from the textbook. Also given are the keystrokes necessary to produce some of the commands shown in the text's examples. In some cases, some suggestions are made for using the calculator more efficiently.

Throughout this section, it is assumed that the textbook is available for reference. The problems from the text are not restated here, and there are frequent references to the calculator screens shown in the text.

Section R.1   Example 2   (page 4)   Evaluating Exponential Expressions

This example discusses how to evaluate 4^3, $(-6)^2$, -6^2, $4 \cdot 3^2$, and $(4 \cdot 3)^2$. To evaluate 4^3, one could type [4][^][3][ENTER], or a superscripted 3 can be produced by pressing [4][MATH][3][ENTER]. Of course, the results are the same either way. (Note: Only reciprocating, squaring, and cubing—that is, the powers -1, 2, and 3—can be displayed as superscripts. All other powers must use the [^] key.)

```
4^3
           64
4³
           64
■
```

All other computations in this example are straightforward with the TI-83, except for this *caveat*: For $(-6)^2$ and -6^2, one must use the [(-)] key rather than the [-] key to enter "negative 6." In the screen shown, the first line was typed as [(][(-)][6][)] [x^2], while the second line was [(][-][6][)][x^2]. When [ENTER] is pressed, the second line produces a syntax error—the calculator's way of saying that the line makes no sense.

```
(-6)²
           36
(-6)²■
```

Section R.1   Example 3   (page 5)   Using Order of Operations

Using the calculator for parts (a) and (b) of this example is straightforward; the expressions are entered as printed. For (c) and (d), we have the expressions

$$\frac{4+3^2}{6-5\cdot 3} \quad \text{and} \quad \frac{-(-3)^3 + (-5)}{2(-8) - 5(3)}.$$

Entering these on the TI-83 requires us to add some additional parentheses to make sure the correct order of operations is followed.

Proper entry of the expression in (d) is shown on the right, in two different forms. The second illustrates some time-saving that can be done in keying in such expressions: The parentheses around -5 in the numerator were omitted, and the denominator $2(-8) - 5(3)$ was typed in as [2][×][(-)][8][-][5][×][3]—the parentheses were exchanged for the multiplication symbol. It would be fine to type the expression unchanged, but the extra parentheses make it somewhat harder to read (and also mean more opportunities to make a mistake).

```
(-(-3)³+(-5))/(2
(-8)-5(3))▶Frac
           -22/31
(-(-3)³+-5)/(2*-
8-5*3)▶Frac
           -22/31
```

The screen shown above also illustrates the command ▶Frac. This command (which simply means "display the result of this computation as a fraction, if possible") is available as [MATH][1].

Section R.2   Example 2   (page 18)   Evaluating Absolute Value

---

Section R.2   Example 3   (page 18)   Finding Absolute Values of Sums and Differences

The absolute value function is typed using MATH ▶ 1, and displays as abs(. Expressions like those in these examples would be entered as abs(-5/8) or abs(-8+2) on the TI-83. Note that the TI-83 automatically supplies the opening parenthesis.

[82] *On the TI-82, the absolute value function is typed using* 2nd x⁻¹, *and the opening parenthesis is not included. Parentheses are optional for expressions like* -abs -2, *but are needed for* abs (-8+2).

Section R.6   Example 4   (page 58)   Using the Definition of $a^{1/n}$

In evaluating these fractional exponents with a calculator, some time can be saved by entering fractions as decimals. The screen on the right performs the computations for (a), (b) and (c) with fewer keystrokes than entering, for example, 36^(1/2). (Of course, as noted in Section R.7 of the text, $36^{1/2} = \sqrt{36}$, which requires even fewer keystrokes.)

Note for (d), the parentheses around -1296 cannot be omitted: The text observes that this is not a real number, but the calculator will display a real result if the parentheses are left out. (See also the next example.) For (e), the decimal equivalent of $1/3$ is $0.\overline{3}$, which can be entered as a sufficiently long string of 3s (at least 12). The last line shows a better way to do this; the TI-83's order of operations is such that 3^{-1} is evaluated before the other exponentiation. This method would also work for the other computations; e.g., (a) could be entered 3 6 ^ 2 x⁻¹.

Section R.6   Example 5   (page 59)   Using the Definition of $a^{m/n}$

For (f), attempting to evaluate $(-4)^{5/2}$ will produce either a NONREAL ANS error, or a complex number result, depending on the Real a+bi re^θi mode setting, described on page 4.

[82] *On the TI-82, the only possible result is a* NONREAL ANS *error, as the TI-82 does not support complex results.*

Section R.7   Example 1   (page 65)   Evaluating Roots

Aside from the square root function, produced with 2nd x², the cube root (³√ () and "x-root" (ˣ√) functions are available as MATH 4 and MATH 5. For example, the input 4ˣ√ (16) computes $\sqrt[4]{16}$. It is worth noting that fourth roots can be typed in more efficiently using two square roots, since $\sqrt[4]{a} = a^{1/4} = (a^{1/2})^{1/2} = \sqrt{a^{1/2}} = \sqrt{\sqrt{a}}$.

Section 1.1   Example 1   (page 87)   Solving a Linear Equation

The TI-83 offers several approaches to solving (or confirming a solution to) an
equation. Aside from graphical approaches to solving equations (which are discussed later, on page 18), here are some non-graphical (numerical) approaches:

```
solve(3(2X-4)-(7
-(X+5)),X,10)
                2
■
```

As illustrated on the right, the TI-83's solve function attempts to find a value of X that makes the given
expression equal to 0, given a guess (10, in this case).

The solve command is accessed through the function catalog: Press 2nd 0, then 4 (which brings up the
commands beginning with "t"). Press ▲ until the triangle cursor (▶) points to solve(, then press ENTER.
For the equations in this section, the "guess" value does not affect the result, but for equations in later
sections, different guesses might produce different results. Full details on how to use this function (found
in the CATALOG) can be found in the TI-83 manual.

Since it is difficult to access this command, it would be a good idea to either use deep recall (see page 3) if
solve is needed several times in a row, or to use the "interactive solver" built-in to the TI-83. This feature
is found by pressing MATH 0.

If Solver has not been used before, the first screen below (a) appears, asking for an expression involving at
least one variable. The TI-83 will attempt to find values of that variable which make the expression equal
to 0. The expression for this example is shown in screen (b). Pressing ENTER brings up screen (c). Type
the guess (this example uses 5), then press ALPHA ENTER and the TI-83 seeks a solution near 5, which is
reported in screen (d).

| (a) | (b) | (c) | (d) |
| Opening screen | Enter expression | Enter guess | Solution |

If Solver *has* been used before, MATH 0 jumps directly to screen (c). To change the expression, press ▲.

Note: In this example, we learned how the TI-83 can be used to support an analytic solution. But the
TI-83 and any other graphing calculator also can be used for solving problems when an analytic solution
is **not** possible—that is, when one cannot solve an equation "algebraically." This is often the case in many
"real-life" applications, and is one of the best arguments for the use of graphing calculators.

82 *The TI-82 does not include this interactive solver; the* solve *function is accessed with* MATH 0.

Section 1.3   Example 1   (page 109)   Writing $\sqrt{-a}$ as $i\sqrt{a}$

Section 1.3   Example 2   (page 109)   Finding Products and Quotients Involving Negative Radicands

Section 1.3   Example 3   (page 110)   Simplifying a Quotient Involving a Negative Radicand

The TI-83 will not do these computations unless it is first put in a+bi mode; see page 4. (One could also
use re^θi mode, but this would report complex numbers in "polar format," rather than the format used in
the text.) See also the comment related to Figure 4 on page 108 of the text.

⟨82⟩ *The TI-82 will not do computations with complex results. See the appendix to the chapter (page 39) for information about how to "fake" these computations.*

| Section 1.3 Example 4 (page 110) | Adding and Subtracting Complex Numbers |

| Section 1.3 Example 5 (page 111) | Multiplying Complex Numbers |

| Section 1.3 Example 6 (page 112) | Simplifying Powers of *i* |

| Section 1.3 Example 7 (page 113) | Dividing Complex Numbers |

The character " ι " is [2nd][.]. Although not completely necessary, it is a good idea to put the TI-83 in a+bι mode; see page 4. (Even in Real mode, the TI-83 will display results for computations in which ι is entered directly; it only complains if asked to find even roots of negative numbers.)

⟨82⟩ *See the appendix to the chapter (page 39) for information about doing these computations on a TI-82.*

| Section 1.5 Example 1 (page 126) | Solving a Problem Involving the Volume of a Box |

A *table* can be a useful tool to solve equations like this. To use the table features of the TI-83, begin by entering the formula ($y = 15x^2 - 200x + 500$) on the [Y=] screen, as one would to create a graph. (The highlighted equals signs determine which formulas will be displayed in the table, just as they do for graphs.)

Next, press [2nd][WINDOW] to access the TABLE SETUP screen. The table will display *y* values for given values of *x*. The TblStart value sets the lowest value of *x*, while ΔTbl determines the "step size" for successive values of *x*. These two values are only used if the Indpnt option is set to Auto—this means, "automatically generate the values of the independent variable (*x*)." The effect of setting this option to Ask is illustrated at the end of this example. (The Depend option should almost always be set to Auto; if it is set to Ask, the *y* values are not displayed until [ENTER] is pressed.)

When the TABLE SETUP options are set satisfactorily, press [2nd][GRAPH] to produce the table. Shown (above, right) is the table generated based on the settings in the above screen; the fact that *y* is negative for *x* = 8 and *x* = 9 supports the restriction *x* > 10 from Step 3 of the example. By pressing [▼] repeatedly, the *x* values are increased, and the *y* values updated. (Pressing [▲] decreases the *x* values, but clearly that is not appropriate for this problem.) After pressing [▼] eleven times, the table looks like the second screen, which shows that Y1 equals 1435 when X equals 17.

Extension: Suppose the specifications called for the box to be 1500 cubic inches (instead of 1435). We see from the table above that *x* must be between 17 and 18 inches. The TI-83's table capabilities provide a convenient way to "zoom in" on the value of *x* (which could also be found with the solve command, or by other methods).

Since $17 < x < 18$, set TblStart to 17 and ΔTbl to 0.1. This produces the table shown on the right, from which we see that $17.2 < x < 17.3$. Now set TblStart to 17.2 and ΔTbl to 0.01, which reveals that x is between 17.2 and 17.21. This process can be continued to achieve any desired degree of accuracy.

Finally, the screen on the right shows the effect of setting Indpnt to Ask. Initially, the table is blank, but as values of x are entered, the y values are computed. Up to seven x values can be entered; if more are desired, the [DEL] key can be used to make room.

Section 1.7   Example 1   (page 147)   Solving a Linear Inequality

---

Section 1.7   Example 2   (page 148)   Solving a Linear Inequality

---

Shown is one way to visualize the solution to inequalities like these. The inequality symbols $>$, $<$, $\geq$, $\leq$ are found in the TEST menu ([2nd][MATH]). The TI-83 responds with 1 when a statement is true and 0 for false statements. This is why the graph of Y₁ appears as it does: For values of x less than 4, the inequality is true (and so Y₁ equals 1), and for $x \geq 4$, the inequality is false (and Y₁ equals 0). Note that this picture does *not* help one determine what happens when $x = 4$.

Section 1.7   Example 3   (page 149)   Solving a Three-Part Inequality

---

To see a "picture" of this inequality like the one shown for the previous two examples requires a little additional work. Setting Y₁=-2<5+3X<20 will *not* work correctly. Instead, one must enter either

    Y₁=(-2<5+3X)(5+3X<20)   or   Y₁=(-2<5+3X) and (5+3X<20)

which will produce the desired results: A function that equals 1 between $-\frac{7}{3}$ and 5, is equals 0 elsewhere. ("and" is found in the TEST:LOGIC menu, [2nd][MATH][▶].)

Section 1.7   Example 5   (page 150)   Solving a Quadratic Inequality

---

Section 1.7   Example 6   (page 151)   Solving a Quadratic Inequality

---

Section 1.7   Example 8   (page 154)   Solving a Rational Inequality

---

Section 1.7   Example 9   (page 155)   Solving a Rational Inequality

---

The methods described above can also be applied to these inequalities.

Extension: Can the calculator be used to solve the inequality $x^2 + 6x + 9 > 0$? Yes—if it is used carefully. Shown is the graph of the expression $x^2 + 6x + 9 > 0$. This suggests that the inequality is true for all x; that is, the solution set is $(-\infty, \infty)$.

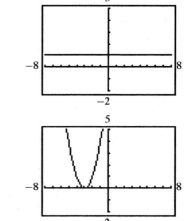

This conclusion is **not correct**: The graph of $y = x^2 + 6x + 9$ (without "> 0") touches the x-axis at $x = -3$, which means that this must be excluded from the solution set, since "> 0" means the graph must be above (not on) the x-axis. The correct solution set is $(-\infty, -3) \cup (-3, \infty)$.

This example should serve as a warning: Sometimes, the TI-83 will mislead you. When possible, try to confirm the calculator's answers in some way.

Section 1.8 Example 1 (page 161) Solving Absolute Value Equations

The "solver" features described on page 14 of this manual can be used for these equations, too. Recall that abs(is entered as $\boxed{\text{MATH}}\boxed{\blacktriangleright}\boxed{1}$.

Section 2.1 Example 5 (page 186) Using the Midpoint Formula

The TI-83 can do midpoint computations nicely by putting coordinates in a list—that is, using braces ($\boxed{\text{2nd}}\boxed{(}$ and $\boxed{\text{2nd}}\boxed{)}$) instead of parentheses. When adding two lists, the calculator simply adds corresponding elements, so the two x-coordinates are added, as are the y-coordinates. Dividing by 2 completes the task.

Section 2.1 Example 10 (page 190) Graphing a Circle

The text suggests graphing $Y_1=4+\sqrt{(36-(X+3)^2)}$ and $Y_2=4-\sqrt{(36-(X+3)^2)}$. Here are three options to speed up entering these formulas:

- After typing the formula in Y_1, move the cursor to Y_2 and press $\boxed{\text{2nd}}\boxed{\text{STO}\blacktriangleright}$ (RCL), then $\boxed{\text{VARS}}\boxed{\blacktriangleright}\boxed{1}$ $\boxed{1}\boxed{\text{ENTER}}$. This will "recall" the formula of Y_1, placing that formula in Y_2. Now edit this formula, changing the first "$+$" to a "$-$."

- After typing the formula in Y_1, enter $Y_2=8-Y_1$. (To type Y_1, press $\boxed{\text{VARS}}\boxed{\blacktriangleright}\boxed{1}\boxed{1}$.) This produces the desired results, since $8 - Y_1 = 8 - (4 + \sqrt{36 - (x+3)^2}) = 8 - 4 - \sqrt{36 - (x+3)^2} = 4 - \sqrt{36 - (x+3)^2}$.

- Enter the single formula $Y_1=4+\{-1,1\}\sqrt{(36-(X+3)^2)}$. (The curly braces { and } are $\boxed{\text{2nd}}\boxed{(}$ and $\boxed{\text{2nd}}$ $\boxed{)}$). When a list (like $\{-1,1\}$) appears in a formula, it tells the TI-83 to graph this formula several times, using each value in the list.

The window chosen in the text is a square window (see section 11 of the introduction of this chapter), so that the graph looks like a circle. (On a non-square window, the graph would look like an ellipse—that is, a squashed circle.) Other square windows would also produce a "true" circle, but some will leave gaps similar to those circles shown in sections 11 and 12 of the introduction (pages 6–7). Shown is the same circle on the square window produced by pressing $\boxed{\text{ZOOM}}\boxed{6}\boxed{\text{ZOOM}}\boxed{5}$.

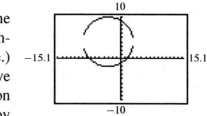

Section 2.2　Example 6　(page 205)　Using Function Notation

Section 2.2　Example 7　(page 205)　Using Function Notation

The TI-83 will do *some* computations in function notation. Simply enter the function in Y₁ (or any other function). Return to the home screen, and press $\boxed{\text{VARS}}$ $\boxed{\blacktriangleright}$ (Y-VARS). Option 1 allows access to all the function (y) variables; parametric and polar variables are also available (as options 2 and 3). Select the appropriate function (Y₁ in this case), then type (2) to evaluate that function with the input 2. The result shown on the screen agrees with (a) in the text.

　The TI-83 is less helpful if asked to evaluate expressions like those given in Example 6(b) or Example 7. Note, for example, that Y₁(Q) produces the result -3, rather than the desired result $-Q^2 + 5Q - 3$. When asked to evaluate an expression using a variable (like Q), the TI-83 simply substitutes the current value of that variable, which in this case was 0.

Section 2.3　Example 3　(page 215)　Graphing a Vertical Line

The text notes that such a line is not a function; therefore, it cannot be graphed by entering the equation on the $\boxed{\text{Y=}}$ screen. However, the TI-83 does provide a fairly straightforward method of graphing vertical lines using the Vertical command.

From the home screen, press $\boxed{\text{2nd}}\boxed{\text{PRGM}}\boxed{4}$ to access the Vertical command, then type the x-coordinate of the line. The command shown on the right was typed as $\boxed{\text{2nd}}\boxed{\text{PRGM}}\boxed{4}\boxed{(-)}\boxed{3}$; when $\boxed{\text{ENTER}}$ is pressed, the line will be drawn.

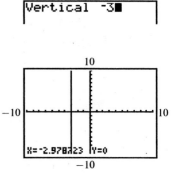

Alternatively, the vertical line can be drawn "interactively" if the Vertical command is issued from the graph screen. This allows the user to move the cursor (and the vertical line) to the desired position using the $\boxed{\blacktriangleleft}$ and $\boxed{\blacktriangleright}$ keys. Pressing $\boxed{\text{ENTER}}$ places the line at that location, then allows more lines to be drawn. (Press $\boxed{\text{GRAPH}}$ to finish drawing vertical lines.) Note that since $x = -3$ does not correspond to a column of pixels on the screen (see page 6), the vertical line is actually located at $x \approx -2.9787$, but the appearance on the screen is the same as if it were at $x = -3$.

Section 2.4   Example 5   (page 230)   Finding Equations of Parallel and Perpendicular Lines

In the discussion following this example (on page 231), the text notes that the lines from part (b) do not appear to be perpendicular unless they are plotted on a square window. See section 11 of the introduction of this chapter (page 6) for more information about square windows.

Section 2.4   Example 6   (page 232)   Finding an Equation of a Line That Models Data

Section 2.4   Example 7   (page 233)   Finding a Linear Equation That Models Data

Aside from the methods described in these two examples, the text refers to the technique of linear regression on page 235. The steps are illustrated in Figure 48; here is a more detailed description of the process (using the data of Example 7).

Given a set of data pairs (x, y), the TI-83 can find various formulas (including linear and quadratic, as well as more complex formulas) that approximate the relationship between x and y. These formulas are called "regression formulas."

The first step in determining the regression formula is to enter the data into the TI-83. This is done by pressing $\boxed{\text{STAT}}$, then choosing option 1 (Edit).

This brings up the list-editing screen. (If the column headings are not L1, L2, L3 as shown on the right, press $\boxed{\text{STAT}}\boxed{5}\boxed{\text{ENTER}}$ to reset the statistics [list] editor to its default. Then return to the list-editing screen.) Enter the year values into the first column (L1) and the percentage of women in the labor force into the second column (L2). If either column already contains data, the $\boxed{\text{DEL}}$ key can be used to delete numbers one at a time, or—to delete the whole column at once—press the $\boxed{\blacktriangle}$ key until the cursor is at the top of the column (on L1 or L2) and press $\boxed{\text{CLEAR}}\boxed{\text{ENTER}}$. Make sure that both columns contain the same number of entries. (The screen shown here is the same as the first screen in Figure 48.)

When all data is entered, press $\boxed{\text{STAT}}\boxed{\blacktriangleright}\boxed{4}$ to choose LinReg(ax+b) from the CALC statistics submenu. This will place the command LinReg(ax+b) on the home screen.

To tell the TI-83 where to find x and y, press $\boxed{\text{2nd}}\boxed{1}\boxed{,}\boxed{\text{2nd}}\boxed{2}$, which adds "L1,L2" to the command. (**Note:** This is not absolutely necessary, since the TI-83 will assume that x is in L1 and y is in L2 unless told otherwise. In other words, "LinReg(ax+b)" (by itself) works the same as "LinReg(ax+b) L1,L2".) Pressing $\boxed{\text{ENTER}}$ should then produce the second screen shown in Figure 48 of the text. (It may also include a value of "R^2," but this can be ignored.)

If it produces an error message, it will likely either be a DIM MISMATCH (meaning that the two lists L1 and L2 have different numbers of entries) or a SYNTAX error, probably because the LinReg(ax+b) command was not on a line by itself. The screen on the right, for example, produces a syntax error.

Section 2.4   Example 8   (page 235)   Solving an Equation with a Graphing Calculator

The text illustrates a graphical process for solving the equation $-2x - 4(2 - x) = 3x + 4$; in this discussion, we will show two graphical methods for solving the equation $\frac{1}{2}x - 6 = \frac{3}{4}x - 9$. (The answer is $x = 12$.)

The first method is the **intersection** method. To begin, set up the TI-83 to graph the left side of the equation as Y1, and the right side as Y2. **Note:** Putting the fractions in parentheses ensures no mistakes with order of operations. This is not crucial for the TI-83, but is a good practice because some other models give priority to implied multiplication. See section 8 of the introduction, page 3.

We are looking for an x value that will make the left and right sides of this equation equal to each other, which corresponds to the x-coordinate of the point of intersection of these two graphs.

Next, select a viewing window which shows the point of intersection; we use $[-15, 15] \times [-10, 10]$ for this example. The TI-83 can automatically locate this point using the CALC menu (2nd TRACE). Choose option 5 (intersect), use ▲, ▼ and ENTER to specify which two functions to use (in this case, the only two being displayed), and then use ◄ or ► to specify a guess. After pressing ENTER, the TI-83 will try to find an intersection of the two graphs. The screens below illustrate these steps.

2nd TRACE 5   ENTER (choose Y1)   ENTER (choose Y2)   ENTER (specify
                                                                            guess)

The final result of this process is the screen shown on the right. The x-coordinate of this point of intersection is calculated to 14 digits of accuracy, so if the solution were some less "convenient" number (say, $\sqrt{3}$ or $1/\pi$), we would have an answer that would be accurate enough for nearly any computation.

Note: An approximation for the point of intersection can be found simply by moving the TRACE cursor as near the intersection as possible. The amount of error can be minimized by "zooming in" on the graph. This is the only method available for graphing calculators such as the TI-81.

The second graphical approach is to use the x**-intercept method**, which seeks the x-coordinate of the point where a graph crosses the x-axis. Specifically, we want to know where the graph of Y1−Y2 crosses the x-axis, where Y1 and Y2 are as defined above. This is because the equation $\frac{1}{2}x - 6 = \frac{3}{4}x - 9$ can only be true when $\frac{1}{2}x - 6 - \left(\frac{3}{4}x - 9\right) = 0$. (This is the approach illustrated in the text for Example 8.)

To find this x-intercept, begin by defining Y3=Y1−Y2 on the Y= screen. We could do this by re-typing the formulas entered for Y1 and Y2, but having typed those formulas once, it is more efficient to do this as shown on the right. To type Y1 and Y2, press VARS ▶ 1 to access the Y-VARS:FUNCTION menu. Note that Y1 and Y2 have been "de-selected" so that they will not be graphed (see section 12 of the introduction, page 7).

We must first select a viewing window which shows the x-intercept; we again use $[-15, 15] \times [-10, 10]$. The TI-83 can automatically locate this point by choosing option 2 from the CALC (2nd TRACE) menu. The TI-83 prompts for left and right bounds and a guess, then attempts to locate the zero between the given bounds. (Provided there is only one zero between the bounds, and the function is "well-behaved"—meaning it has some nice properties like continuity—the calculator will find it.) The screens below illustrate these steps.

(move cursor)   (move cursor)   (move cursor)   Here is the result.
ENTER   ENTER   ENTER

Section 2.5   Example 2   (page 246)   Graphing Piecewise-Defined Functions

The text shows two methods for entering piecewise-defined functions on the TI-83. Recall that the inequality symbols $>, <, \geq, \leq$ are found in the TEST menu (2nd MATH). The use of DOT mode is not crucial to the graphing process, as long as one remembers that vertical line segments connecting the "pieces" of the graph (in this case, at $x = 2$) are not really part of the graph.

The advantage of the method used in (b)—placing the piecewise definition in a single formula—is that Y1 will act exactly like the function f. For example, to evaluate $f(5)$ in (a), one would first have to check which formula to use (Y1 or Y2). To evaluate $f(5)$ in (b), simply enter Y1(5). Also, when a single formula is used, TRACE will properly show the behavior of the function as the trace cursor moves left and right.

Extension: For more complicated piecewise-defined functions, a similar procedure can be used. Consider

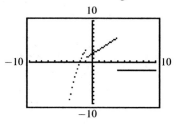

$$f(x) = \begin{cases} 4 - x^2 & \text{if } x < -1 \\ 2 + x & \text{if } -1 \leq x \leq 4 \\ -2 & \text{if } x > 4 \end{cases}$$

shown on the right in DOT mode on the standard window.

It might be tempting to enter Y1=(4−X2)(X<−1)+(2+X)(−1≤X≤4)+(−2)(X>4), but this does not work. Instead, use either

    Y1=(4−X2)(X<−1)+(2+X)(−1≤X and X≤4)+(−2)(X>4),   or

    Y1=(4−X2)(X<−1)+(2+X)(−1≤X)(X≤4)+(−2)(X>4)

(the "and" in the first formula is found using 2nd MATH ▶ 1).

Section 2.5   Example 3   (page 247)   Graphing a Greatest Integer Function

We wish to graph the step function $y = [\![\frac{1}{2}x + 1]\!]$. This is entered on the TI-83 as shown on the right (either Y₁ or Y₂). int (is found in the MATH:NUM menu, MATH ▶ 5 .

```
Plot1 Plot2 Plot3
\Y1▪int(X/2+1)
\Y2▪int((1/2)X+1
)▪
```

Section 2.6   Example 1   (page 253)   Stretching or Shrinking a Graph

---

Section 2.6   Example 2   (page 254)   Reflecting a Graph Across an Axis

---

Section 2.6   Example 6   (page 259)   Translating a Graph Vertically

---

Section 2.6   Example 7   (page 260)   Translating a Graph Horizontally

See page 8 for information on setting the thickness of a graph. Note that the symbol next to Y₂ in the calculator screens shown in the text indicates that the graph should be thick.

It is possible to distinguish between two graphs without having them drawn using different styles. When two or more graphs are drawn, the TRACE feature can be used to determine which graphs correspond to which formulas: By pressing ▲ and ▼, the trace cursor jumps from one graph to another, and the upper right corner displays the number of the current formula. On the right, the trace cursor is on graph 2—that is, the graph of $g(x) = 2|x|$.

Alternatively, when ExprOn is selected on the TI-83's graph format screen (2nd ZOOM —see page 5), the calculator will display in the upper left corner the formula for the graph currently being traced. The screen on the right illustrates this feature.

Section 2.7   Example 5   (page 272)   Evaluating Composite Functions

To type Y₁, Y₂, . . . on the home screen, press VARS ▶ 1 .

Section 3.1   Example 1   (page 295)   Graphing Quadratic Functions

---

Section 3.1   Example 2   (page 297)   Graphing a Parabola by Completing the Square

---

Section 3.1   Example 3   (page 298)   Graphing a Parabola by Completing the Square

The TI-83 can automatically locate the vertex of the parabola (to a reasonable degree of accuracy) using the CALC menu (2nd TRACE).

We illustrate this procedure for the function in Example 1(c). After defining Y₁=-(1/2)(X-4)²+3 and choosing a suitable window, press 2nd TRACE and select option 4 for a downward opening parabola, or option 3 for an upward opening parabola. Next, specify left and right bounds (numbers that are, respectively, less than and greater than the location of the vertex) and a guess, and the TI-83 will try to find the highest (or lowest) point on the graph between the given bounds. (For some functions, it might not always find the correct maximum or minimum, but for parabolas, it should succeed.) The screens below illustrate these steps.

| [2nd][TRACE][4] | (move cursor)
[ENTER] | ...then twice more | ...and *voilà!* |

Section 3.1   Example 6   (page 302)   Modeling the Number of Hospital Outpatient Visits

See page 17 for information about using the TI-83 for regression computations.

Section 3.2   Example 3   (page 317)   Deciding whether a Number is a Zero

The TI-83's "function notation" evaluation method (page 16 of this manual) can also be used to check for zeros: In the screen on the right, Y_1, Y_2, and Y_3 have been defined (respectively) as the functions in (a), (b), and (c). While this method fails for complex numbers—$Y_3(1+2i)$ results in an error—one can evaluate Y_3 at $1 + 2i$ by first storing that value in X, then requesting the value of Y_3 (with no parentheses, which means "evaluate using the current value of X"). The screen on the right shows the output of this sequence of commands. While the TI-83 does not report the value as 0, it lends support to the belief that $1 + 2i$ is a zero since both the real and complex parts are very small. (The difference is due to roundoff error.)

Section 3.3   Example 6   (page 327)   Finding All Zeros of a Polynomial Given One Zero

Calculator programs can be downloaded from the Internet to automate the process of synthetic division, and even the determination of zeros for polynomials. See section 13 of the introduction (page 8) for details about calculator programs.

Section 3.5   Example 2   (page 352)   Graphing a Rational Function

Note that this function is entered as $Y_1=2/(X+1)$, **not** $Y_1=2/X+1$.

The issue of incorrectly drawn asymptotes is also addressed in section 12 of the introduction to this chapter (page 7). Changing the window to $Xmin = -5$ and $Xmax = 3$ (or any choice of $Xmin$ and $Xmax$ which has -1 halfway between them) eliminates this vertical line because it forces the TI-83 to attempt to evaluate the function at $x = -1$. Since f is not defined at -1, it cannot plot a point there, and as a result, it does not attempt to connect the dots across the "break" in the graph.

Section 4.1   Example 7   (page 396)   Finding the Inverse of a Function with a Restricted Domain

Note that Figure 10 shows a square viewing window (see page 6); the mirror-image property of the inverse function would not be as clear on a non-square window.

Section 4.2   Example 11   (page 412)   Using Data to Model Exponential Growth

See page 17 for information about using the TI-83 for regression computations.

Section 4.4   Example 1   (page 433)   Finding pH

For (a), the text shows $-\log(2.5*10^{\wedge}(-4))$, but this could also be entered as shown on the first line of the screen on the right, since "E" (produced with 2nd ,) and "$*10^{\wedge}$" are nearly equivalent. The two are not completely interchangeable, however; in particular, in part (b), "$10^{\wedge}$" **cannot** be replaced with "E", because "E" is only valid when followed by an *integer*. That is, E-7 produces the same result as $10^{\wedge}-7$, but the last line shown on the screen produces a syntax error.

(Incidentally, "$10^{\wedge}$" is 2nd LOG, but 1 0 ∧ produces the same results.)

Section 4.5   Example 8   (page 448)   Modeling Coal Consumption in the U.S.

The modeling function given in the text was found using a regression procedure (LnReg, or logarithmic regression) similar to that described on page 17.

Section 5.1   Example 2   (page 476)   Calculating with Degrees, Minutes, and Seconds

---

Section 5.1   Example 3   (page 476)   Converting between Decimal Degrees and Degrees, Minutes, and Seconds

See section 9 of this chapter's introduction (page 4) for information about selecting Degree mode. The alternative to putting the calculator in Degree mode is to use the degree symbol (2nd MATRX 1) following each angle measure.

The degrees and minutes symbols, and the ▶DMS operator (which causes an angle to be displayed in degrees, minutes, and seconds, rather than as a decimal), are all found in the ANGLE (2nd MATRX) menu, shown on the right. The "seconds" symbol is simply the double quotes, entered as ALPHA +.

82 *The TI-82 uses only the minutes symbol "'" for entering angles in degrees, minutes, and seconds (output uses all the symbols). For example, to convert* $74°8'14''$ *to decimal degrees, one would type* 74'8'12'.

Section 5.2   Example 4   (page 484)   Finding Function Values of Quadrantal Angles

The alternative to putting the calculator in Degree mode is to use the degree symbol ([2nd][MATRX][1]) following each angle measure; e.g., enter sin(90°) rather than just sin(90).

Since the cotangent, secant, and cosecant functions are the reciprocals of the tangent, cosine, and sine, they can be entered as (e.g.) 1/sin(90). (This is illustrated in Figure 21 on page 485 of the text.) Note, though, that this will not properly compute cot 90°, since 1/tan(90) produces a domain error. Entering cot x as cos x/ sin x will produce the correct result at 90°.

One might guess that the other three trigonometric functions are accessed with [2nd] followed by [SIN], [COS], or [TAN] (which produce, e.g., sin^{-1}). This is **not** what these functions do; in this case, the exponent -1 does not mean "reciprocal," but instead indicates that these are inverse functions (which are discussed in Sections 5.3 and 7.5 of the text). The text comments on this distinction at th bottom of page 485.

Section 5.3   Example 6   (page 500)   Finding Function Values with a Calculator

The screen on the right shows how computations like the secant in part (b) and the cotangent in (c) can be entered on a single line. These computations were done in Degree mode.

```
sin(49°12'
          .7569950557
(cos(97.977))-1
         -7.205879213
■
```

The screen on the right (with computations done in Radian mode) illustrates a somewhat unexpected behavior: Even if an angle is entered in DMS format, the TI-83 assumes that the angle is in radians. In order to remedy this, either put the calculator in Degree mode, or use the degree symbol ([2nd][MATRX][1]) as was done in the second entry.

```
sin(49°12'
         -.875022579
sin(49°12'°
          .7569950557
■
```

82 *On a TI-82, the computation in part (a) would be entered* sin⁻ 49'12'.

Section 5.3   Example 7   (page 500)   Using an Inverse Trigonometric Function to Find an Angle

---

Section 5.3   Example 8   (page 501)   Finding Angle Measures

The sin^{-1} ("inverse sine," or "arcsine") function is [2nd][SIN], while cos^{-1} is [2nd][COS]. The computations shown in Figures 34 and 36 in the text were done in Degree mode; the screen on the right shows the result for Example 7 when done in Radian mode. Note that in the second entry, an attempt was made to get the TI-83 to report the result in degrees (by placing the degree symbol at the end of the entry), but this does not have the desired result.

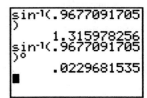

```
sin-1(.9677091705
)
           1.315978256
sin-1(.9677091705
)°
           .0229681535
■
```

Section 5.4	Example 1	(page 510)	Solving a Right Triangle Given an Angle and a Side

Section 5.4	Example 2	(page 511)	Solving a Right Triangle Given Two Sides

For problems like these, the Ans variable can be used to avoid loss of accuracy from rounding off intermediate results. Shown are computations for Example 1. (Be sure the TI-83 is in Degree mode. Also, recall that the arcsine (or inverse sine) function is [2nd][SIN] — *not* [SIN][x^{-1}].)

Section 5.4	Example 7	(page 514)	Solving a Problem Involving Angles of Elevation

The TI-83 can automatically locate the intersection of two graphs using the CALC menu ([2nd][TRACE]). This feature was previously illustrated on page 18, but we repeat the description here: Choose option 5 (intersect), use [▲], [▼] and [ENTER] to specify which two functions to use (in this case, the only two being displayed), and then use [◄] or [►] to specify a guess. After pressing [ENTER], the TI-83 will try to find an intersection of the two graphs. The screens below illustrate these steps; the final result is the screen shown as Figure 51 of the text. The guessing step in the fourth screen below is not crucial in this case, since the calculator would locate the intersection even if a very poor guess was given.

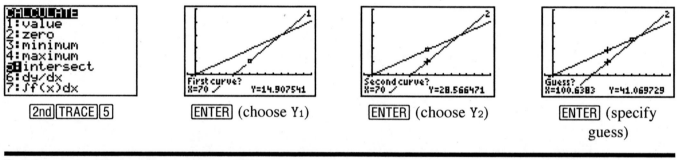

[2nd][TRACE][5]   [ENTER] (choose Y₁)   [ENTER] (choose Y₂)   [ENTER] (specify guess)

Section 6.1	Example 1	(page 535)	Converting Degrees to Radians

The number π is available as [2nd][∧], and the degree symbol is [2nd][MATRX][1]. With the calculator in Radian mode (see page 4), entering $45°$ causes the TI-83 to automatically convert to radians.

A useful technique to aid in recognizing when an angle is a multiple of π is to divide the result by π. This approach is illustrated in the screen on the right, showing that $45°$ is $\pi/4$ radians, and $30°$ is $\pi/6$ radians. This screen also makes use of the ►Frac command ([MATH][1]), which simply means "display the result of this computation as a fraction, if possible."

An alternative to using the degree symbol is to store $\pi/180$ in the calculator variable D (see page 3). Then typing, for example, 45D [ENTER] will multiply 45 by $\pi/180$. This approach will work regardless of whether the calculator is in Degree or Radian mode. (A value stored in a variable will remain there until it is replaced by a new value.)

Section 6.1   Example 2   (page 535)   Converting Radians to Degrees

With the TI-83 in Degree mode (see page 4), the radian symbol (a superscripted r), produced with 2nd MATRX 3, will automatically change a radian angle measurement to degrees.

Alternatively, with the value $180/\pi$ stored in the calculator variable R (see page 3), typing (9π/4)R ENTER will convert from radians to degrees regardless of whether the calculator is in Degree or Radian mode. (The same result can be achieved by *dividing by* the calculator variable D as defined in the previous example.)

Section 6.2   Example 4   (page 549)   Finding a Number Given Its Circular Function Value

The arccosine (or inverse cosine) function is 2nd COS — *not* COS x^{-1}. Likewise, $\tan^{-1}$ is 2nd TAN.

Section 6.3   Example 1   (page 559)   Graphing $y = a\sin x$

Note that the TI-83 must be in Radian mode in order to produce the desired graph. See page 8 for information on setting the thickness of a graph.

The graphs in the text, and those below, are shown in the "trig viewing window," described on the top of page 558. This window can be selected automatically by pressing ZOOM 7. (If the TI-83 is in Degree mode, Xmin and Xmax will be ±360 instead of ±2π.)

It is possible to distinguish between the two graphs without having them drawn using different styles by using the TRACE feature. On the right, the trace cursor is on graph 2—that is, the graph of $y_2 = \sin x$. This approach is discussed on page 20 of this manual.

Alternatively, when ExprOn is selected on the TI-83's graph format screen, the expression is displayed in the upper left corner of the screen. (This approach is also discussed on page 20.)

82 *The TI-82 has neither graph styles nor* ExprOn, *so the* TRACE *feature mentioned above is the only option.*

Section 6.3   Example 8   (page 566)   Modeling Temperature with a Sine Function

The "sine regression" illustrated at the end of this example is a built-in feature of the TI-83. See page 17 for information about using the TI-83 for regression computations.

82 *The TI-82 does not support sine regression. It might be possible to find a program to do this; see section 13 of this chapter's introduction, on page 8.*

Section 6.4 Example 1 (page 578)	Graphing $y = a \sec bx$

Section 6.4 Example 2 (page 579)	Graphing $y = a \csc(x - d)$

See section 9 of the introduction (page 4) for information about Connected versus Dot mode. The function in Example 1 can be entered as Y₁=2cos(X/2)⁻¹ (or as shown in the text). The function in Example 2 can be entered as Y₁=(3/2)(1/sin(X-π/2)) or Y₁=3/(2sin(X-π/2)). A reminder: sin⁻¹ ([2nd][SIN]) is *not* the cosecant function.

Section 7.1 Example 3 (page 609)	Rewriting an Expression in Terms of Sine and Cosine

The top screen on the right shows how these expressions are entered on the [Y=] screen. As an alternative to graphing these two functions, the TI-83's table feature (see page 13 of this manual) can be used: If the y values are the same for a reasonably large sample of x values, one can be fairly sure (though not certain) that the two expressions are equal. To make this approach more reliable, be sure to choose x values that are not, for example, all multiples of π.

Section 7.3 Example 1 (page 622)	Finding Exact Cosine Function Values

---

Section 7.3 Example 4 (page 626)	Finding Exact Sine and Tangent Function Values

The TI-83 can graphically and numerically support exact value computations such as $\cos 15° = \frac{\sqrt{6}+\sqrt{2}}{4}$. Starting with a graph of Y₁=cos(X), the TI-83 makes it possible to trace to any real number value for x between Xmin and Xmax. Simply type a number or expression (like 1/π or √(2)) while in TRACE mode. The number appears at the bottom of the window in a larger font size than the TRACE coordinates. Pressing [ENTER] causes the TRACE cursor to jump to that x-coordinate. This same result can be achieved using option 1 (value) from the [2nd][TRACE] (CALC) menu.

[82] *This latter approach is also available on the TI-82.*

Alternatively, a table of values like those shown here can be used to find the value of $\cos 15°$. Of course, the screen shown in the text in support of Example 1(b) shows the other part of this process: Computing the decimal value of $(\sqrt{6}+\sqrt{2})/2$ and observing that it agrees with those found here.

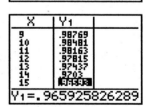

Note that Example 8 in Section 7.4 (page 639) shows that $\cos 15°$ can also be written as $\frac{\sqrt{2+\sqrt{3}}}{2}$.

Section 7.5 Example 1 (page 646)	Finding Inverse Sine Values

Section 7.5 Example 2 (page 646)	Finding Inverse Cosine Values

Of course, it is not necessary to graph $y = \sin^{-1} x$ or $y = \cos^{-1} x$ to find these values; one can simply enter, e.g., $\sin^{-1}(1/2)$ on the home screen. The first entry of the screen on the right shows what happens when the calculator is in Degree mode; note that the result is not in $[-\pi/2, \pi/2]$. With the calculator in Radian mode, results similar to those in the text are found, and the method employed on page 24 of this manual (in the discussion of text Example 1 from Section 6.1) confirms that these values are $\pi/6$ and $3\pi/4$.

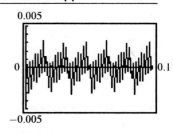

Section 7.5 Example 4 (page 651)	Finding Inverse Function Values with a Calculator

Note that the answer given for (b), $109.499054°$, overrepresents the accuracy of that value. A typical rule for doing computations involving decimal values (like -0.3541) is to report only as many digits in the result as were present in the original number—in this case, four. This means the reported answer should be "about $109.5°$," and in fact, any angle θ between about $109.496°$ and $109.501°$ has a cotangent which rounds to -0.3541.

Section 7.6 Example 9 (page 663)	Describing a Musical Tone from a Graph

Section 7.6 Example 10 (page 664)	Analyzing Pressures of Upper Harmonics

Note that the calculator screens shown in Figures 27–30 illustrate the importance of choosing a "good" viewing window. If we choose the wrong vertical scale (Ymin and Ymax), we might not be able to see the graph at all—it might be squashed against the x-axis. If we make the window too wide—that is, if Xmax minus Xmin is too large—we might see the "wrong" picture, like the one on the right (for Example 10): We seem to see six periods in this view, when in fact there are 44. Each of the six "pseudo-cycles" is made of parts of seven or eight full periods.

This observation—that a periodic function, viewed at fixed intervals, can appear to be a *different* periodic function—is the same effect that causes wagon wheels to appear to run backwards in old movies.

Section 8.3 Example 1 (page 716)	Finding Magnitude and Direction Angle

The R▸Pr(and R▸Pθ(conversion functions (illustrated in Figure 26) are in the TI-83's ANGLE menu ([2nd] [MATRX]) as options 5 and 6. R▸Pθ(x,y) returns an angle in degrees if the TI-83 is in Degree mode.

"R" and "P" stand for "rectangular" and "polar" coordinates. Rectangular coordinates are the familiar x and y values. Polar coordinates, described in Section 8.7 of the text, are r (which corresponds to the magnitude of a vector) and θ (the direction angle).

Section 8.3   Example 2   (page 716)   Finding Horizontal and Vertical Components

The P▸Rx(and P▸Ry(conversion functions are in the ANGLE menu (2nd MATRX)
as options 7 and 8. Note that the screen shown in the text was created with the
calculator set to display only one digit after the decimal, and in Degree mode. If the
TI-83 is in Radian mode, the degree symbol (also in the ANGLE menu) can specify
that the angle is in degrees.

"R" and "P" stand for "rectangular" and "polar" coordinates. Rectangular coordinates are the familiar x and
y values. Polar coordinates, described in Section 8.7 of the text, are r (which corresponds to the magnitude
of a vector) and θ (the direction angle).

Section 8.3   Example 5   (page 718)   Performing Vector Operations

Section 8.3   Example 6   (page 719)   Finding the Dot Product

Vector operations might be performed with a program (see page 8), or the vectors
can be entered as lists, as Figure 33 shows. If a vector is to be used more than
once, it may be useful to store it in one of the TI-83's list variables L_1, L_2, ...,
L_6. For dot products, one can use the sum command, found in the LIST:MATH menu
(2nd STAT ◄).

Section 8.5   Example 2   (page 734)   Converting from Trigonometric Form to Rectangular Form

While the TI-83 must be in a+bi or re^θi mode in order to compute (e.g.) square roots of negative numbers,
it will perform computations involving i (2nd .) even while in Real mode (see page 4).

Section 8.5   Example 3   (page 734)   Converting from Rectangular Form to Trigonometric Form

The TI-83 can convert from rectangular to trigonometric
form in several ways. Aside from the ANGLE (2nd MATRX)
menu commands R▸Pr(and R▸Pθ(, shown in the text,
one can use the MATH:CPX menu commands angle(and
abs(. The angle(command gives the angle θ in radians
or degrees (depending on the mode setting), and the abs(
function (also found in the MATH:NUM menu) gives the modulus r. These functions are shown on page 737
of the text.

Furthermore, with the calculator placed in re^θi mode (see page 4), the conversion can be done all at once, as the screen on the right shows (the TI-83 was
also in Degree mode, so the angles are reported in degrees). As the name of the
mode suggests, the values of r and θ can be read directly from the output: r is the
leading coefficient, and θ is in the exponent.

Additionally, using the ▸Polar command (option 7 in the MATH CPX menu; MATH
▸ ▸ 7), and with the TI-83 in **any** mode (Real, a+bi, or re^θi), the output is
displayed in this polar format, as the screen on the right shows. Note: Polar format
is equivalent to trigonometric format because of the (fairly deep) mathematical
fact that $e^{i\theta} = \cos\theta + i\sin\theta = \operatorname{cis}\theta$.

Section 8.5   Example 4   (page 735)

Converting Between Trigonometric and Rectangular Forms
Using Calculator Approximations

Aside from entering the expression in (a) as it is shown in the text (using the cos
and sin functions), one can use the polar format (re^θi), but note that *regardless
of the TI-83's* Degree/Radian *mode setting,* all such computations are done with the
angle θ in radians.   Thus, the first result on the right is incorrect, because the
cosine and sine were computed for 115 radians (this is true even if the TI-83 is in Degree mode). The second
entry, with the degree symbol included, gives the correct result, but *this will only work if the TI-83 is in*
Radian *mode!*

Section 8.6   Example 1   (page 743)

Finding a Power of a Complex Number

The screen on the right shows several options for computing $(1 + i\sqrt{3})^8$ with the
TI-83 (in a+bi mode). The first is fairly straightforward, but the reported result
shows the complex part of the answer ($128i\sqrt{3}$) given in decimal form.   For an
"exact" answer, the TI-83's polar format (re^θi) can be used. The TI-83 was in
Degree mode for the first of the two polar-format answers, and in Radian mode for
the second.

Section 8.7   Example 3   (page 751)

Examining Polar and Rectangular Equations
of Lines and Circles

Section 8.7   Example 4   (page 753)

Graphing a Polar Equation (Cardioid)

Section 8.7   Example 5   (page 753)

Graphing a Polar Equation (Rose)

Section 8.7   Example 6   (page 754)

Graphing a Polar Equation (Lemniscate)

To produce these polar graphs, the TI-83 should be set to Degree and Polar modes
(see the screen on the right). In this mode, the Y= key allows entry of up to six
polar equations (r as a function of θ).   One could also use Radian mode, adjusting
the values of θmin, θmax, and θstep accordingly (e.g., use 0, 2π, and $\pi/30$
instead of 0, 360, and 5).

For the cardioid, rose, and lemniscate, the window settings shown in the text show these graphs on "square"
windows (see section 11 of the introduction, page 6), so one can see how their proportions compare to
those of a circle.

For the cardioid, the value of θstep does not need to be 5, although that choice
works well for this graph. Too large a choice of θstep produces a graph with
lots of sharp "corners," like the one shown on the right (drawn with θstep=30).
Setting θstep too small, on the other hand, produces a smooth graph, but it is
drawn very slowly. Sometimes it may be necessary to try different values of θstep
to choose a good one.

The lemniscate can be drawn by setting θmin=0 and θmax=180, or θmin=−45 and θmax=45. In fact, with θ
ranging from −45 to 225, the graph of $r_1 = \int(\cos(2\theta))$ (alone) will produce the entire lemniscate. (θstep
should be about 5.)

The rose can be produced by setting θmin=0 and θmax=360, or using any 360°-range of θ values (with
θstep about 5).

Section 8.7   Example 7   (page 755)   Graphing a Polar Equation (Spiral of Archimedes)

To produce this graph on the viewing window shown in the text, the TI-83 must be in Radian mode. (In
Degree mode, it produces the same shape, but magnified by a factor of $180/\pi$ — meaning that the viewing
window needs to be larger by that same factor.)

Section 8.8   Example 1   (page 761)   Graphing a Plane Curve Defined Parametrically

Place the TI-83 in Parametric mode, as the screen on the right shows. In this mode,
the Y= key allows entry of up to six pairs of parametric equations (*x* and *y* as
functions of *t*). No graph is produced unless both functions in the pair are entered
and selected (that is, both equals signs are highlighted).

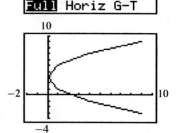

The value of Tstep does not need to be 0.05, although that choice works well
for this graph. Too large a choice of Tstep produces a less-smooth graph,
like the one shown on the right (drawn with Tstep=1). Setting Tstep too
small, on the other hand, produces a smooth graph, but it is drawn very slowly.
Sometimes it may be necessary to try different values of Tstep to choose a
good one.

Section 8.8   Example 3   (page 762)   Graphing a Plane Curve Defined Parametrically

This curve can be graphed in Degree mode with Tmin=0 and Tmax=360, or in Radian mode with Tmax=2π.
In order to see the proportions of this ellipse, it might be good to graph it on a square window. This can be
done most easily by pressing ZOOM 5. On a TI-83, initially with the window settings shown in the text,
this would result in the window $[-6, 6] \times [-4, 4]$.

Section 8.8   Example 5   (page 763)   Graphing a Cycloid

The TI-83 *must* be in Radian mode in order to produce this graph.

Section 8.8   Example 6   (page 764) Simulating Motion with Parametric Equations

---

Section 8.8   Example 8   (page 765) Analyzing the Path of a Projectile

---

Parametric mode is particularly nice for analyzing motion, because one can picture the motion by watching the calculator create the graph, or by pressing $\boxed{\text{TRACE}}$ and watching the motion of the trace cursor. (When tracing in parametric mode, the $\boxed{\blacktriangleright}$ and $\boxed{\blacktriangleleft}$ keys increase and decrease the value of t, and the trace cursor shows the location (x, y) at time t.) Figure 80 illustrates tracing on the projectile path in Example 8. Note that the value of t changes by $\pm$Tstep each time $\boxed{\blacktriangleright}$ or $\boxed{\blacktriangleleft}$ is pressed, so obviously the choice of Tstep affects which points can be traced.

The TI-83's graph styles (see page 8) can be useful, too. The screen on the right shows the three paths for Example 6 being plotted in "ball path" style.

Section 9.1   Example 8   (page 792) Using Curve Fitting to Find an Equation Through Three Points

---

Note that the equation found in this example by algebraic methods can also be found very quickly on the TI-83 by performing a quadratic regression (see page 17) on the three given points.

Section 9.2   Example 1   (page 802) Using the Gauss-Jordan Method

---

Section 9.2   Example 2   (page 804) Using the Gauss-Jordan Method

---

Before describing the row operations, a few words about entering matrices into the TI-83: The TI-83 has ten matrices, named [A] through [J]. One way to enter a matrix is by "storing" the contents on the home screen; an example is shown on the right. "[B]" is typed by pressing $\boxed{\text{MATRX}}\boxed{2}$, while the other square brackets [and] are $\boxed{\text{2nd}}\boxed{\times}$ and $\boxed{\text{2nd}}\boxed{-}$.

Alternatively, press $\boxed{\text{MATRX}}\boxed{\blacktriangleleft}$, then choose one of the matrices, specify the number of rows and columns, and type in the entries, moving around by pressing the arrow keys and $\boxed{\text{ENTER}}$. The screen on the right shows the process of editing matrix [A]. Press $\boxed{\text{2nd}}\boxed{\text{MODE}}$ (QUIT) when finished.

The formats for the matrix row-operation commands are:

- rowSwap(*matrix*,*A*,*B*) produces a new matrix that has row *A* and row *B* swapped.

- row+(*matrix*,*A*,*B*) produces a new matrix with row *A* added to row *B*.

- *row(*number*,*matrix*,*A*) produces a new matrix with row *A* multiplied by *number*.

- *row+(*number*,*matrix*,*A*,*B*) produces a new matrix with row *A* multiplied by *number* and added to row *B* (row *A* is unchanged).

Shown below are examples of each of these operations on the matrix $[E] = \begin{bmatrix} 1 & 4 & 7 \\ 2 & 5 & 8 \\ 3 & 6 & 9 \end{bmatrix}$.

Keep in mind that these row operations leave the matrix [E] untouched. To perform a sequence of row operations, each result must either be stored in a matrix, or use the result variable Ans as the matrix. For example, with [A] equal to the augmented matrix for the system given in this example, the following screens illustrate the initial steps in the Gauss-Jordan method. Note the use of Ans in the last two screens.

As we see in Figure 7(d), the rref command (MATRX ▶ ALPHA MATRX) will do all the necessary row operations at once, making these individual steps seem tedious.

82 *The TI-82 will perform the individual row operations, but does not have the* rref *command.*

Section 9.3   Example 1   (page 813)   Evaluating a 2×2 Determinant

---

Section 9.3   Example 3   (page 816)   Evaluating a 3×3 Determinant

To type "det([A])," press MATRX ▶ 1 (since det is under the MATRX:MATH submenu) then MATRX 1, then) (although this command will work correctly without the closing parenthesis).

The determinant of a 3 × 3 — or larger — matrix is as easy to find with a calculator as that of a 2 × 2 matrix. (At least, it is as easy for the user; the calculator is doing all the work!) Note, however, that trying to find the determinant of a non-square matrix (for example, a 3 × 4 matrix) results in an INVALID DIM error.

Section 9.5   Example 2   (page 832)   Solving a Nonlinear System by Elimination

See the discussion of Example 10 from Section 2.1 on page 15 of this manual for tips on entering formulas like these.

The text shows the intersections as found by the procedure built in to the calculator (described on page 18 of this manual). However, that is somewhat misleading; for these equations, the TI-83 can only find these intersections if the "guesses" supplied by the user are the exact x coordinates of the intersections (that is, -2 and 2). This is because the two circle equations are only valid for $-2 \leq x \leq 2$, while the hyperbola equations are only valid for $x \leq -2$ and $x \geq 2$. Since only ± 2 fall in both of these domains, any guess other than these two values results in a BAD GUESS error.

Section 9.6   Example 1   (page 843)   Graphing a Linear Inequality

With the TI-83, there are two ways to shade above or below a function. The simpler way is to use the "shade above" graph style (see page 8). The screen on the right shows the "shade above" symbol next to Y₁, which produces the graph shown in the text

The other way to shade is the Shade(command, found as option 7 in the 2nd PRGM (DRAW) menu. The format is

Shade(*lower*,*upper*,*min X*,*max X*,*pattern*,*resolution*)

Here *lower* and *upper* are the functions between which the TI-83 will draw the shading (above *lower* and below *upper*). The last four options can be omitted. *min X* and *max X* specify the starting and ending *x* values for the shading. If omitted, the TI-83 uses Xmin and Xmax.

The last two options specify how the shading should look. *pattern* determines the direction of the shading: 1 (vertical—the default), 2 (horizontal), 3 (negative-slope 45°—that is, upper left to lower right), or 4 (positive-slope 45°—that is, lower left to upper right). *resolution* is a positive integer (1,2,3,...) which specifies how dense the shading should be (1 = shade every column of pixels, 2 = shade every other column, 3 = shade every third column, etc.). If omitted, the TI-83 shades every column; i.e., it uses *resolution* = 1.

To produce a graph like the one accompanying Example 1 in the text, the appropriate command (typed on the home screen) would be something like

Shade(-(1/4)X+1,10,-2,6,1,2).

The use of 10 for the *upper* function simply tells the TI-83 to shade up as high as necessary; this could be replaced by any number greater than 4 (the value of Ymax for the viewing window shown). Also, if the function Y₁ had previously been defined as -(1/4)X+1, this command could be shortened to Shade(Y₁,10,-2,6,1,2).

One more useful piece of information: Suppose one makes a mistake in typing the Shade(command (e.g., switching *upper* and *lower*, or using the wrong value of *resolution*), resulting in the wrong shading. The screen on the right, for example, arose from typing Shade(-(1/4)X+1,1,-2,6,1,2). In order to achieve the desired results, the mistake must be erased using the Clr-Draw command (2nd PRGM 1 ENTER). Then—perhaps using deep recall (see page 3)—correct the mistake in the Shade(command and try again.

Section 9.6   Example 2   (page 844)   Graphing Systems of Inequalities

The easiest way to produce (essentially) the same graph as that shown in the text is to use the "shade above" graph style (see page 8). The screen on the right (above) shows the "shade above" symbol next to Y_1 and Y_2, with the results shown on the graph below. When more than one function is graphed with shading, the TI-83 rotates through the four shading patterns (see page 33); that is, it graphs the first with vertical shading, the second with horizontal, and so on. All shading is done with a resolution of 2 (every other pixel).

The Shade command can be used to produce this from the home screen. If $Y_1=(6-X)/2$ and $Y_2=X^2/2$, the commands at right produce the graph shown in the text.

A nicer picture can be created, with a little more work, by making the observation that if y is greater than both $x^2/2$ and $(6-x)/2$, then for any x, y must be greater than the larger of these two expressions. The TI-83 provides a convenient way to find the larger of two numbers with the max(function ([2nd][STAT][◄][2]), so that max(Y_1,Y_2) will return the larger of Y_1 and Y_2, and the functions shown on the [Y=] screen on the right (above) will produce the graph shown below it. (Note the graph style settings: Y_1 and Y_2 display as solid curves, while Y_3 has the "shade above" style.) Similar results would result from the home-screen command Shade(max(Y_1,Y_2),11,-10,10,1,2).

Extension: The table below shows how (using graph styles or home-screen commands) to shade regions that arise from variations on the inequalities in this example, assuming that $Y_1=(6-X)/2$ and $Y_2=X^2/2$. (The results of these commands are not shown here.)

For the system...	or equivalently...	the command would be...
$x < 6 - 2y$ $x^2 < 2y$	$y < (6-x)/2$ $y > x^2/2$	shade below Y_1 and above Y_2, or enter Shade(Y_2,Y_1,-10,10,1,2)
$x > 6 - 2y$ $x^2 > 2y$	$y > (6-x)/2$ $y < x^2/2$	shade above Y_1 and below Y_2, or enter Shade(Y_1,Y_2,-10,10,1,2)
$x < 6 - 2y$ $x^2 > 2y$	$y < (6-x)/2$ $y < x^2/2$	shade below Y_1 and below Y_2, or enter Shade(-10,min(Y_1,Y_2),-10,10,1,2)

Section 9.7	Example 2	(page 854)	Adding Matrices

Section 9.7	Example 3	(page 855)	Subtracting Matrices

Section 9.7	Example 4	(page 856)	Multiplying Matrices by Scalars

Section 9.7	Example 6	(page 859)	Multiplying Matrices

See page 31 for information about matrices on the TI-83.

Section 9.8	Example 1	(page 868)	Verifying the Identity Property of I_3

The `identity` function is option 5 under the MATRX:MATH submenu. To produce the 3×3 identity matrix, for example, press $\boxed{\text{MATRX}}\boxed{\blacktriangleright}\boxed{5}\boxed{3}\boxed{)}\boxed{\text{ENTER}}$.

Section 9.8	Example 2	(page 870)	Finding the Inverse of a 3×3 Matrix

Section 9.8	Example 3	(page 872)	Identifying a Matrix with No Inverse

An inverse matrix is found using $\boxed{x^{-1}}$. For example, to find the inverse of matrix $[\text{A}]$, press $\boxed{\text{MATRX}}\boxed{1}\boxed{x^{-1}}$ $\boxed{\text{ENTER}}$. An error will occur if the matrix is not square, or if it is a singular matrix (as in Example 3).

Section 10.1	Example 1	(page 893)	Graphing a Parabola with Horizontal Axis

Section 10.1	Example 2	(page 894)	Graphing a Parabola with Horizontal Axis

Section 10.2	Example 1	(page 904)	Graphing Ellipses Centered at the Origin

Section 10.3	Example 1	(page 914)	Using Asymptotes to Graph a Hyperbola

See the discussion of Example 10 from Section 2.1 on page 15 of this manual for tips on entering formulas like these.

When entering these formulas, make sure to use enough parentheses, so that operations are performed in the correct order; e.g., for Example 2 of Section 10.1, the formula in Y_1 should look like this:

```
Y₁=-1.5+√((X-.5)/2)
```

Also, when looking at a calculator graph like the one shown in Figure 18 (page 595), keep in mind that the apparent gap between this graph and the x-axis is not really there; it is a flaw that arises from the calculator's method of plotting functions (see discussion on page 8 of this manual).

Section 11.1   Example 3   (page 939)   Modeling Insect Population Growth

One way to produce this sequence (and similar recursively defined sequences) is with the Ans variable, as shown on the right. After pressing $\boxed{1}\boxed{\text{ENTER}}$, then typing the next line and pressing $\boxed{\text{ENTER}}$, we simply press $\boxed{\text{ENTER}}$ over and over to generate successive terms in the sequence. Each time, Ans is replaced by the previous result.

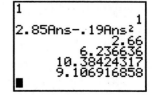

Figure 4 of the text shows a table of values created by putting the TI-83 into Sequence mode, and making the definitions shown on the right. (This screen is accessed with the $\boxed{\text{Y=}}$ key.) The plot in Figure 5(b) was also created in this way; see the discussion of Example 7 from Section 11.3 (below) for details.

Section 11.1   Example 4   (page 941)   Using Summation Notation

Section 11.2   Example 9   (page 953)   Using Summation Notation

The seq(command is item 5 in the $\boxed{\text{2nd}}\boxed{\text{STAT}}\boxed{\blacktriangleright}$ (LIST:OPS) menu. Given a formula a_n for the nth term in a sequence, the command

   seq(*formula*, *variable*, *start*, *end*, *step*)

produces the list $\{a_{start}, a_{start+step}, \ldots, a_{end}\}$. In most uses, the value of *step* is 1, which is the assumed value if this is omitted. The resulting list can have no more than 999 items (or possibly fewer, if memory is low).

Note that *variable* can be any letter—K and I are used in the text, but X is more convenient (since it can be typed with $\boxed{\text{X,T,}\Theta,n}$). Also, in each of the commands shown on the right, the final ", 1)" could be omitted.

The sum command found by pressing $\boxed{\text{2nd}}\boxed{\text{STAT}}\boxed{\blacktriangleleft}\boxed{5}$. sum can be applied to any list—either one of the built-in lists L1,..., L6, or a list created with the seq(command, or a user-defined list.

Section 11.3   Example 7   (page 960)   Summing the Terms of an Infinite Geometric Series

The plot shown in the text can be produced in at least two ways. The first method involves putting the TI-83 in sequence mode, then entering the formula for S_n on the u(n) line of the $\boxed{\text{Y=}}$ screen, as on the right. Note that the graph style is set to "dotted," based on the symbol to the left of u(n). Also, the value of u(nMin)=u(1) must be specified.

Next, press WINDOW and make the settings shown on the right. The viewing window is as shown in the text ($\text{Xmin} = 0$, $\text{Xmax} = 6$, $\text{Ymin} = 0$, $\text{Ymax} = 2$).

Finally, press 2nd ZOOM and check that the first option (which only appears in sequence mode) is set to Time. Pressing GRAPH should produce a plot like that shown in the text.

The second method begins by storing lists in L1 and L2 as shown on the right, so that L1 contains values of n, and L2 contains the corresponding values of S_n. (The slightly shorter command $(1-(1/3)^{\wedge}\text{L1})/(2/3) \rightarrow \text{L2}$ has the same effect as the second command shown.) Note that this approach is less appealing for recursively defined sequences.

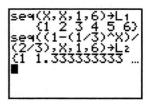

Next press 2nd Y= and 1 and make the settings for a STAT PLOT shown on the right.

Finally, set up the viewing window, and check that nothing else will be plotted; that is, press Y= and make sure that the only thing highlighted is Plot1. Pressing GRAPH should produce a plot like that shown in the text.

Note: When finished with a STAT PLOT, it is a good idea to turn all statistics plots off so that the TI-83 will not attempt to display them the next time GRAPH is pushed. This is most easily done by executing the PlotsOff command, using the key sequence 2nd Y= 4 ENTER.

Section 11.4 Example 1 (page 971)	Evaluating Binomial Coefficients

Section 11.6 Example 4 (page 984)	Using the Permutations Formula

The nCr and nPr commands are found by pressing MATH ◄, then either 3 or 2. (Also located in that menu is the factorial operator "!.")

Section 11.7   Example 6   (page 999)   Finding Probabilities in a Binomial Experiment

Statistical distribution functions are found by pressing 2nd VARS ; binompdf is
option 0 in this menu. As the text explains, the format for this function is

binompdf (*# of trials , prob. of success , # of successes*)

[82] *The TI-82 has no such functions.*

```
DISTR DRAW
4↑tpdf(
5:tcdf(
6:X²pdf(
7:X²cdf(
8:Fpdf(
9:Fcdf(
0↓binompdf(
```

Appendix: Simulating complex numbers with a TI-82

The TI-82 does not support complex numbers; however, it can be made (using matrices) to add, subtract, multiply, and divide complex numbers in rectangular format. Here are the details:

Enter two matrices in the TI-82 by reproducing the screen on the right. The "[" character is ‹2nd›‹×›, and "]" is ‹2nd›‹-›. Enter "[A]" as ‹MATRX›‹1›, and "[B]" as ‹MATRX›‹2› (do not use ‹2nd›‹×› and ‹2nd›‹-› for these brackets). The screen is shown just before pressing ‹ENTER›.

```
[[1,0][0,1]]→[A]
              [[1  0]
               [0  1]]
[[0,1][-1,0]]→[B
]■
```

The matrix [A] stands for "1", and [B] stands for "i." To enter $2 - 3i$, for example, type 2[A]-3[B] (**not** just 2-3[B]). Addition and subtraction are simply performed; the screen on the right shows the computation of the addition problem $(3+5i)+(6-2i)$. To obtain the answer—$9+3i$—simply read the first row of the resulting matrix; the first number is the real part, and the second is the imaginary part.

```
3[A]+5[B]
              [[3   5]
               [-5  3]]
Ans+(6[A]-2[B])
              [[9   3]
               [-3  9]]
■
```

Multiplication is no more complicated than addition and subtraction. Shown below are the calculator entries and outputs for some sample multiplication problems.

$$(2-3i)(3+4i)$$
$$=18-i$$

$$(5-4i)(7-2i)$$
$$=27-38i$$

$$(6+5i)(6-5i)$$
$$=61$$

$$(4+3i)^2$$
$$=7+24i$$

For division problems, do not use the ‹÷› key. Instead, *multiply* by the inverse (‹x⁻¹›) of the denominator.

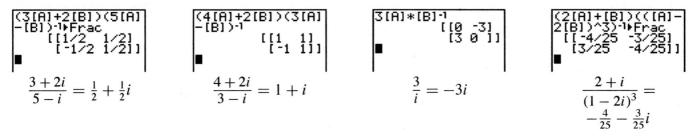

$$\frac{3+2i}{5-i} = \tfrac{1}{2}+\tfrac{1}{2}i$$

$$\frac{4+2i}{3-i} = 1+i$$

$$\frac{3}{i} = -3i$$

$$\frac{2+i}{(1-2i)^3} =$$
$$-\tfrac{4}{25}-\tfrac{3}{25}i$$

Introduction

The information in this section is essentially a summary of material that can be found in the TI-85 manual. Consult that manual for more details.

---

1   Power

To power up the calculator, simply press the ⟨ON⟩ key. This should bring up the "home screen"—a flashing block cursor, and possibly the results of any previous computations that might have been done.

If the home screen does not appear, one may need to adjust the contrast (see the next section).

To turn the calculator off, press ⟨2nd⟩⟨ON⟩ (note that the "second function" of ⟨ON⟩—written in yellow type above the key—is "OFF"). The calculator will automatically shut off if no keys are pressed for several minutes.

---

2   Adjusting screen contrast

If the screen is too dark (all black), decrease the contrast by pressing ⟨2nd⟩ then pressing and holding ⟨▼⟩. If the screen is too light, increase the contrast by pressing ⟨2nd⟩ and then press and hold ⟨▲⟩.

As one adjusts the contrast, the numbers 1 through 9 will appear in the upper right corner of the screen. If the contrast setting reaches 8 or 9, or if the screen never becomes dark enough to see, the batteries should be replaced.

---

3   Replacing batteries

To replace the four AAA batteries, first turn the calculator off (⟨2nd⟩⟨ON⟩), then remove the back cover, remove and replace each battery, replace the back cover, then turn the calculator on again. (After replacing batteries, one may need to adjust the contrast down as described above.)

4   Basic operations

Simple computations are entered in essentially the same way they would be written. For example, to compute $2 + 17 \times 5$, press $\boxed{2}\boxed{+}\boxed{1}\boxed{7}\boxed{\times}\boxed{5}\boxed{\text{ENTER}}$ (the $\boxed{\text{ENTER}}$ key tells the calculator to act on what has been typed). Standard order of operations (including parentheses) is followed.

```
2+17*5
            87
■
```

The result of the most recently entered expression is stored in Ans, which is typed by pressing $\boxed{\text{2nd}}\boxed{(-)}$ (the word "ANS" appears in yellow above this key). For example, $\boxed{5}\boxed{+}\boxed{\text{2nd}}\boxed{(-)}\boxed{\text{ENTER}}$ will add 5 to the result of the previous computation.

```
2+17*5
            87
5+Ans
            92
■
```

After pressing $\boxed{\text{ENTER}}$, the TI-85 automatically produces Ans if the first key pressed is one which requires a number before it; the most common of these are $\boxed{+}$, $\boxed{-}$, $\boxed{\times}$, $\boxed{\div}$, $\boxed{\wedge}$, $\boxed{x^2}$, and $\boxed{\text{STO}\blacktriangleright}$. For example, $\boxed{+}\boxed{5}\boxed{\text{ENTER}}$ would accomplish the same thing as the keystrokes above (that is, it adds 5 to the previous result).

```
2+17*5
            87
5+Ans
            92
Ans+5
            97
■
```

Pressing $\boxed{\text{ENTER}}$ by itself evaluates the previously typed expression again. This can be especially useful in conjunction with Ans. The screen on the right shows the result of pressing $\boxed{\text{ENTER}}$ a second time.

```
2+17*5
            87
5+Ans
            92
Ans+5
            97
           102
■
```

Several expressions can be evaluated together by separating them with colons ($\boxed{\text{2nd}}\boxed{.}$). When $\boxed{\text{ENTER}}$ is pressed, the result of the *last* computation is displayed. The screen shown illustrates the computation $2(5 + 1)^2$.

```
3+2
             5
Ans+1:Ans²:2 Ans
            72
■
```

5   Cursors

When typing, the appearance of the cursor indicates the behavior of the next keypress. When the standard cursor (a flashing solid block, ■) is visible, the next keypress will produce its standard action—that is, the command or character printed on the key itself.

If $\boxed{\text{2nd}}\boxed{\text{DEL}}$ is pressed, the TI-85 is placed in INSERT mode and the standard cursor will appear as a flashing underscore. If the arrow keys ($\boxed{\blacktriangle}$, $\boxed{\blacktriangledown}$, $\boxed{\blacktriangleright}$, $\boxed{\blacktriangleleft}$) are used to move the cursor around within the expression, and the TI-85 is placed in INSERT mode, subsequent characters and commands will be inserted in the line at the cursor's position. When the cursor appears as a block, the TI-85 is in DELETE (or OVERWRITE) mode, and subsequent keypresses will replace the character(s) at the cursor's position. (When the cursor is at the end of the expression, this is irrelevant.)

The TI-85 will return to DELETE mode when any arrow key is pressed. It can also be returned to DELETE mode by pressing $\boxed{\text{2nd}}\boxed{\text{DEL}}$ a second time.

Pressing $\boxed{\text{2nd}}$ causes an arrow to appear in the cursor: ◨ (or an underscored arrow). The next keypress will produce its "second function"—the command or character printed in yellow above the key. (The cursor will then return to "standard.") If $\boxed{\text{2nd}}$ is pressed by mistake, pressing it a second time will return the cursor to standard.

Pressing ALPHA places the letter "A" in the cursor: ▯ (or an underscored "A"). The next keypress will produce the letter or other character printed in blue above that key (if any), and the cursor will then return to standard. Pressing 2nd ALPHA puts the calculator in lowercase ALPHA mode, changing the cursor to ▮ and producing the lowercase version of a letter. Pressing ALPHA twice (or 2nd ALPHA ALPHA) "locks" the TI-85 in ALPHA (or lowercase ALPHA) mode, so that all of the following keypresses will produce characters until ALPHA is pressed again.

6   Accessing previous entries

By pressing 2nd ENTER ("ENTRY"), the last expression can be recalled to the home screen for editing and/or re-execution. This can be useful if a fairly complicated sequence of commands must be executed several times, with slight variations each time.

7   Menus

Keys such as STAT , GRAPH and 2nd 7 (MATRX) bring up a menu line at the bottom of the screen with a variety of options. These options can be selected by pressing one of the function keys (F1 , F2 , . . . , F5). If the menu ends with a small triangle ("▸"), it means that more options are available in this menu, which can be viewed by pressing MORE . Shown is the menu produced by pressing 2nd × (MATH).

This screen shows the result of pressing F1 (the "NUM" option, which lists a variety of numerical functions). Note that the MATH menu still appears (with NUM highlighted) and the bottom line now lists the functions available in this sub-menu—including, for example, the absolute value function (abs), which is accessed by pressing F5 . The command line abs (-5) was typed by pressing F5 ((-) 5) ENTER .

This manual will use (e.g.) MATH:NUM to indicate commands accessed through menus like this. Sometimes the keypresses will be included as well; for this example, it would be 2nd × F1 F5 .

The various commands in these menus are too numerous to be listed here. They will be mentioned as needed in the examples.

One last comment is worthwhile, however. Some functions that may be used frequently are buried several levels deep in the menus, and may take many keystrokes to access. Worse, the location of the function might be forgotten (is it MATH:NUM or MATH:MISC?), necessitating a search through the menus. It is useful to remember three things:

- Any command can be typed one letter at a time, in either upper- or lowercase; e.g., ALPHA ALPHA LOG SIN 6 (-) will type the letters "ABS ", which has the same effect as 2nd × F1 F5 .

- Any command can be found in the CATALOG menu (2nd CUSTOM). Since the commands appear in alphabetical order, it may take some time to locate the desired function (although abs is easy to find!). Pressing any letter key brings up commands starting with that letter (it is not necessary to press ALPHA first); e.g., pressing , shows commands starting with "P."

- Frequently used commands can be placed in the CUSTOM menu, and will then be available simply by pressing CUSTOM. To do this, scroll through the CATALOG to find the desired function, then press F3 (CUSTM) followed by one of F1–F5 to place that command in the CUSTOM menu. In the screen shown, F1 was pressed, so that pressing CUSTOM F1 will type "Solver(." The commands in the MATH:ANGLE menu (2nd × F3), used frequently for problems in this text, could be made more accessible by placing them in this menu.

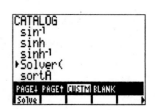

8   Variables

The uppercase letters A through Z, as well as some (but not all) lowercase letters, and also sequences of letters (like "High" or "count") can be used as variables (or "memory") to store numerical values. To store a value, type the number (or an expression) followed by STO▶, then a letter or letters (note that the TI-85 automatically goes into ALPHA mode when STO▶ is pressed), then ENTER. That variable name can then be used in the same way as a number, as demonstrated at right.

Note: The TI-85 interprets 2A as "2 times A"—the "*" symbol is not required (this is consistent with how we interpret mathematical notation). However, the various Texas Instruments calculators are not consistent in how they interpret an expression like 1/2A. The TI-82 and TI-85 perform "implied multiplication" *before* the division (see the screen on the right), while the other (newer) models follow the standard order of operations. Owners of the TI-82 and TI-85 need to aware of this quirk.

9   Setting the modes

By pressing 2nd MORE (MODE), one can change many aspects of how the calculator behaves. For most of the examples in this manual, the "default" settings should be used; that is, the MODE screen should be as shown on the right. Each of the options is described below; consult the TI-85 manual for more details. Changes in the settings are made using the arrows keys and ENTER.

The Normal Sci Eng setting specifies how numbers should be displayed. The screen on the right shows the number 12345 displayed in Normal mode (which displays numbers in the range ±999, 999, 999, 999 with no exponents), Sci mode (which displays all numbers in scientific notation), and Eng mode (which uses only exponents that are multiples of 3). Note: "E" is short for "times 10 to the power," so $1.2345E4 = 1.2345 \times 10^4 = 1.2345 \times 10000 = 12345$.

The Float 012345678901 setting specifies how many places after the decimal should be displayed (the 0 and 1 at the end mean 10 and 11 decimal places). The default, Float, means that the TI-85 should display all non-zero digits (up to a maximum of 12).

Radian Degree indicates whether angle measurements should be assumed to be in radians or degrees. (A right angle measures $\frac{\pi}{2}$ radians, which is equivalent to 90°.) Most of the examples in the text include reminders to set the calculator in the appropriate mode, in cases where this is important.

<u>RectC</u> PolarC specifies whether complex numbers should be displayed in rectangular or polar format. The TI-85's rectangular format is similar to the $a + bi$ format used by the text (beginning in Section 1.3); polar format is not discussed in this text, but is closely related to trigonometric format (see page 69 of this manual).

<u>Func</u> Pol Param DifEq specifies whether formulas to be graphed are functions (y as a function of x), polar equations (r as a function of θ), parametric equations (x and y as functions of t), or differential equations ($Q'(t)$ as a function of Q and t). The text accompanying this manual uses the first three of these settings.

The <u>RectV</u> CylV SphereV setting indicates the default display format for vectors (see page 68 of this manual).

The other two mode settings deal with issues that are beyond the scope of the textbook, and are not discussed here.

A group of settings related to the graph screen are found by pressing $\boxed{\text{GRAPH}}\boxed{\text{MORE}}$ $\boxed{\text{F3}}$ (GRAPH:FORMT). The default settings are shown in the screen on the right, and are generally the best choices for most examples in this book (although the last setting could go either way).

<u>RectGC</u> PolarGC specifies whether graph coordinates should be displayed in rectangular (x, y) or polar (r, θ) format. Note that this choice is independent of the Func Pol Param DifEq mode setting.

The <u>CoordOn</u> CoordOff setting determines whether or not graph coordinates should be displayed.

When plotting a graph, the <u>DrawLine</u> DrawDot setting tells the TI-85 whether or not to connect the individually plotted points. (The text refers to these as Connected and Dot modes.) <u>SeqG</u> SimulG specifies whether individual expressions should be graphed one at a time (sequentially), or all at once (simultaneously).

<u>GridOff</u> GridOn specifies whether or not to display a grid of dots on the graph screen, while <u>AxesOn</u> AxesOff and <u>LabelOff</u> LabelOn do the same thing for the axes and labels (y and x) on the axes.

---

10   Setting the graph window

Pressing $\boxed{\text{GRAPH}}\boxed{\text{F2}}$ brings up the RANGE settings. (**Note:** These are more appropriately called WINDOW settings; they have nothing to do with the "range" of a function, meaning the set of possible output values.) The exact contents of the RANGE (WINDOW) menu vary depending on whether the calculator is in function, polar, parametric, or DifEq mode; below are four examples showing this menu in each of these modes.

Function mode

Polar mode

Parametric mode

DifEq mode

All these menus include the values xMin, xMax, xScl, yMin, yMax, and yScl. When GRAPH F5 (GRAPH) is pressed, the TI-85 will show a portion of the Cartesian (x-y) plane determined by these values. The other settings in this screen allow specification of the smallest, largest, and step values of θ (for polar mode) or t (for parametric mode), or initial conditions for the differential equation.

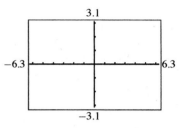

With settings as in the example screens shown above, the TI-85 would display the screen at right: x values from -6.3 to 6.3 (that is, from xMin to xMax), and y values between -3.1 to 3.1 (yMin to yMax). Since xScl = yScl = 1, the TI-85 places tick marks on both axes every 1 unit; thus the x-axis ticks are at -6, -5, ..., 5, and 6, and the y-axis ticks fall on the integers from -3 to 3. This window is called the "decimal" window, and is most quickly set by pressing GRAPH F3 (ZOOM) MORE F4 (ZDECM).

Note: If the graph screen has a menu on the bottom (like that shown on the right), possibly obscuring some important part of the graph, it can be removed by pressing CLEAR. The menu can be restored later by pressing EXIT.

Below are four more sets of window settings, and the graph screens they produce. Note that the first graph on the left has tick marks every 10 units on both axes. The second window is called the "standard" viewing window, and is most quickly set by pressing GRAPH F3 (ZOOM) F4 (ZSTD). The setting yScl = 0 in the final graph means that no tick marks are placed on the y-axis.

11   The graph screen

The TI-85 screen is made up of an array of rectangular dots (pixels) with 63 rows and 127 columns. All the pixels in the leftmost column have x-coordinate xMin, while those in the rightmost column have x-coordinate xMax. The x-coordinate changes steadily across the screen from left to right, which means that the coordinate for the nth column (counting the leftmost column as column 0) must be $xMin + n\Delta x$, where $\Delta x = (xMax - xMin)/126$. Similarly, the nth row of the screen (counting up from the bottom row, which is row 0) has y-coordinate $yMin + n\Delta y$, where $\Delta y = (yMax - yMin)/62$.

It is not necessary to memorize the formulas for Δx and Δy. Should they be needed, they can be determined by pressing GRAPH F5 and then the arrow keys. When pressing ▶ or ◀ successively, the displayed x-coordinate changes by Δx; meanwhile, when pressing ▲ or ▼, the y-coordinate changes by Δy. Alternatively, the values can be found by typing "Δx" and "Δy" on the home screen; this

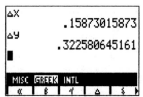

is most easily done by pressing 2nd 0 F2 F4 to access the CHAR:GREEK menu and type the "Δ" character, then typing lowercase x or y. This produces results like those shown on the right; the CHAR:GREEK menu remains on the bottom of the screen.

In the decimal window $\texttt{xMin} = -6.3$, $\texttt{xMax} = 6.3$, $\texttt{yMin} = -3.1$, $\texttt{yMax} = 3.1$, note that $\Delta x = 0.1$ and $\Delta y = 0.1$. Thus, the individual pixels on the screen represent x-coordinates -6.3, -6.2, -6.1, ..., 6.1, 6.2, 6.3 and y-coordinates -3.1, -3, -2.9, ..., 2.9, 3, 3.1. This is where the decimal window gets its name.

It happens that the pixels on the TI-85 screen are about 1.2 times taller than they are wide, so if $\Delta y/\Delta x$ is approximately 1.2 (the exact value is $1.19565\ldots$), the window will be a "square" window (meaning that the scales on the x- and y-axes are equal). For example, the decimal window (with $\Delta y/\Delta x = 1$) is not square, so that one unit on the x-axis is not the same length as one unit on the y-axis. (Specifically, one y-axis unit is about 20% longer than one x-axis unit.)

Any window can be made square be pressing GRAPH F3 (ZOOM) MORE F2 (ZSQR). To see the effect of a square window, observe the two pairs of graphs below. In each pair, the first graph is on the standard window, and the second is on a square window (after choosing ZOOM:ZSQR). The first pair shows the lines $y = 2x - 3$ and $y = 3 - \frac{1}{2}x$; note that on the square window, these lines look perpendicular (as they should). The second pair shows a circle centered at the origin with a radius of 8. On the standard window, this looks like an oval since the screen is wider than it is tall. (The reason for the gaps in the circle will be addressed in the next section.)

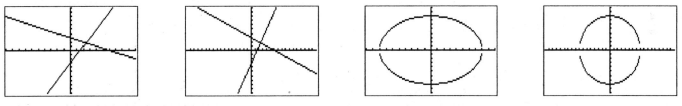

12   Graphing a function

This introductory section only addresses creating graphs in function mode. Procedures for creating parametric and polar graphs are very similar; they are covered beginning on page 70 of this manual, in material related to Chapter 8 of the text. Sequence plotting is covered on page 77 of this manual, in the material related to Section 11.3 from the text.

To see the graph of $y = 2x - 3$, begin by entering the formula into the calculator. This is done by pressing GRAPH F1 to access the "y equals" screen of the calculator. Enter the formula as y1 (or any other yn); note that the letter x can be typed by pressing F1 or x-VAR (as well as 2nd ALPHA +). If another y variable has a formula, position the cursor on that line and press either F4 (DELf—to delete the

function) or F5 (SELCT). The latter has the effect of toggling the "highlighting" for the equals sign "=" for that line (an "unhighlighted" equals sign tells the TI-85 not to graph that formula). In the screen on the right, only y1 will be graphed.

The next step is to choose a viewing window (or "range," in the terminology of the TI-85). See the previous section for more details on this. This example uses the standard window ([GRAPH][F3][F4]).

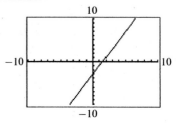

If the graph has not been displayed, press [GRAPH][F5], and the line should be drawn. In order to produce this graph, the TI-85 considers 127 values of x, ranging from xMin to xMax in steps of Δx. For each value of x, it computes the corresponding value of y, then plots that point (x, y) and (if the calculator is in Connected [DrawLine] mode) draws a line between this point and the previous one.

Note: If the line does not appear, or the TI-85 reports an error, double-check all the previous steps. Also, check the mode settings (discussed in section 9, page 44).

Once the graph is visible, the window can be changed using [F2] (RANGE) or [F3] (ZOOM). Pressing [F4] (TRACE) brings up the "trace cursor," and displays the x- and y-coordinates for various points on the line as the [◄] and [►] keys are pressed. Tracing beyond the left or right columns causes the TI-85 to adjust the values of xMin and xMax and redraw the graph.

To graph the function

$$y = \frac{1}{x - 3},$$

enter that formula into the "y equals" screen (note the use of parentheses). As before, this example uses the standard viewing window.

For this function, the TI-85 produces the graph shown on the right. This illustrates one of the pitfalls of the connect-the-dots method used by the calculator: The nearly-vertical line segment drawn at $x = 3$ *should not be there*, but it is drawn because the calculator connects the points

$$x = 2.85714, \ y = -6.99999 \ \text{and} \ x = 3.01587, \ y = 62.99999.$$

Calculator users must learn to recognize these flaws in calculator-produced graphs.

The graph of a circle centered at the origin with radius 8 (shown on the square window ZOOM:ZSTD - ZOOM:ZSQR) shows another problem that arises from connecting the dots. When $x = -8.093841$, y is undefined, so no point is plotted (that is, there is no point on this circle that has x-coordinate less than -8, or greater than 8). The next point plotted on the upper half of the circle is $x = -7.824046$ and $y = 1.668619$; since no point had been plotted for the previous x-coordinate, this is not connected to anything, so there appears to be a gap between the circle and the x-axis. The calculator is not "smart" enough to know that the graph should extend from -8 to 8.

13   Adding programs to the TI-85

The TI-85's capabilities can be extended by downloading or entering programs into the calculator's memory. Instructions for writing a program are beyond the scope of this manual, but programs written by others and downloaded from the Internet (or obtained as printouts) can be transferred to the calculator in one of three ways:

1. If one TI-85 already has a program, it can be transferred to another using the calculator-to-calculator link cable. To do this, first make sure the cable is firmly inserted in both calculators. On the sending calculator, press [2nd][x-VAR] (LINK), then [F1][F2] (SEND:PRGM), and then select (by using the [▲] and [▼] keys and [F2]) the program(s) to be transferred. *Before* pressing [F1] (SEND) on the sending calculator, prepare the receiving calculator by pressing [2nd][x-VAR][F2], and *then* press [F1] on the sending calculator.

2. If a computer with the TI-Graph Link is available, and the program file is on that computer (e.g., after having been downloaded from the Internet), the program can be transferred to the calculator using the TI Graph Link software. This transfer is done in a manner similar to the calculator-to-calculator transfer described above; specific instructions can be found in the documentation that accompanies the Graph Link software. (They are not given here because of slight differences between platforms and software versions.)

3. View a listing of the program and type it in manually. (**Note:** Even if the TI-Graph Link cable is not available, the Graph Link software can be used to view program listings on a computer.) While this is the most tedious method, studying programs written by others can be a good way to learn programming. To enter a program, start by choosing [PRGM][F2] (EDIT), then type a name for the new program (up to eight letters, like "QuadForm" or "Midpoint")—note that the TI-85 is automatically put into ALPHA mode. Then type each command in the program, and press [2nd][EXIT] (QUIT) to return to the home screen when finished.

To run the program, make sure there is nothing on the current line of the home screen, then press [PRGM][F1], select the program using one of the keys [F1]–[F5] and [MORE] (a sample screen is shown; only the first four to six characters of each program name are shown), and press [ENTER]. If the program was entered manually (option 3 above), errors may be reported; in that case, choose GOTO, correct the mistake and try again.

Programs can be found at many places on the Internet, including:

- http://www.awl.com/lhs—the Web site for the text;

- http://www.bluffton.edu/~nesterd—the Web site of the author of this manual;

- http://tifaq.calc.org—A "Frequently Asked Questions" page maintained by Ray Kremer; and

- http://www.ticalc.org.

Examples

Here are the details for using the TI-85 for several of the examples from the textbook. Also given are the keystrokes necessary to produce some of the commands shown in the text's examples. In some cases, some suggestions are made for using the calculator more efficiently.

Throughout this section, it is assumed that the textbook is available for reference. The problems from the text are not restated here, and there are frequent references to the calculator screens shown in the text.

Section R.1   Example 2   (page 4)   Evaluating Exponential Expressions

This example discusses how to evaluate 4^3, $(-6)^2$, -6^2, $4 \cdot 3^2$, and $(4 \cdot 3)^2$.

To evaluate 4^3 with a TI-85, type $\boxed{4}\boxed{\wedge}\boxed{3}\boxed{\text{ENTER}}$; the TI-85 does not have a super-scripted 3 for cubing. Only squaring and reciprocating—that is, the powers 2 and -1—can be displayed as superscripts (using $\boxed{x^2}$ and $\boxed{\text{2nd}}\boxed{\text{EE}}$, respectively). All other powers must use the $\boxed{\wedge}$ key. The other computations in this example are straightforward with the TI-85, except for this *caveat*: For $(-6)^2$ and -6^2, one must use the $\boxed{(-)}$ key rather than the $\boxed{-}$ key to enter "negative 6." In the screen shown, the second line was typed as $\boxed{(}\boxed{(-)}\boxed{6}\boxed{)}\boxed{x^2}$, while the fourth line was $\boxed{(}\boxed{-}\boxed{6}\boxed{)}\boxed{x^2}$. When $\boxed{\text{ENTER}}$ is pressed, the fourth line produces a syntax error—the calculator's way of saying that the line makes no sense.

```
4^3
              64
(-6)²
              36
-6²
             -36
(-6)²■
```

Section R.1   Example 3   (page 5)   Using Order of Operations

Using the calculator for parts (a) and (b) of this example is straightforward; the expressions are entered as printed. For (c) and (d), we have the expressions

$$\frac{4+3^2}{6-5\cdot 3} \quad \text{and} \quad \frac{-(-3)^3 + (-5)}{2(-8) - 5(3)}.$$

Entering these on the TI-85 requires us to add some additional parentheses to make sure the correct order of operations is followed.

Proper entry of the expression in (d) is shown on the right, in two different forms. The second illustrates some time-saving that can be done in keying in such expressions: The parentheses around -5 in the numerator were omitted, and the denominator $2(-8) - 5(3)$ was typed in as $\boxed{2}\boxed{\times}\boxed{(-)}\boxed{8}\boxed{-}\boxed{5}\boxed{\times}\boxed{3}$—the parentheses were exchanged for the multiplication symbol. It would be fine to type the expression unchanged, but the extra parentheses make it somewhat harder to read (and also mean more opportunities to make a mistake).

```
(-(-3)^3+(-5))/(2(-8)
-5(3))▶Frac
             -22/31
(-(-3)^3+-5)/(2*-8-5*
3)▶Frac
             -22/31
■
```

The screen shown above also illustrates the command ▶Frac at the end of the line. This command (which simply means "display the result of this computation as a fraction, if possible") is available in the MATH:MISC menu ($\boxed{\text{2nd}}\boxed{\times}\boxed{\text{F5}}\boxed{\text{MORE}}\boxed{\text{F1}}$). This is a useful enough command that one may wish to put it in the CUSTOM menu (see page 44).

Section R.2   Example 2   (page 18)   Evaluating Absolute Value

---

Section R.2   Example 3   (page 18)   Finding Absolute Values of Sums and Differences

The absolute value function abs is found in the MATH:NUM menu ([2nd][×][F1][F5]).
See the discussion of typing commands on page 43; the screen on the right illustrates that the TI-85 does not pay attention to upper- and lowercase.

```
abs (-5/8)▶Frac
                5/8
ABS (-5/8)▶Frac
                5/8
aBs (-5/8)▶Frac
                5/8
■
```

Section R.6   Example 4   (page 58)   Using the Definition of $a^{1/n}$

In evaluating these fractional exponents with a calculator, some time can be saved
by entering fractions as decimals. The screen on the right performs the computations for (a), (b) and (c) with fewer keystrokes than entering, for example,
$36^{\wedge}(1/2)$. (Of course, as noted in Section R.7 of the text, $36^{1/2} = \sqrt{36}$, which
requires even fewer keystrokes.)

```
36^.5
            6
-100^.5
           -10
625^.25
            5
■
```

Note for (d), the parentheses around -1296 cannot be omitted: The text observes
that this is not a real number, but the calculator will display a real result if the
parentheses are left out. (See also the next example.) For (e), the decimal equivalent of $1/3$ is $0.\overline{3}$, which can be entered as a sufficiently long string of 3s (at least
12). The last line shows a better way to do this; the TI-85's order of operations

```
-1296^.25
            -6
(-27)^.333333333333
            -3
(-27)^3-1
            -3
■
```

is such that 3^{-1} is evaluated before the other exponentiation. This method would also work for the other
computations; e.g., (a) could be entered [3][6][^][2][2nd][EE].

Section R.6   Example 5   (page 59)   Using the Definition of $a^{m/n}$

For (f), attempting to evaluate $(-4)^{5/2}$ will produce the result shown on the right.
This is the TI-85's way of displaying complex numbers (which are discussed in
the text beginning in Section 1.3); the result $(0,32)$ would be written as $0 + 32i$
in the format used by the text.

```
(-4)^(5/2)
            (0,32)
■
```

Section R.7   Example 1   (page 65)   Evaluating Roots

Aside from the square root function $\int$ ([2nd][x²]), the TI-85 has an "x-root" function ($^x\!\sqrt{\ }$), found in the
MATH:MISC menu ([2nd][×][F5][MORE][F4]). For example, "3$^x\!\sqrt{\ }$ 1000" would compute $\sqrt[3]{1000}$ for part (d) . It is
worth noting that fourth roots can be typed in more efficiently using two square roots, since $\sqrt[4]{a} = a^{1/4} = (a^{1/2})^{1/2} = \sqrt{a^{1/2}} = \sqrt{\sqrt{a}}$.

Section 1.1   Example 1   (page 87)   Solving a Linear Equation

The TI-85 offers several approaches to solving (or confirming a solution to) an equation. Aside from graphical approaches to solving equations (which are discussed later, on page 58), here are some non-graphical (numerical) approaches: As illustrated on the right, the TI-85's Solver function (found in the CATALOG) attempts to find a value of x that makes the given expression equal to 0, given a guess (5, in this case). The solution is stored in the variable x (or whatever variable is used in the equation), but as the screen shows, this solution is not automatically displayed. A colon can be used to place the two lines shown on a single line.

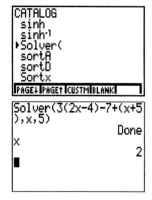

For the equations in this section, the "guess" value does not affect the result, but for equations in later sections, different guesses might produce different results. Full details on how to use this function can be found in the TI-85 manual.

Since it is difficult to access the Solver command, it might be a good idea to place Solver in the CUSTOM menu (see page 44), or to use the "interactive solver" built-in to the TI-85. This feature is found by pressing 2nd GRAPH.

Solver begins with the first screen below (a), requesting an equation, which must include at least one variable. (The "eqn:" line might not be blank, since Solver remembers the most recent equation entered into it.) The menu at the bottom of the screen lists any user-defined variables in the calculator's memory. The expression for this example is shown in screen (b); use ALPHA STO▶ to type the equals sign. Pressing ENTER or ▼ brings up screen (c). Type the guess (this example uses 5), then press F5 (SOLVE) and the TI-85 seeks a solution near 5, which is reported in screen (d). (Make sure the cursor is on the "x=" line when F5 is pressed.)

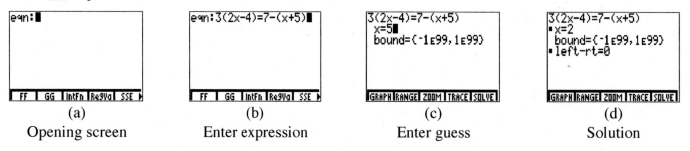

(a)	(b)	(c)	(d)
Opening screen	Enter expression	Enter guess	Solution

From screen (c) or (d), pressing ▲ returns to screen (b), so that the equation can be edited.

The Solver can also be used with equations containing more than one variable; simply provide values for all but one variable, then place the cursor on the line containing the variable for which a value is needed and press F2.

Note: In this example, we learned how the TI-85 can be used to support an analytic solution. But the TI-85 and any other graphing calculator also can be used for solving problems when an analytic solution is **not** possible—that is, when one cannot solve an equation "algebraically." This is often the case in many "real-life" applications, and is one of the best arguments for the use of graphing calculators.

Section 1.3	Example 1	(page 109)	Writing $\sqrt{-a}$ as $i\sqrt{a}$

Section 1.3	Example 2	(page 109)	Finding Products and Quotients Involving Negative Radicands

Section 1.3	Example 3	(page 110)	Simplifying a Quotient Involving a Negative Radicand

The TI-85 does these computations almost as shown in the text, except that it reports the results differently. The screen on the right illustrates the output from the computations for parts (b) and (d) of Example 2. The TI-85 uses the format (a, b) for the complex number $a + bi$; whenever the TI-85 does a computation involving square roots of negative numbers, it reports the results in this format *even if the result is real*. Thus $(-7.74596669241, 0)$ represents the real number $-7.74596669241 \approx -2\sqrt{15}$, and $(0, 1.41421356237)$ is $i\sqrt{2}$.

While the calculator always reports complex *results* in this format*, it can recognize *input* typed in using the text's format by first defining a variable i as the complex number $(0, 1) = 0 + 1i$. Shown on the right is a computation using this definition. One could also use I (uppercase), which can be typed with one less keystroke, but i will be used in these examples.

*Results can also be reported in "polar format" by changing the "RectC PolarC" mode setting, but this format is even further removed from the $a + bi$ format used in the text.

Section 1.3	Example 4	(page 110)	Adding and Subtracting Complex Numbers

Section 1.3	Example 5	(page 111)	Multiplying Complex Numbers

Section 1.3	Example 6	(page 112)	Simplifying Powers of i

Section 1.3	Example 7	(page 113)	Dividing Complex Numbers

Using the variable i defined to be $(0, 1)$ — as was described in the previous example — computations like these can be done in a manner similar to those illustrated in the text's calculator screens. The screens on the right show (in the TI-85's format) the same results as those in the text accompanying Examples 5 and 7.

| Section 1.4 | Example 5 | (page 120) | Using the Quadratic Formula (Real Solutions) |

| Section 1.4 | Example 6 | (page 120) | Using the Quadratic Formula (Nonreal Complex Solutions) |

| Section 1.4 | Example 7 | (page 121) | Solving a Cubic Equation |

The TI-85 can solve quadratic and cubic equations (as well as higher-degree polynomial equations) using its built-in polynomial solver, accessed through [2nd] [PRGM] (POLY). This first prompts the user for the "order" (degree) of the polynomial, meaning the highest power of x. For the quadratic equations of Examples 5 and 6, this should be 2; for Example 7, the order is 3.

Pressing [ENTER] then brings up the screen on the right, requesting the coefficients of the equation. Note that the top line of the screen contains a reminder that the expression must be equal to 0. The menu at the bottom indicates that [F1] will clear the coefficients, while [F5] solves the equation.

Pressing [F5] reports the solutions in much the same way as the program shown in the text (although it does not specify that the roots are real). [F1] allows the user to change the coefficient values (that is, it goes back to the previous screen), and [F2] provides a way to store the coefficients in a variable (as a list).

For Example 6, the TI-85 reports the solutions (using its complex number format) as approximately $0.25 \pm 1.3919i$ — the decimal equivalents of the answers given in the text. Note in the results for Example 7, the real solution -2 is displayed as $(-2, 0) = -2 + 0i$; if any of the solutions are complex, the TI-85 displays all of them in its complex format.

| Section 1.7 | Example 1 | (page 147) | Solving a Linear Inequality |

| Section 1.7 | Example 2 | (page 148) | Solving a Linear Inequality |

Shown is one way to visualize the solution to inequalities like these. The inequality symbols $>$, $<$, $\geq$, $\leq$ are found in the TEST menu ([2nd] [2nd] [×]). The TI-85 responds with 1 when a statement is true and 0 for false statements. This is why the graph of y1 appears as it does: For values of x less than 4, the inequality is true (and so y1 equals 1), and for $x \geq 4$, the inequality is false (and y1 equals 0). Note that this picture does *not* help one determine what happens when $x = 4$.

Section 1.7   Example 3   (page 149)   Solving a Three-Part Inequality

To see a "picture" of this inequality like the one shown for the previous two examples requires a little additional work. Setting y1=-2<5+3x<20 will *not* work correctly. Instead, one must enter

    y1=(-2<5+3x)(5+3x<20)

which will produce the desired results: A function that equals 1 between $-\frac{7}{3}$ and 5, is equals 0 elsewhere.

Section 1.7   Example 5   (page 150)   Solving a Quadratic Inequality

Section 1.7   Example 6   (page 151)   Solving a Quadratic Inequality

Section 1.7   Example 8   (page 154)   Solving a Rational Inequality

Section 1.7   Example 9   (page 155)   Solving a Rational Inequality

The methods described above can also be applied to these inequalities.

Extension: Can the calculator be used to solve the inequality $x^2 + 6x + 9 > 0$? Yes—if it is used carefully. Shown is the graph of the expression $x^2 + 6x + 9 > 0$. This suggests that the inequality is true for all x; that is, the solution set is $(-\infty, \infty)$.

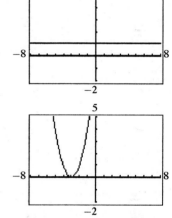

This conclusion is **not correct**: The graph of $y = x^2 + 6x + 9$ (without "> 0") touches the x-axis at $x = -3$, which means that this must be excluded from the solution set, since "> 0" means the graph must be above (not on) the x-axis. The correct solution set is $(-\infty, -3) \cup (-3, \infty)$.

This example should serve as a warning: Sometimes, the TI-85 will mislead you. When possible, try to confirm the calculator's answers in some way.

Section 1.8   Example 1   (page 161)   Solving Absolute Value Equations

The "solver" features described on page 54 of this manual can be used for these equations, too. Recall that abs is entered as [2nd][×][F1][F5].

Section 2.1   Example 5   (page 186)   Using the Midpoint Formula

The TI-85 can do midpoint computations nicely by putting coordinates in parentheses, as shown on the right. (The TI-85 interprets an ordered pair such as (8,-4) as the complex number $8 - 4i$, but since adding two complex numbers means adding their corresponding parts, the computations are done in the correct way to find the midpoint.)

Section 2.1   Example 10   (page 190)   Graphing a Circle

The text suggests graphing y1=4+∫(36-(x+3)²) and y2=4-∫(36-(x+3)²). Here are three options to speed up entering these formulas:

- After typing the formula in y1, move the cursor to y2 and press [2nd][STO▶] (RCL), then type y1 [ENTER] (note that [F2] will produce the lowercase y). This will "recall" the formula of y1, placing that formula in y2. Now edit this formula, changing the first "+" to a "−."

- After typing the formula in y1, enter y2=8-y1. This produces the desired results, since $8 - \text{y1} = 8 - (4 + \sqrt{36 - (x+3)^2}) = 8 - 4 - \sqrt{36 - (x+3)^2} = 4 - \sqrt{36 - (x+3)^2}$.

- Enter the single formula y1=4+{-1,1}∫(36-(x+3)²). (The curly braces { and } are [F1] and [F2] in the LIST menu, [2nd][-]). When a list (like {-1,1}) appears in a formula, it tells the TI-85 to graph this formula several times, using each value in the list.

The window chosen in the text is a square window (see Section 11 of the introduction of this chapter), so that the graph looks like a circle. (On a non-square window, the graph would look like an ellipse—that is, a distorted circle.) Note, however, that on the TI-85, this window is not square. Other square windows would also produce a "true" circle, but some will leave gaps similar to those circles shown in Sections 11 and 12 of the introduction (pages 46–47). Shown is the same circle on the square window produced by "squaring up" the standard window— GRAPH:ZOOM:ZSTD - ZOOM:ZSQR.

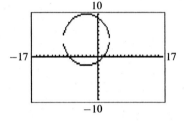

Section 2.2   Example 6   (page 205)   Using Function Notation

Section 2.2   Example 7   (page 205)   Using Function Notation

The TI-85 has a feature that is similar to function notation. Enter the function $(-x^2 + 5x - 3)$ in y1 (or any other function). Return to the home screen, and type either of the expressions on the right. The first simply places 2 in x then computes y1 (which always returns the value based on the current value of x). The second uses the evalF ("evaluate formula") function, found in the CALC menu ([2nd][÷]), which requires three arguments: the expression to be evaluated, the variable, and the value to be used in place of that variable. The result shown on the screen

agrees with (a) in the text. [The more natural entry "y1(2)" does not work; it is interpreted as (the value of y1 with the current value of x) times 2.]

    The TI-85 is less helpful if asked to evaluate expressions like those given in Example 6(b) or Example 7. For example, "q→x:y1" or "evalF(y1,x,q)" produces an error message or an unpredictable result (depending on how the variable q is defined), rather than the desired result $-q^2 + 5q - 3$.

Section 2.3   Example 3   (page 215)   Graphing a Vertical Line

The text notes that such a line is not a function; therefore, it cannot be graphed by entering the equation on the GRAPH:y(x)= screen. However, the TI-85 does provide a fairly straightforward method of graphing vertical lines using the Vert command.

From the home screen, type the Vert command one letter at a time, or using the function catalog (see page 44), then type the x-coordinate of the line. When ENTER is pressed, the line will be drawn.

Alternatively, the vertical line can be drawn "interactively" if the VERT command is accessed through the GRAPH:DRAW menu (GRAPH MORE F2 F3). This allows the user to move the cursor (and the vertical line) to the desired position using the ◀ and ▶ keys. Pressing ENTER places the line at that location, then allows more lines to be drawn. (Press GRAPH to finish drawing vertical lines.) Note that since $x = -3$ does not correspond to a column of pixels on the screen (see page 46), the vertical line is actually located at $x \approx -3.0159$, but the appearance on the screen is the same as if it were at $x = -3$.

Section 2.4   Example 5   (page 230)   Finding Equations of Parallel and Perpendicular Lines

In the discussion following this example (on page 231), the text notes that the lines from part (b) do not appear to be perpendicular unless they are plotted on a square window. See Section 11 of the introduction of this chapter (page 47) for more information about square windows.

Section 2.4   Example 6   (page 232)   Finding an Equation of a Line That Models Data

Section 2.4   Example 7   (page 233)   Finding a Linear Equation That Models Data

Aside from the methods described in these two examples, the text refers to the technique of linear regression on page 235. Figure 48 illustrates the steps on a TI-83; here is a more detailed description of the process on a TI-85 (using the data of Example 7).

Given a set of data pairs (x, y), the TI-85 can find various formulas (including linear and quadratic, as well as more complex formulas) that approximate the relationship between x and y. These formulas are called "regression formulas."

The first step in determining the regression formula is to enter the data into the TI-85. This is done by pressing STAT F2, producing the screen on the right, requesting which lists should be used to store the values of x and y. The defaults, xStat and yStat, can be selected by pressing ENTER twice.

This brings up the data-entry screen shown on the right. If any data (x and y values) are listed here, it is best to press F5 to clear the old data. Then enter each pair (x, y), with the year as x and the percentage of women as y.

When all data is entered, the screen will look like the one on the right. Note that the last values are x_{10} and y_{10}, so ten pairs have been entered, and the table in the text lists ten pairs. It is a good idea to check the number of entries, and also to proofread the numbers entered.

Now to do the computation, press EXIT F1 (CALC), at which point the calculator once again asks which lists contain the data (as shown on the right). As before, press ENTER twice to accept the defaults.

The bottom of the screen now lists the various options for the type of calculation to be done. We want to do a linear regression, which is F2 (LINR).

The results of the LINR are shown on the right. These numbers agree (after rounding) with those in the text, except that the roles of a and b have been switched; these numbers are for a model of the form y=a+bx, rather than y=ax+b.

Section 2.4   Example 8   (page 235)   Solving an Equation with a Graphing Calculator

The text illustrates a graphical process for solving the equation $-2x - 4(2-x) = 3x+4$; in this discussion, we will show two graphical methods for solving the equation $\frac{1}{2}x - 6 = \frac{3}{4}x - 9$. (The answer is $x = 12$.)

The first method is the **intersection** method. To begin, set up the TI-85 to graph the left side of the equation as y1, and the right side as y2. **Note:** Putting the fractions in parentheses ensures no mistakes with order of operations. This is important for the TI-85, since it performs implied multiplication before division; see section 8 of the introduction, page 44.

We are looking for an x value that will make the left and right sides of this equation equal to each other, which corresponds to the x-coordinate of the point of intersection of these two graphs.

After selecting a viewing window which shows the point of intersection—in this example, $[-15, 15] \times [-10, 10]$ is a convenient choice—the TI-85 can automatically locate this point using GRAPH:MATH:ISECT (GRAPH MORE F1 MORE F5). Use ▲, ▼ and ENTER to specify which two functions to use (in this case, the only two being displayed). After pressing ENTER to select the second function, the TI-85 will try to find an intersection of the two graphs. The screens below illustrate these steps.

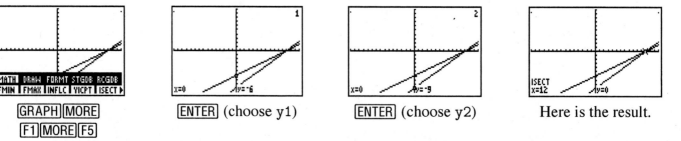

GRAPH MORE   ENTER (choose y1)   ENTER (choose y2)   Here is the result.
F1 MORE F5

The x-coordinate of this point of intersection is calculated to 14 digits of accuracy, so if the solution were some less "convenient" number (say, $\sqrt{3}$ or $1/\pi$), we would have an answer that would be accurate enough for nearly any computation.

Note: An approximation for the point of intersection can be found simply by moving the TRACE cursor as near the intersection as possible. The amount of error can be minimized by "zooming in" on the graph. This is the only method available for graphing calculators such as the TI-81.

The second graphical approach is to use the *x*-**intercept method**, which seeks the *x*-coordinate of the point where a graph crosses the *x*-axis. Specifically, we want to know where the graph of y1−y2 crosses the *x*-axis, where y1 and y2 are as defined above. This is because the equation $\frac{1}{2}x - 6 = \frac{3}{4}x - 9$ can only be true when $\frac{1}{2}x - 6 - \left(\frac{3}{4}x - 9\right) = 0$. (This is the approach illustrated in the text for Example 8.)

To find this *x*-intercept, begin by defining y3=y1−y2 on the GRAPH:y(x)= screen. We could do this by re-typing the formulas entered for y1 and y2, but having typed those formulas once, it is more efficient to do this as shown on the right. The simplest way to type "y1" and "y2" is to use the [F2] key to produce "y." Note that y1 and y2 have been "de-selected" so that they will not be graphed (see section 12 of the introduction, page 47).

We must first select a viewing window which shows the *x*-intercept; we again use [−15, 15] × [−10, 10]. The TI-85 can automatically locate this point with the GRAPH:MATH:ROOT ([GRAPH][MORE][F1][F3]) feature ("root" is a synonym for "*x*-intercept"). Simply select the function for which a root is sought, and after pressing [ENTER], the TI-85 will attempt to find that root. (Provided there is only one root between the bounds, and the function is "well-behaved"—meaning it has some nice properties like continuity—the calculator will find it.) The screens on the right illustrate these steps.

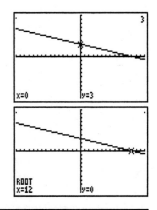

Section 2.5   Example 2   (page 246)   Graphing Piecewise-Defined Functions

---

The text shows two methods for entering piecewise-defined functions on the TI-85. Recall that the inequality symbols >, <, ≥, ≤ are found in the TEST menu ([2nd][2]). The use of DOT (DrawDot) mode is not crucial to the graphing process, as long as one remembers that vertical line segments connecting the "pieces" of the graph (in this case, at *x* = 2) are not really part of the graph.

The advantage of the method used in (b)—placing the piecewise definition in a single formula—is that y1 will act exactly like the function *f*. For example, to evaluate *f*(5) in (a), one would first have to check which formula to use (y1 or y2). To evaluate *f*(5) in (b), simply enter 5→x:y1. Also, when a single formula is used, TRACE will properly show the behavior of the function as the trace cursor moves left and right.

Extension: Use a similar procedure for more complicated piecewise-defined functions, such as

$$f(x) = \begin{cases} 4 - x^2 & \text{if } x < -1 \\ 2 + x & \text{if } -1 \leq x \leq 4 \\ -2 & \text{if } x > 4 \end{cases}$$

shown here in DOT (DrawDot) mode on the standard viewing window. It does not work to define y1=(4−x²)(x<−1)+(2+x)(−1≤x≤4)+(−2)(x>4). Instead, use

y1=(4−x²)(x<−1)+(2+x)(−1≤x)(x≤4)+(−2)(x>4)

Section 2.5   Example 3   (page 247)   Graphing a Greatest Integer Function

We wish to graph the step function $y = [\![\frac{1}{2}x + 1]\!]$. This is entered on the TI-85
as shown on the right (any one of y1, y2, or y3). int is found in the MATH:NUM
menu, [2nd][×][F1].

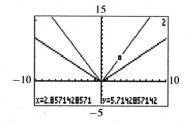

Section 2.6   Example 1   (page 253)   Stretching or Shrinking a Graph

---

Section 2.6   Example 2   (page 254)   Reflecting a Graph Across an Axis

---

Section 2.6   Example 6   (page 259)   Translating a Graph Vertically

---

Section 2.6   Example 7   (page 260)   Translating a Graph Horizontally

Note that the TI-85 does not support varying the thickness of graphs; all graphs
appear the same. However, when two or more graphs are drawn, the TRACE
feature can be used to determine which graphs correspond to which formulas:
By pressing [▲] and [▼], the trace cursor jumps from one graph to another, and
the upper right corner displays the number of the current formula. On the right,
the trace cursor is on graph 2—that is, the graph of $g(x) = 2|x|$.

Also note that the TI-85 does not support split-screen mode, which was used to produce the screens shown
in the text (with a graph above, and the "y equals" screen below).

Section 2.7   Example 5   (page 272)   Evaluating Composite Functions

Because the TI-85 does not understand function notation, it would compute
y1(y2(2)) as (the current value of y1) times (the current value of y2) times 2.
These composite function values can be found by more roundabout approaches.
The screen on the right shows two methods for (a), but only the shorter method
for (b).

Compositions like $y = f \circ g(x)$ can be graphed by adapting the second (longer) method shown above: Set
y3=evalF(y1,x,y2).

Section 3.1   Example 1   (page 295)   Graphing Quadratic Functions

---

Section 3.1   Example 2   (page 297)   Graphing a Parabola by Completing the Square

---

Section 3.1   Example 3   (page 298)   Graphing a Parabola by Completing the Square

The TI-85 can automatically locate the vertex of the parabola (to a reasonable degree of accuracy). We
illustrate this procedure for the function in Example 1(c). After defining y1=-(1/2)(x-4)²+3 and choosing
a suitable window, go to the GRAPH:MATH menu ([MORE][F1]), shown on the first screen below. Pressing [MORE]
again brings up the menu shown in the second screen; choose [F1] for an upward-opening parabola, or [F2]

for a downward-opening parabola (like the one in this example). Then (see the third screen below) the TI-85 prompts the user to select the function for which a maximum (or minimum) is to be sought (in this case there is only the one). When ENTER is pressed, the TI-85 will try to find a "peak" (or a "valley") on the graph between xMin and xMax, which is reported on the last screen. Note that the *x*-coordinate rounds to 4; the degree of accuracy depends on the value of tol set on the TOLER screen (2nd CLEAR). The results shown arose from tol=1E-6.

GRAPH MORE F1   MORE F2   ENTER   . . . *and voilà!*

Note: Some functions may have two or more high points (called "local maxima") or low points ("local minima"). Since the TI-85 seeks the highest peak (or lowest valley) between xMin and xMax, one can find the coordinates of these other points by changing xMin and xMax, but they can also be found by using LOWER and UPPER (options F1 and F2 in the GRAPH:MATH menu). These let the user specify lower and/or upper bounds (numbers that are, respectively, less than and greater than the location of the high or low point), and cause the TI-85 to search between those bounds. In the screen on the right, for example, the triangle ▸ indicates the location of a user-specified lower bound; when MATH:FMAX was selected, the TI-85 looked for a peak between this lower bound and xMax, with the results shown.

Section 3.1   Example 6   (page 302)   Modeling the Number of Hospital Outpatient Visits

See page 57 for information about using the TI-85 for regression computations. On the TI-85, a quadratic regression is called a "P2REG" (polynomial-degree-2 regression.)

Section 3.2   Example 3   (page 317)   Deciding whether a Number is a Zero

Page 56 of this manual describes how to evaluate functions on the TI-85; this method works equally well with complex numbers, as the screen on the right shows. This screen assumes that i has been defined as (0, 1), as described on page 53; the command (1,2)→x:y3 would also work. While the TI-85 does not report the value of this last computation as 0, it lends support to the belief that $1 + 2i$ is a zero since both the real and complex parts are very small. (The difference is due to roundoff error.)

Section 3.3   Example 6   (page 327)   Finding All Zeros of a Polynomial Given One Zero

---

Section 3.4   Example 7   (page 340)   Approximating Real Zeros of a Polynomial Function

The TI-85's POLY feature (described on page 54) can determine *all* the zeros—not just the real zeros. The result of using this feature is shown on the right for Example 6, using the TI-85's complex number format.

```
a₄x^4+...+a₁x+a₀=0
x1■(3,0)
x2=(2,0)
x3=(1,1)
x4=(1,-1)


COEFS STOa
```

The TI-85 does not have a built-in capability to generate tables like the one shown in the screen on the right in Figure 32. However, calculator programs can be downloaded from the Internet to do this; see Section 13 of the introduction (page 48) for details about calculator programs.

Section 3.5   Example 2   (page 352)   Graphing a Rational Function

Note that this function is entered as y1=2/(1+x), **not** y1=2/1+x.

The issue of incorrectly drawn asymptotes is also addressed in Section 12 of the introduction to this chapter (page 47). Changing the window to xMin $= -5$ and xMax $= 3$ (or any choice of xMin and xMax which has -1 halfway between them) eliminates this vertical line because it forces the TI-85 to attempt to evaluate the function at $x = -1$. Since f is not defined at -1, it cannot plot a point there, and as a result, it does not attempt to connect the dots across the "break" in the graph.

Section 4.1   Example 7   (page 396)   Finding the Inverse of a Function with a Restricted Domain

Note that Figure 10 shows a square viewing window (see page 47); the mirror-image property of the inverse function would not be as clear on a non-square window. Note also that although this window is square on a TI-83, it is not quite square on a TI-85.

Section 4.2   Example 11   (page 412)   Using Data to Model Exponential Growth

See page 57 for information about using the TI-85 for regression computations.

Section 4.4   Example 1   (page 433)   Finding pH

For (a), the text shows -log(2.5*10^(-4)), but this could also be entered as shown on the first line of the screen on the right, since "E" (produced with [EE]) and "*10^" are nearly equivalent. The two are not completely interchangeable, however; in particular, in part (b), "10^" **cannot** be replaced with "E", because "E"

```
-log (2.5E-4)
          3.60205999133
E-7
               1E-7
E-7.1■
```

is only valid when followed by an *integer*. That is, E-7 produces the same result as 10^-7, but the last line shown on the screen produces a syntax error.

(Incidentally, "10^" is [2nd][LOG], but [1][0][^] produces the same results.)

Section 4.5   Example 8   (page 448)   Modeling Coal Consumption in the U.S.

The modeling function given in the text was found using a regression procedure (LNR, or logarithmic regression) similar to that described on page 57.

Section 5.1   Example 2   (page 476)   Calculating with Degrees, Minutes, and Seconds

---

Section 5.1   Example 3   (page 476)   Converting between Decimal Degrees and Degrees, Minutes, and Seconds

See section 9 of this chapter's introduction (page 44) for information about selecting Degree mode. The alternative to putting the calculator in Degree mode is to use the degree symbol following each angle measure.

The MATH:ANGLE menu ([2nd][×][F3]) is shown on the right. It includes the degrees and minutes symbols, and the ▸DMS operator (which causes an angle to be displayed in degrees, minutes, and seconds, rather than as a decimal).

Entering angles on a TI-85, however, is different than on a TI-83 (which was used to create the screens shown in the text.) The degree and seconds symbols (° and ") are not used; the minutes symbol is used for all three positions, as in the screen on the right. (The results of the computations are displayed with the "usual" symbols.)

The screen on the right shows the proper way to enter the angles from Example 3 for computation on the TI-85.

Section 5.2   Example 4   (page 484)   Finding Function Values of Quadrantal Angles

The alternative to putting the calculator in Degree mode is to use the degree symbol ([2nd][×][F3][F1]) following each angle measure; e.g., enter $\sin 90°$ rather than just $\sin 90$. (However, see the comment in the next example.)

Since the cotangent, secant, and cosecant functions are the reciprocals of the tangent, cosine, and sine, they can be entered as (e.g.) $1/\sin 90$. (This is illustrated in Figure 21 on page 485 of the text.) Note, though, that this will not properly compute $\cot 90°$, since $1/\tan 90$ produces a domain error. Entering $\cot x$ as $\cos x / \sin x$ will produce the correct result at $90°$.

One might guess that the other three trigonometric functions are accessed with [2nd] followed by [SIN], [COS], or [TAN] (which produce, e.g., $\sin^{-1}$). This is **not** what these functions do; in this case, the exponent -1 does not mean "reciprocal," but instead indicates that these are inverse functions (which are discussed in Sections 5.3 and 7.5 of the text). The text comments on this distinction at th bottom of page 485.

Section 5.3   Example 6   (page 500)   Finding Function Values with a Calculator

Recall that the TI-85 uses a slightly different format for entering angles in degrees and minutes, as illustrated on the right. This screen also shows how computations like the secant in part (b) can be entered on a single line. These computations were done in Degree mode.

```
sin 49'12'
         .756995055652
(cos 97.977)⁻¹
         -7.2058792129
■
```

The screen on the right (with computations done in Radian mode) illustrates a somewhat unexpected behavior: Even if an angle is entered in DMS format, the TI-85 assumes that the angle is in radians. In order to remedy this, either put the calculator in Degree mode, or use the degree symbol ([2nd][×][F3][F1]) as was done in the second entry.

```
sin 49'12'
         -.87502257899
sin 49'12'°
         .756995055652
■
```

Section 5.3   Example 7   (page 500)   Using an Inverse Trigonometric Function to Find an Angle

Section 5.3   Example 8   (page 501)   Finding Angle Measures

The sin⁻¹ ("inverse sine," or "arcsine") function is [2nd][SIN], while cos⁻¹ is [2nd] [COS]. The computations shown in Figures 34 and 36 in the text were done in Degree mode; the screen on the right shows the result for Example 7 when done in Radian mode. Note that in the second entry, an attempt was made to get the TI-85 to report the result in degrees (by placing the degree symbol at the end of the entry), but this does not have the desired result.

```
sin⁻¹ .9677091705
         1.31597825608
(sin⁻¹ .9677091705)°
         .022968153453
■
```

Section 5.4   Example 1   (page 510)   Solving a Right Triangle Given an Angle and a Side

Section 5.4   Example 2   (page 511)   Solving a Right Triangle Given Two Sides

For problems like these, the Ans variable can be used to avoid loss of accuracy from rounding off intermediate results. Shown are computations for Example 1. (Be sure the TI-85 is in Degree mode. Also, recall that the arcsine (or inverse sine) function is [2nd][SIN] —*not* [SIN][2nd][EE].)

```
12.7 sin 34'30'
         7.19335920895
√(12.7²-Ans²)
         10.4664025955
sin⁻¹ (Ans/12.7)▶DMS
         55°30'0"
■
```

Section 5.4   Example 7   (page 514)   Solving a Problem Involving Angles of Elevation

The TI-85's GRAPH:MATH:ISECT ([GRAPH][MORE][F1][MORE][F5]) feature will automatically locate the intersection of two graphs. This feature was previously illustrated on page 58, but we repeat the description here: Use [▲], [▼] and [ENTER] to specify which two functions to use (in this case, the only two being displayed). After [ENTER] is pressed the second time, the TI-85 will try to find an intersection of the two graphs. The screens below illustrate these steps.

GRAPH:MATH:ISECT

[ENTER] (choose y1)

[ENTER] (choose y2)

and that's it.

Section 6.1   Example 1   (page 535)   Converting Degrees to Radians

The number π is available as $\boxed{\text{2nd}}\boxed{\wedge}$, and the degree symbol is $\boxed{\text{2nd}}\boxed{\times}\boxed{\text{F3}}\boxed{\text{F1}}$. With the calculator in Radian mode (see page 44), entering $45°$ causes the TI-85 to automatically convert to radians.

A useful technique to aid in recognizing when an angle is a multiple of π is to divide the result by π. This approach is illustrated in the screen on the right, showing that $45°$ is $\pi/4$ radians, and $30°$ is $\pi/6$ radians. This screen also makes use of the $\blacktriangleright$Frac command from the MATH:MISC menu ($\boxed{\text{2nd}}\boxed{\times}\boxed{\text{F5}}\boxed{\text{MORE}}\boxed{\text{F1}}$), which simply means "display the result of this computation as a fraction, if possible." This is a useful enough command that one may wish to put it in the CUSTOM menu (see page 44).

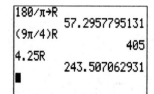

An alternative to using the degree symbol is to store $\pi/180$ in the calculator variable D (see page 44). Then typing, for example, 45D $\boxed{\text{ENTER}}$ will multiply 45 by $\pi/180$. This approach will work regardless of whether the calculator is in Degree or Radian mode. (A value stored in a variable will remain there until it is replaced by a new value.)

Section 6.1   Example 2   (page 535)   Converting Radians to Degrees

With the TI-85 in Degree mode (see page 44), the radian symbol (a superscripted r), produced with $\boxed{\text{2nd}}\boxed{\times}$ $\boxed{\text{F3}}\boxed{\text{F2}}$, will automatically change a radian angle measurement to degrees.

Alternatively, with the value $180/\pi$ stored in the calculator variable R (see page 44), typing $(9\pi/4)$R $\boxed{\text{ENTER}}$ will convert from radians to degrees regardless of whether the calculator is in Degree or Radian mode. (The same result can be achieved by *dividing by* the calculator variable D as defined in the previous example.)

Section 6.2   Example 4   (page 549)   Finding a Number Given Its Circular Function Value

The arccosine (or inverse cosine) function is $\boxed{\text{2nd}}\boxed{\text{COS}}$ — *not* $\boxed{\text{COS}}\boxed{\text{2nd}}\boxed{\text{EE}}$. Likewise, $\tan^{-1}$ is $\boxed{\text{2nd}}\boxed{\text{TAN}}$.

Section 6.3   Example 1   (page 559)   Graphing $y = a \sin x$

Note that the TI-85 must be in Radian mode in order to produce the desired graph.

The graphs in the text are shown in the "trig viewing window," described on the top of page 558. The TI-85's default trig window (selected with $\boxed{\text{GRAPH}}\boxed{\text{F3}}\boxed{\text{MORE}}\boxed{\text{F3}}$) is slightly wider than that shown in the text; it shows x from -2.625π to 2.625π. (If the TI-85 is in Degree mode, xMin and xMax will be ±472.5 instead of $\pm2.625\pi$.) The graph below is shown using the text's trig window, rather than the TI-85's.

The TI-85 does not support varying the thickness of graphs; all graphs appear the same. However, the TRACE ($\boxed{\text{GRAPH}}\boxed{\text{F4}}$) feature can be used to determine which graphs correspond to which formulas: On the right, the trace cursor is on graph 2 — that is, the graph of $y_2 = \sin x$. This approach is discussed on page 60 of this manual.

Section 6.3   Example 8   (page 566)   Modeling Temperature with a Sine Function

The "sine regression" illustrated at the end of this example is not a built-in feature of the TI-85. It might be possible to find a program to do this; see section 13 of this chapter's introduction, on page 48.

Section 6.4   Example 1   (page 578)   Graphing $y = a \sec bx$

Section 6.4   Example 2   (page 579)   Graphing $y = a \csc(x - d)$

See section 9 of the introduction (page 44) for information about DrawLine versus Dot (DrawDot) mode. The function in Example 1 can be entered as `y1=2cos (x/2)`$^{-1}$ (or as shown in the text). The function in Example 2 can be entered as `y1=(3/2)(1/sin (x-π/2))` or `y1=3/(2sin (x-π/2))`. A reminder: `sin`$^{-1}$ (`2nd` `SIN`) is *not* the cosecant function.

Section 7.1   Example 3   (page 609)   Rewriting an Expression in Terms of Sine and Cosine

The screen on the right shows how these expressions are entered on the "y equals" screen.

```
y1▤tan x+1/tan x
y2▤1/(cos x*sin x)
```

Section 7.3   Example 1   (page 622)   Finding Exact Cosine Function Values

Section 7.3   Example 4   (page 626)   Finding Exact Sine and Tangent Function Values

The TI-85 can graphically and numerically support exact value computations such as $\cos 15° = \frac{\sqrt{6}+\sqrt{2}}{4}$. Starting with a graph of `y1=cos x`, the TI-85 makes it possible to evaluate `y1` (or any function) for any value of x between xMin and xMax using the TI-85's GRAPH:EVAL (`GRAPH` `MORE` `MORE` `F1`) option. GRAPH:EVAL prompts for a value of x, which can be either a number like 15 or expression (like $1/\pi$ or $\sqrt{2}$). Pressing `ENTER` causes the cursor to jump to that x-coordinate.

```
Eval x=15▮
 EVAL  STPIC  RCPIC
```

```
                    1

x=15        y=.9659258629
```

Note that Example 8 in Section 7.4 (page 639) shows that $\cos 15°$ can also be written as $\frac{\sqrt{2+\sqrt{3}}}{2}$.

Section 7.5   Example 1   (page 646) Finding Inverse Sine Values

---

Section 7.5   Example 2   (page 646) Finding Inverse Cosine Values

Of course, it is not necessary to graph $y = \sin^{-1} x$ to find these values; one can simply enter, e.g., $\sin^{-1} (1/2)$ on the home screen. The first entry of the screen on the right shows what happens when the calculator is in Degree mode; note that the result is not in $[-\pi/2, \pi/2]$. With the calculator in Radian mode, results similar to those in the text are found, and the method employed on page 65 of this manual (in the discussion of text Example 1 from Section 6.1) confirms that these values are $\pi/6$ and $3\pi/4$.

```
sin⁻¹ (1/2)
                    30
sin⁻¹ (1/2)
          .523598775598
Ans/π▶Frac
                   1/6
■
```

```
cos⁻¹ (-√2/2)
          2.35619449019
Ans/π▶Frac
                   3/4
■
```

Note that the TI-85 does *not* give an error for the input $\sin^{-1} -2$, but instead gives a complex result: $-\pi/2 + i \ln(2 + \sqrt{3})$. The reason that this is technically a correct result is beyond the scope of the textbook; TI-85 owners should recognize that a complex answer is not appropriate for this problem, and so should ignore this result.

```
sin⁻¹ -2
    (-1.57080,1.31696)
■
```

Section 7.5   Example 4   (page 651) Finding Inverse Function Values with a Calculator

Note that the answer given for (c), $109.499054°$, overrepresents the accuracy of that value. A typical rule for doing computations involving decimal values (like -0.3541) is to report only as many digits in the result as were present in the original number—in this case, four. This means the reported answer should be "about $109.5°$," and in fact, any angle θ between about $109.496°$ and $109.501°$ has a cotangent which rounds to -0.3541.

Section 7.6   Example 9   (page 663) Describing a Musical Tone from a Graph

---

Section 7.6   Example 10   (page 664) Analyzing Pressures of Upper Harmonics

Note that the calculator screens shown in Figures 27–30 illustrate the importance of choosing a "good" viewing window. If we choose the wrong vertical scale (yMin and yMax), we might not be able to see the graph at all—it might be squashed against the x-axis. If we make the window too wide—that is, if xMax minus xMin is too large—we might see the "wrong" picture, like the one on the right (for Example 10): We seem to see six periods in this view, when in fact there are 44. Each of the six "pseudo-cycles" is made of parts of seven or eight full periods.

This observation—that a periodic function, viewed at fixed intervals, can appear to be a *different* periodic function—is the same effect that causes wagon wheels to appear to run backwards in old movies.

Section 8.3   Example 1   (page 716)   Finding Magnitude and Direction Angle

---

Section 8.3   Example 2   (page 716)   Finding Horizontal and Vertical Components

---

The TI-85 does not have the conversion functions shown in Figures 26 and 28, but can do the desired conversions in a manner that is perhaps even more convenient. The TI-85 recognizes vectors entered in either of two formats:

[*horizontal component, vertical component*]   or   [*magnitude ∠ angle*]

(The square brackets are [2nd][(] and [2nd][)], and "∠" is [2nd][,].) Regardless of how the vector is entered, the TI-85 displays it according to the <u>RectV CylV SphereV</u> mode setting (see page 44); specifically, it displays the vector in component form in RectV mode, and in magnitude/angle form for either of the other two modes.

For Example 1, then, either put the TI-85 in CylV or SphereV mode, or (perhaps more conveniently), use the ▸Pol command ([2nd][8][F4][F3]), as the screen on the right illustrates. This causes a vector to be displayed in magnitude/direction angle format regardless of the mode setting. On the fourth line, we see the results of pressing [▸] to see all the digits of the angle. (With the TI-85 in Degree mode, the angle returned is in degrees.)

```
[3,-2]▸Pol
[3.605551275462-33.6…
[3,-2]▸Pol
…275462-33.690067526]
■
```

For Example 2, both the horizontal and vertical components can be found at once, as the screen on the right shows. (The vertical component is too long to fit on the screen, but the other digits can be seen by pressing [▸]. Note that the screen shown in the text was created with the calculator set to display only one digit after the decimal.) These computations were done with the TI-85 in Degree mode,

```
[25.0∠41.7]
[18.6659545571 16.63…
[25.0∠41.7]
…45571 16.6307588664]
[25.0∠41.7]▸Rec
[18.6659545571 16.63…
■
```

so it was not necessary to include the degree symbol on the angle. The third entry shown uses the ▸Rec command, which forces the vector to be displayed in component form regardless of the mode setting. (It was unnecessary in this case, because the TI-85 with in RectV mode.)

Section 8.3   Example 3   (page 717)   Writing Vectors in the Form ⟨*a, b*⟩

Note how easily these conversions are done in the TI-85's polar vector format. (The TI-85 was in Degree mode.)

```
[5∠60]
    [2.5 4.33012701892]
[2∠180]
              [-2 0]
[6∠280]
[1.041889066 -5.9088…
■
```

Section 8.3   Example 5   (page 718)   Performing Vector Operations

---

Section 8.3   Example 6   (page 719)   Finding the Dot Product

---

Using the TI-85's vector notation, the vectors can be stored in calculator variables (see page 44) which can then be used to do the desired operations. Shown are the commands to compute 5(c): 4**u** − 3**v**, and 6(a): ⟨2, 3⟩ · ⟨4, −1⟩ (the dot command is [2nd][8][F3][F4]).

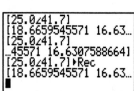
```
[-2,1]→U:[4,3]→V
              [4 3]
4U-3V
         [-20 -5]
dot([2,3],[4,-1])
              5
■
```

Section 8.5   Example 2   (page 734)   Converting from Trigonometric Form to Rectangular Form

Complex numbers can be entered in trigonometric form in a manner similar to
the polar format for vectors (see page 68); the screen on the right illustrates how
to quickly convert from the TI-85's trigonometric form to its rectangular form
(assuming the calculator is in RectC mode; see page 44). "∠" is [2nd][,].

```
(2∠300)
        (1,-1.73205080757)
■
```

Section 8.5   Example 3   (page 734)   Converting from Rectangular Form to Trigonometric Form

Although the TI-85 does not have the conversion functions shown on page 735,
the same thing can be accomplished with the abs and angle commands, found
in the TI-85's CPLX menu ([2nd][9]), and shown on page 737 of the text. On the
screen on the right, note that if one makes use of the variable i defined as (0, 1),
the angle and abs functions require parentheses; the third output is incorrect
because it first computes the "angle" of the real number $-\sqrt{3}$ (which is 0, although it really should be π)
and then adds this to i.

```
angle (-√3,1)
                  150
abs (-√3,1)
                    2
angle -√3+i
                (0,1)
■
conj│real│imag│ abs │angle▶
```

More convenient is the TI-85's ▶Pol command, found by pressing [MORE] in the
CPLX menu. (This command is also found in the VECTR:OPS menu.) This gives
both the magnitude and angle at the same time.

```
(-√3,1)▶Pol
               (2∠150)
-√3+i▶Pol
               (2∠150)
-3i▶Pol
               (3∠-90)
■
▶Rec│▶Pol│    │    │
```

Section 8.5   Example 4   (page 735)   Converting Between Trigonometric and Rectangular Forms Using Calculator Approximations

Aside from entering the expression in (a) as it is shown in the text (using the cos
and sin functions), one can use the TI-85's polar format ($r \angle \theta$), but be sure to
either put the TI-85 in the correct mode (Degree or Radian) or use the degrees or
radians symbol from the MATH:ANGLE menu. Both computations on the right were
done in Radian mode, and the first result is incorrect.

```
(6∠115)
(-1.95485883132,5.67…
(6∠115°)
(-2.53570957044,5.43…
■
```

Section 8.6   Example 1   (page 743)   Finding a Power of a Complex Number

The screen on the right shows several options for computing $(1 + i\sqrt{3})^8$ with the
TI-85. The first is fairly straightforward, but the reported result shows the complex
part of the answer ($128i\sqrt{3}$) given in decimal form. For an "exact" answer, the
TI-85's polar format can be used. The TI-85 was in Degree mode for the first of
the two polar-format answers, and in Radian mode for the second.

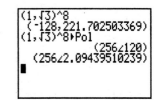

```
(1,√3)^8
(-128,221.702503369)
(1,√3)^8▶Pol
            (256∠120)
(256∠2.09439510239)
■
```

Section 8.6   Example 4   (page 746)   Solving an Equation by Finding Complex Roots

The TI-85's POLY polynomial solver (see page 54) can be
used to see the pattern of these roots, if the calculator is in
PolarC and Degree modes. The two negative angles shown
in the second screen are coterminal with the angles $216°$
and $288°$ given in the text.

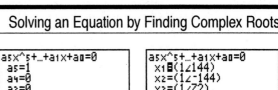

```
a5x^5+…+a1x+a0=0
a5=1
a4=0
a3=0
a2=0
a1=0
a0=-1■
CLRq│    │    │    │SOLVE
```
```
a5x^5+…+a1x+a0=0
x1■(1∠144)
x2=(1∠-144)
x3=(1∠72)
x4=(1∠-72)
x5=(1∠0)
COEFS│STOq│    │    │
```

Section 8.7	Example 3	(page 751)	Examining Polar and Rectangular Equations of Lines and Circles
Section 8.7	Example 4	(page 753)	Graphing a Polar Equation (Cardioid)
Section 8.7	Example 5	(page 753)	Graphing a Polar Equation (Rose)
Section 8.7	Example 6	(page 754)	Graphing a Polar Equation (Lemniscate)

To produce these polar graphs, the TI-85 should be set to Degree and Polar modes (see the screen on the right). In this mode, GRAPH F1 allows entry of polar equations (r as a function of θ). One could also use Radian mode, adjusting the values of θMin, θMax, and θStep accordingly (e.g., use 0, 2π, and $\pi/30$ instead of 0, 360, and 5).

For the cardioid, rose, and lemniscate, the window settings shown in the text show these graphs on "square" windows (see section 11 of the introduction, page 46), so one can see how their proportions compare to those of a circle. Note, however, that on the TI-85, these window are not square; the ZOOM:ZSQR option can be used to adjust the window dimensions to make it square.

For the cardioid, the value of θStep does not need to be 5, although that choice works well for this graph. Too large a choice of θStep produces a graph with lots of sharp "corners," like the one shown on the right (drawn with θStep=30). Setting θStep too small, on the other hand, produces a smooth graph, but it is drawn very slowly. Sometimes it may be necessary to try different values of θStep to choose a good one.

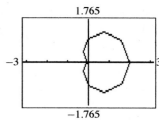

The lemniscate can be drawn by setting θMin=0 and θMax=180, or θMin=-45 and θMax=45. In fact, with θ ranging from -45 to 225, the graph of r1=$\sqrt{}$cos (2θ) (alone) will produce the entire lemniscate. (θStep should be about 5.)

The rose can be produced by setting θMin=0 and θMax=360, or using any 360°-range of θ values (with θStep about 5).

Section 8.7	Example 7	(page 755)	Graphing a Polar Equation (Spiral of Archimedes)

To produce this graph on the viewing window shown in the text, the TI-85 must be in Radian mode. (In Degree mode, it produces the same shape, but magnified by a factor of $180/\pi$ —meaning that the viewing window needs to be larger by that same factor.)

Section 8.8   Example 1   (page 761)   Graphing a Plane Curve Defined Parametrically

Place the TI-85 in Parametric mode, as the screen on the right shows. In this mode, [GRAPH][F1] allows entry of pairs of parametric equations (x and y as functions of t). No graph is produced unless both functions in the pair are entered and selected (that is, both equals signs are highlighted).

The value of tStep does not need to be 0.05, although that choice works well for this graph. Too large a choice of tStep produces a less-smooth graph, like the one shown on the right (drawn with tStep=1). Setting tStep too small, on the other hand, produces a smooth graph, but it is drawn very slowly. Sometimes it may be necessary to try different values of tStep to choose a good one.

Section 8.8   Example 3   (page 762)   Graphing a Plane Curve Defined Parametrically

This curve can be graphed in Degree mode with tMin=0 and tMax=360, or in Radian mode with tMax=2π. In order to see the proportions of this ellipse, it might be good to graph it on a square window. This can be done most easily with the ZOOM:ZSQR option ([GRAPH][F3][MORE][F2]). On a TI-85, initially with the window settings shown in the text, this would result in the window $[-6.8, 6.8] \times [-4, 4]$.

Section 8.8   Example 5   (page 763)   Graphing a Cycloid

The TI-85 *must* be in Radian mode in order to produce this graph.

Section 8.8   Example 6   (page 764)   Simulating Motion with Parametric Equations

Section 8.8   Example 8   (page 765)   Analyzing the Path of a Projectile

Parametric mode is particularly nice for analyzing motion, because one can picture the motion by watching the calculator create the graph, or by using TRACE ([GRAPH][F4]) and watching the motion of the trace cursor. (When tracing in parametric mode, the [▶] and [◀] keys increase and decrease the value of t, and the trace cursor shows the location (x, y) at time t.) Figure 80 illustrates tracing on the projectile path in Example 8. Note that the value of t changes by $\pm$tStep each time [▶] or [◀] is pressed, so obviously the choice of tStep affects which points can be traced.

Section 9.1   Example 1   (page 785)   Solving a System by Substitution

Section 9.1   Example 4   (page 787)   Solving a System with Infinitely Many Solutions

Section 9.1   Example 6   (page 790)   Solving a System of Three Equations with Three Variables

The TI-85's built-in SIMULT feature can be used to solve linear systems with up to 30 unknowns. Pressing [2nd][STAT] causes the TI-85 to prompt for the number of equations, after which it prompts for the coefficients, one equation at a time. The screens below show the first and third equations being entered; the arrow keys (or [F1] and [F2]) allow the user to move from one coefficient to another. When all the constants have been entered, pressing [F5] solves for the three unknowns (which the TI-85 calls x_1, x_2, and x_3, rather than x, y, and z).

For systems with no solutions, or infinitely many solutions (as in Example 4), the TI-85 gives a SINGULAR MAT error ("MAT" stands for "matrix"; these are discussed in Section 9.2 of the text).

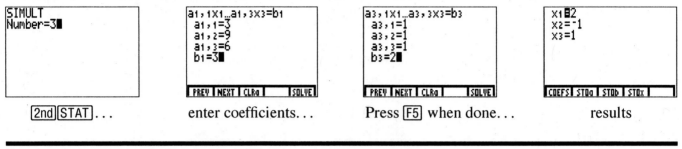

[2nd][STAT]...   enter coefficients...   Press [F5] when done...   results

---

Section 9.1   Example 8   (page 792)   Using Curve Fitting to Find an Equation Through Three Points

Note that the equation found in this example by algebraic methods can also be found very quickly on the TI-85 by performing a quadratic regression (P2REG— see page 57) on the three given points. In the screen shown, PRegC is the list of "polynomial regression coefficients." These agree with the coefficients found in the text.

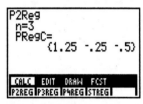

Section 9.2   Example 1   (page 802)   Using the Gauss-Jordan Method

Section 9.2   Example 2   (page 804)   Using the Gauss-Jordan Method

The menu shown in the text (Figure 7) is from a TI-83. The TI-85 has the four matrix row operations, but they are located in the MATRX:OPS menu (not MATRX:MATH), and the names are slightly different. The screen on the right shows this menu (visible after pressing [2nd][7][F4][MORE]).

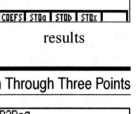

Before describing these operations, a few words about entering matrices into the TI-85: The matrix in the text has the name "[A]." On the TI-82 and TI-83, all matrices have names of the form [*letter*]; on the TI-85, matrices can have any variable name. (In fact, variable names *cannot* include the bracket characters on the TI-85.)

To change the entries in a matrix (e.g., to enter the augmented matrix for this example), either store the matrix using a home screen command (similar to the form used in the screen above), or use the MATRX:EDIT feature, then choose the name of a matrix (or type a name for a new matrix), specify the number of rows and columns, and type in the entries. The screen on the right shows the process of entering the final column of MAT.

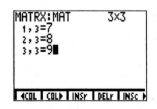

The formats for the matrix row-operation commands are:

- rSwap(*matrix*, *A*, *B*) produces a new matrix that has row *A* and row *B* swapped.

- rAdd(*matrix*, *A*, *B*) produces a new matrix with row *A* added to row *B*.

- multR(*number,matrix,A*) produces a new matrix with row *A* multiplied by *number*.

- mRAdd(*number,matrix,A,B*) produces a new matrix with row *A* multiplied by *number* and added to row *B* (row *A* is unchanged).

Shown below are examples of each of these operations on the matrix MAT$=\begin{bmatrix} 1 & 4 & 7 \\ 2 & 5 & 8 \\ 3 & 6 & 9 \end{bmatrix}$.

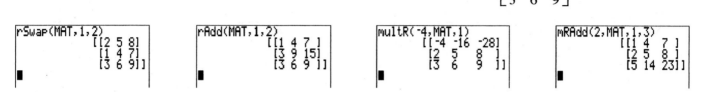

Keep in mind that these row operations leave the matrix MAT untouched. To perform a sequence of row operations, each result must either be stored in a matrix, or use the result variable Ans as the matrix. For example, with MAT equal to the augmented matrix for the system given in this example, the following screens illustrate the initial steps in the Gauss-Jordan method. Note the use of Ans in the last two screens.

As we see in Figure 7(d), the rref command (2nd 7 F4 F5) will do all the necessary row operations at once, making these individual steps seem tedious. On the TI-85, the parentheses are not needed, so the necessary command is rref MAT.

Section 9.3   Example 1   (page 813)   Evaluating a 2×2 Determinant

---

Section 9.3   Example 3   (page 816)   Evaluating a 3×3 Determinant

On a TI-85, the parentheses around the matrix name are not needed. The function "det" is available in the MATRX:MATH menu (2nd 7 F3 F1). Shown on the right is the TI-85 version of the screen in the text.

  The determinant of a 3×3—or larger—matrix is as easy to find with a calculator as that of a 2×2 matrix. (At least, it is as easy for the user; the calculator is doing all the work!) Note, however, that trying to find the determinant of a non-square matrix (for example, a 3×4 matrix) results in a DIMENSION error.

Section 9.5   Example 2   (page 832)   Solving a Nonlinear System by Elimination

See the discussion of Example 10 from Section 2.1 on page 56 of this manual for tips on entering formulas like these.

The text shows the intersections as found by the procedure built in to the calculator (described on page 58 of this manual, called "ISECT" on the TI-85). However, for these equations, the TI-85 fails to locate the intersections, because the two circle equations are only valid for $-2 \le x \le 2$, while the hyperbola equations are only valid for $x \le -2$ and $x \ge 2$. When the TI-85 looks for an intersection, it finds that either one function or the other is undefined for every x (except ± 2), which results in a BAD GUESS error. (The TI-85 always checks several different x values, even if the very first value it tries happens to be a point of intersection.)

Section 9.6   Example 1   (page 843)   Graphing a Linear Inequality

The appropriate command to shade with a TI-85 is the Shade(command, accessed in the GRAPH:DRAW menu (GRAPH MORE F2 F1). The format is

    Shade(*lower*, *upper*, *min X*, *max X*)

Here *lower* and *upper* are the functions between which the TI-85 will draw the shading (above *lower* and below *upper*). *min X* and *max X* specify the starting and ending *x* values for the shading. These are optional; if omitted, the TI-85 uses xMin and xMax.

The TI-85 does not have as many shading options as the other TI graphing calculators. Most notably, the TI-85 only does "solid" shading; it cannot shade every other column of pixels like the screen shown in the text.

To produce a graph like the one accompanying Example 1 in the text, the appropriate command (typed on the home screen) would be something like

    Shade(-(1/4)x+1,10).

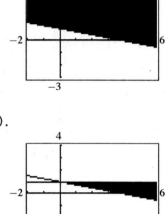

The use of 10 for the *upper* function simply tells the TI-85 to shade up as high as necessary; this could be replaced by any number greater than 4 (the value of yMax for the viewing window shown). Also, if the function y1 had previously been defined as -(1/4)x+1, this command could be shortened to Shade(y1,10).

One more useful piece of information: Suppose one makes a mistake in typing the Shade(command (e.g., switching *upper* and *lower*, or using the wrong value of *resolution*), resulting in the wrong shading. The screen on the right, for example, arose from typing Shade(-(1/4)x+1,1). In order to achieve the desired results, the mistake must be erased using the CLDRW (clear drawing) command, found in the GRAPH:DRAW menu (GRAPH MORE F2 MORE F5). Then, press 2nd ENTER, correct the mistake in the Shade(command, and try again.

Section 9.6   Example 2   (page 844)   Graphing Systems of Inequalities

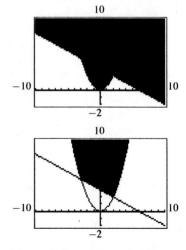

Since the TI-85 only supports solid shading, regions like the one in this example cannot be depicted by simply shading the two inequalities individually and then looking for the region where they overlap. If y1=(6-x)/2 and y2=x²/2, issuing the command Shade(y1,10):Shade(y2,10) produces the results on the right, which are not useful.

A useful picture can be created, with a little more work, by making the observation that if y is greater than both $x^2/2$ and $(6 - x)/2$, then for any x, y must be greater than the larger of these two expressions. The TI-85 provides a convenient way to find the larger of two numbers with the max(function, located in the LIST:OPS menu (2nd − F5 F5). Then max(y1,y2) will return the larger of y1 and y2, and the command Shade(max(y1,y2),11) will shade from the larger of y1 and y2 up to 11 (again, any number greater than yMax would work here), producing the screen on the right.

Extension: The table below gives the appropriate commands to shade regions that arise from variations on the inequalities in this example. (The results of these commands are not shown here.)

For the system...	or equivalently...	the command would be...
$x < 6 - 2y$ $x^2 < 2y$	$y < (6-x)/2$ $y > x^2/2$	`Shade(y2,y1)`
$x > 6 - 2y$ $x^2 > 2y$	$y > (6-x)/2$ $y < x^2/2$	`Shade(y1,y2)`
$x < 6 - 2y$ $x^2 > 2y$	$y < (6-x)/2$ $y < x^2/2$	`Shade(-3,min(y1,y2))`

Section 9.7   Example 2   (page 854)   Adding Matrices

Section 9.7   Example 3   (page 855)   Subtracting Matrices

Section 9.7   Example 4   (page 856)   Multiplying Matrices by Scalars

---

Section 9.7   Example 6   (page 859)   Multiplying Matrices

See page 72 for information about matrices on the TI-85.

Section 9.8   Example 1   (page 868)   Verifying the Identity Property of I_3

On the TI-85, the function to produce identity matrices is `ident`, which does not require parentheses, and is located in the MATRX:OPS menu (2nd 7 F4 F3). The screen on the right shows the 3×3 identity matrix.

```
ident 3
           [[1 0 0]
            [0 1 0]
            [0 0 1]]
```

Section 9.8   Example 2   (page 870)   Finding the Inverse of a 3×3 Matrix

---

Section 9.8   Example 3   (page 872)   Identifying a Matrix with No Inverse

---

An inverse matrix is found using 2nd EE —the same method used to find the inverse of a real number. For example, to find the inverse of matrix MAT, type MAT (or choose that name from the MATRX:NAMES menu) then press 2nd EE ENTER. An error will occur if the matrix is not square, or if it is a singular matrix (as in Example 3).

Section 10.1	Example 1	(page 893)	Graphing a Parabola with Horizontal Axis

Section 10.1	Example 2	(page 894)	Graphing a Parabola with Horizontal Axis

Section 10.2	Example 1	(page 904)	Graphing Ellipses Centered at the Origin

Section 10.3	Example 1	(page 914)	Using Asymptotes to Graph a Hyperbola

See the discussion of Example 10 from Section 2.1 on page 56 of this manual for tips on entering formulas like these.

When entering these formulas, make sure to use enough parentheses, so that operations are performed in the correct order; e.g., for Example 2 of Section 10.1, the formula in y1 should look like this:

    y1=-1.5+√((x-.5)/2)

Also, when looking at a calculator graph like the one shown in Figure 18 (page 595), keep in mind that the apparent gap between this graph and the *x*-axis is not really there; it is a flaw that arises from the calculator's method of plotting functions (see discussion on page 48 of this manual).

Section 11.1	Example 3	(page 939)	Modeling Insect Population Growth

One way to produce this sequence (and similar recursively defined sequences) is with the Ans variable, as shown on the right. (After pressing [1][ENTER], then typing the next line and pressing [ENTER], we simply press [ENTER] over and over to generate successive terms in the sequence.)

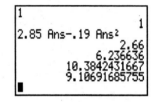

Figure 4 of the text shows a table of sequence terms, while Figure 5(b) shows a plot of the terms. The TI-85 has neither table generation capability nor a "sequence mode" used to create these screens. See the discussion of Example 7 from Section 11.3 (below) for information on creating a plot like Figure 5(b), but note that on the TI-85, recursive sequences are tedious to plot. (Non-recursive sequences are a bit easier.)

Section 11.1	Example 4	(page 941)	Using Summation Notation

Section 11.2	Example 9	(page 953)	Using Summation Notation

The seq(command can be found in the LIST:OPS menu ([2nd][−][F5][MORE][F3]). Given a formula a_n for the *n*th term in a sequence, the command

    seq(*formula*, *variable*, *start*, *end*, *step*)

produces the list $\{a_{start}, a_{start+step}, \ldots, a_{end}\}$. In most uses, the value of *step* is 1. The size of the resulting list can have no more than 99 items.

Note that *variable* can be any letter (or letters)—K and I are used in the text, but x is more convenient (since it can be typed with [x-VAR]).

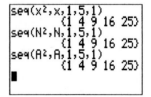

The sum command can be found in the LIST:OPS menu (2nd – F5 MORE F1). On the TI-85, the parentheses are not required. sum can be applied to any list—either to a list variable (called "list" in the example screen on the right), or directly to a list created with the seq(command.

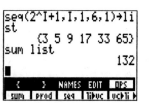

Note: On the TI-85, list variables can be given any kind of legal variable name (see page 44).

Section 11.3   Example 7   (page 960)   Summing the Terms of an Infinite Geometric Series

To produce the plot from Figure 10 on the TI-85, begin by storing values in the lists xStat and yStat as shown on the right, so that xStat contains values of n, and yStat contains the corresponding values of S_n. (The slightly shorter command (1-(1/3)^xStat)/(2/3)→yStat has the same effect as the second command shown.) This step is tedious for recursively defined sequences, but fairly simple in this case.

Set up the viewing window (GRAPH:RANGE) to match that shown in the text, check that nothing else will be plotted (press GRAPH F1 and make sure that all the equals signs are not highlighted), then press STAT F3 F2 (STAT:DRAW:SCAT) to produce the graph (called a "scatterplot").

Note: This description assumes that xStat and yStat were the two lists most recently edited (using STAT:EDIT). If the plot does not appear, it could be because the TI-85 is making a scatterplot with a different pair of lists. To remedy this, simply choose STAT:EDIT and specify the two lists xStat and yStat, then choose STAT:DRAW:SCAT again.

Section 11.4   Example 1   (page 971)   Evaluating Binomial Coefficients

---

Section 11.6   Example 4   (page 984)   Using the Permutations Formula

The nCr and nPr commands are found in the MATH:PROB menu (2nd × F2). (Also located in that menu is the factorial operator "!.")

Section 11.7   Example 6   (page 999)   Finding Probabilities in a Binomial Experiment

The TI-85 does not have statistical distribution functions like binompdf. The computations shown in this example must be done by manually entering the entire binomial probability formula (or by obtaining a program to automate such computations.)

Introduction

The information in this section is essentially a summary of material that can be found in the TI-86 manual. Consult that manual for more details.

1   Power

To power up the calculator, simply press the [ON] key. This should bring up the "home screen"—a flashing block cursor, and possibly the results of any previous computations that might have been done.

If the home screen does not appear, one may need to adjust the contrast (see the next section).

To turn the calculator off, press [2nd][ON] (note that the "second function" of [ON]—written in yellow type above the key—is "OFF"). The calculator will automatically shut off if no keys are pressed for several minutes.

2   Adjusting screen contrast

If the screen is too dark (all black), decrease the contrast by pressing [2nd] then pressing and holding [▼]. If the screen is too light, increase the contrast by pressing [2nd] and then press and hold [▲].

As one adjusts the contrast, the numbers 1 through 9 will appear in the upper right corner of the screen. If the contrast setting reaches 8 or 9, or if the screen never becomes dark enough to see, the batteries should be replaced.

3   Replacing batteries

To replace the four AAA batteries, first turn the calculator off ([2nd][ON]), then remove the back cover, remove and replace each battery, replace the back cover, then turn the calculator on again. (After replacing batteries, one may need to adjust the contrast down as described above.)

4   Basic operations

Simple computations are entered in essentially the same way they would be written. For example, to compute $2 + 17 \times 5$, press ⟨2⟩⟨+⟩⟨1⟩⟨7⟩⟨×⟩⟨5⟩⟨ENTER⟩ (the ⟨ENTER⟩ key tells the calculator to act on what has been typed). Standard order of operations (including parentheses) is followed.

```
2+17*5
                87
■
```

The result of the most recently entered expression is stored in Ans, which is typed by pressing ⟨2nd⟩⟨(-)⟩ (the word "ANS" appears in yellow above this key). For example, ⟨5⟩⟨+⟩⟨2nd⟩⟨(-)⟩⟨ENTER⟩ will add 5 to the result of the previous computation.

```
2+17*5
                87
5+Ans
                92
■
```

After pressing ⟨ENTER⟩, the TI-86 automatically produces Ans if the first key pressed is one which requires a number before it; the most common of these are ⟨+⟩, ⟨−⟩, ⟨×⟩, ⟨÷⟩, ⟨^⟩, ⟨x²⟩, and ⟨STO▸⟩. For example, ⟨+⟩⟨5⟩⟨ENTER⟩ would accomplish the same thing as the keystrokes above (that is, it adds 5 to the previous result).

```
2+17*5
                87
5+Ans
                92
Ans+5
                97
■
```

Pressing ⟨ENTER⟩ by itself evaluates the previously typed expression again. This can be especially useful in conjunction with Ans. The screen on the right shows the result of pressing ⟨ENTER⟩ a second time.

```
2+17*5
                87
5+Ans
                92
Ans+5
                97
               102
■
```

Several expressions can be evaluated together by separating them with colons (⟨2nd⟩⟨.⟩). When ⟨ENTER⟩ is pressed, the result of the *last* computation is displayed. The screen shown illustrates the computation $2(5 + 1)^2$.

```
3+2
                 5
Ans+1:Ans²:2 Ans
                72
■
```

5   Cursors

When typing, the appearance of the cursor indicates the behavior of the next keypress. When the standard cursor (a flashing solid block, ■) is visible, the next keypress will produce its standard action—that is, the command or character printed on the key itself.

If ⟨2nd⟩⟨DEL⟩ is pressed, the TI-86 is placed in INSERT mode and the standard cursor will appear as a flashing underscore. If the arrow keys (⟨▲⟩, ⟨▼⟩, ⟨▶⟩, ⟨◀⟩) are used to move the cursor around within the expression, and the TI-86 is placed in INSERT mode, subsequent characters and commands will be inserted in the line at the cursor's position. When the cursor appears as a block, the TI-86 is in DELETE (or OVERWRITE) mode, and subsequent keypresses will replace the character(s) at the cursor's position. (When the cursor is at the end of the expression, this is irrelevant.)

The TI-86 will return to DELETE mode when any arrow key is pressed. It can also be returned to DELETE mode by pressing ⟨2nd⟩⟨DEL⟩ a second time.

Pressing ⟨2nd⟩ causes an arrow to appear in the cursor: ↑ (or an underscored arrow). The next keypress will produce its "second function"—the command or character printed in yellow above the key. (The cursor will then return to "standard.") If ⟨2nd⟩ is pressed by mistake, pressing it a second time will return the cursor to standard.

Pressing ALPHA places the letter "A" in the cursor: ▣ (or an underscored "A"). The next keypress will produce the letter or other character printed in blue above that key (if any), and the cursor will then return to standard. Pressing 2nd ALPHA puts the calculator in lowercase ALPHA mode, changing the cursor to ▣ and producing the lowercase version of a letter. Pressing ALPHA twice (or 2nd ALPHA ALPHA) "locks" the TI-86 in ALPHA (or lowercase ALPHA) mode, so that all of the following keypresses will produce characters until ALPHA is pressed again.

---

6   Accessing previous entries ("deep recall")

By repeatedly pressing 2nd ENTER ("ENTRY"), previously typed expressions can be retrieved for editing and re-evaluation. Pressing 2nd ENTER once recalls the most recent entry; pressing 2nd ENTER again brings up the second most recent, etc. The number of previous entries thus displayed varies with the length of each expression (the TI-86 allocates 128 bytes to store previous expressions).

---

7   Menus

Keys such as TABLE, GRAPH and 2nd 7 (MATRX) bring up a menu line at the bottom of the screen with a variety of options. These options can be selected by pressing one of the function keys (F1, F2, …, F5). If the menu ends with a small triangle ("▶"), it means that more options are available in this menu, which can viewed by pressing MORE. Shown is the menu produced by pressing 2nd × (MATH).

This screen shows the result of pressing F1 (the "NUM" option, which lists a variety of numerical functions). Note that the MATH menu still appears (with NUM highlighted) and the bottom line now lists the functions available in this sub-menu—including, for example, the absolute value function (abs), which is accessed by pressing F5. The command line abs (-5) was typed by pressing F5 ((-) 5) ENTER.

This manual will use (e.g.) MATH:NUM to indicate commands accessed through menus like this. Sometimes the keypresses will be included as well; for this example, it would be 2nd × F1 F5.

The various commands in these menus are too numerous to be listed here. They will be mentioned as needed in the examples.

One last comment is worthwhile, however. Some functions that may be used frequently are buried several levels deep in the menus, and may take many keystrokes to access. Worse, the location of the function might be forgotten (is it MATH:NUM or MATH:MISC?), necessitating a search through the menus. It is useful to remember three things:

- Any command can be typed one letter at a time, in either upper- or lowercase; e.g., ALPHA ALPHA LOG SIN 6 (-) will type the letters "ABS ", which has the same effect as 2nd × F1 F5.

- Any command can be found in the CATALOG menu ([2nd][CUSTOM][F1]). Since the commands appear in alphabetical order, it may take some time to locate the desired function. Pressing any letter key brings up commands starting with that letter (it is not necessary to press [ALPHA] first); e.g., pressing [LOG] brings up the list on the right, while pressing [,] shows commands starting with "P."

- Frequently used commands can be placed in the CUSTOM menu, and will then be available simply by pressing [CUSTOM]. To do this, scroll through the CATALOG to find the desired function, then press [F3] (CUSTM) followed by one of [F1]–[F5] to place that command in the CUSTOM menu. In the screen shown, [F1] was pressed, so that pressing [CUSTOM][F1] will type "Solver(." The commands in the MATH:ANGLE menu ([2nd][×][F3]), used frequently for problems in this text, could be made more accessible by placing them in this menu.

8   Variables

The uppercase letters A through Z, as well as some (but not all) lowercase letters, and also sequences of letters (like "High" or "count") can be used as variables (or "memory") to store numerical values. To store a value, type the number (or an expression) followed by [STO▸], then a letter or letters (note that the TI-86 automatically goes into ALPHA mode when [STO▸] is pressed), then [ENTER]. That variable name can then be used in the same way as a number, as demonstrated at right.

Note: The TI-86 interprets 2A as "2 times A"—the "*" symbol is not required (this is consistent with how we interpret mathematical notation). As for order of operations, this kind of multiplication is treated the same as "*" multiplication.

9   Setting the modes

By pressing [2nd][MORE] (MODE), one can change many aspects of how the calculator behaves. For most of the examples in this manual, the "default" settings should be used; that is, the MODE screen should be as shown on the right. Each of the options is described below; consult the TI-86 manual for more details. Changes in the settings are made using the arrows keys and [ENTER].

The Normal Sci Eng setting specifies how numbers should be displayed. The screen on the right shows the number 12345 displayed in Normal mode (which displays numbers in the range $\pm 999,999,999,999$ with no exponents), Sci mode (which displays all numbers in scientific notation), and Eng mode (which uses only exponents that are multiples of 3). Note: "E" is short for "times 10 to the power," so $1.2345\text{E}4 = 1.2345 \times 10^4 = 1.2345 \times 10000 = 12345$.

The <u>Float 012345678901</u> setting specifies how many places after the decimal should be displayed (the 0 and 1 at the end mean 10 and 11 decimal places). The default, Float, means that the TI-86 should display all non-zero digits (up to a maximum of 12).

<u>Radian Degree</u> indicates whether angle measurements should be assumed to be in radians or degrees. (A right angle measures $\frac{\pi}{2}$ radians, which is equivalent to $90°$.) Most of the examples in the text include reminders to set the calculator in the appropriate mode, in cases where this is important.

<u>RectC PolarC</u> specifies whether complex numbers should be displayed in rectangular or polar format. The TI-86's rectangular format is similar to the $a + bi$ format used by the text (beginning in Section 1.3); polar format is not discussed in this text, but is closely related to trigonometric format (see page 108 of this manual).

<u>Func Pol Param DifEq</u> specifies whether formulas to be graphed are functions (y as a function of x), polar equations (r as a function of θ), parametric equations (x and y as functions of t), or differential equations ($Q'(t)$ as a function of Q and t). The text accompanying this manual uses the first three of these settings.

The <u>RectV CylV SphereV</u> setting indicates the default display format for vectors (see page 107 of this manual).

The other two mode settings deal with issues that are beyond the scope of the textbook, and are not discussed here.

A group of settings related to the graph screen are found by pressing $\boxed{\text{GRAPH}}\boxed{\text{MORE}}$ $\boxed{\text{F3}}$ (GRAPH:FORMT). The default settings are shown in the screen on the right, and are generally the best choices for most examples in this book (although the last setting could go either way).

<u>RectGC PolarGC</u> specifies whether graph coordinates should be displayed in rectangular (x, y) or polar (r, θ) format. Note that this choice is independent of the Func Pol Param DifEq mode setting.

The <u>CoordOn CoordOff</u> setting determines whether or not graph coordinates should be displayed.

When plotting a graph, the <u>DrawLine DrawDot</u> setting tells the TI-86 whether or not to connect the individually plotted points. <u>SeqG SimulG</u> specifies whether individual expressions should be graphed one at a time (sequentially), or all at once (simultaneously).

<u>GridOff GridOn</u> specifies whether or not to display a grid of dots on the graph screen, while <u>AxesOn AxesOff</u> and <u>LabelOff LabelOn</u> do the same thing for the axes and labels (y and x) on the axes.

10   Setting the graph window

Pressing GRAPH F2 brings up the WINDOW settings. The exact contents of the WINDOW menu vary depending on whether the calculator is in function, polar, parametric, or DifEq mode; below are four examples showing this menu in each of these modes.

Function mode   Polar mode   Parametric mode   DifEq mode

All these menus include the values xMin, xMax, xScl, yMin, yMax, and yScl. When GRAPH F5 (GRAPH) is pressed, the TI-86 will show a portion of the Cartesian (x-y) plane determined by these values. In function mode, this menu also includes xRes, the behavior of which is described in section 12 of this manual (page 86). The other settings in this screen allow specification of the smallest, largest, and step values of θ (for polar mode) or t (for parametric mode), or initial conditions for the differential equation.

With settings as in the "Function mode" screen shown above, the TI-86 would display the screen at right: x values from -6.3 to 6.3 (that is, from xMin to xMax), and y values between -3.1 to 3.1 (yMin to yMax). Since xScl = yScl = 1, the TI-86 places tick marks on both axes every 1 unit; thus the x-axis ticks are at -6, -5, ..., 5, and 6, and the y-axis ticks fall on the integers from -3 to 3. This window is called the "decimal" window, and is most quickly set by pressing GRAPH F3 (ZOOM) MORE F4 (ZDECM).

Note: If the graph screen has a menu on the bottom (like that shown on the right), possibly obscuring some important part of the graph, it can be removed by pressing CLEAR. The menu can be restored later by pressing EXIT.

Below are four more sets of window settings, and the graph screens they produce. Note that the first graph on the left has tick marks every 10 units on both axes. The second window is called the "standard" viewing window, and is most quickly set by pressing GRAPH F3 (ZOOM) F4 (ZSTD). The setting yScl = 0 in the final graph means that no tick marks are placed on the y-axis.

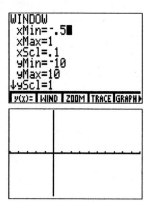

11   The graph screen

The TI-86 screen is made up of an array of rectangular dots (pixels) with 63 rows and 127 columns. All the pixels in the leftmost column have x-coordinate xMin, while those in the rightmost column have x-coordinate xMax. The x-coordinate changes steadily across the screen from left to right, which means that the coordinate for the nth column (counting the leftmost column as column 0) must be $xMin + n\Delta x$, where $\Delta x = (xMax - xMin)/126$. Similarly, the nth row of the screen (counting up from the bottom row, which is row 0) has y-coordinate $yMin + n\Delta y$, where $\Delta y = (yMax - yMin)/62$.

It is not necessary to memorize the formulas for Δx and Δy. Should they be needed, they can be determined by pressing GRAPH F5 and then the arrow keys. When pressing ▶ or ◀ successively, the displayed x-coordinate changes by Δx; meanwhile, when pressing ▲ or ▼, the y-coordinate changes by Δy. Alternatively, the values can be found by typing "Δx" and "Δy" on the home screen; this is most easily done by pressing 2nd 0 F2 F4 to access the CHAR:GREEK menu and type the "Δ" character, then typing lowercase x or y. This produces results like those shown on the right; the CHAR:GREEK menu remains on the bottom of the screen.

In the decimal window $xMin = -6.3$, $xMax = 6.3$, $yMin = -3.1$, $yMax = 3.1$, note that $\Delta x = 0.1$ and $\Delta y = 0.1$. Thus, the individual pixels on the screen represent x-coordinates $-6.3, -6.2, -6.1, \ldots, 6.1,$ $6.2, 6.3$ and y-coordinates $-3.1, -3, -2.9, \ldots, 2.9, 3, 3.1$. This is where the decimal window gets its name.

It happens that the pixels on the TI-86 screen are about 1.2 times taller than they are wide, so if $\Delta y/\Delta x$ is approximately 1.2 (the exact value is $1.19565\ldots$), the window will be a "square" window (meaning that the scales on the x- and y-axes are equal). For example, the decimal window (with $\Delta y/\Delta x = 1$) is not square, so that one unit on the x-axis is not the same length as one unit on the y-axis. (Specifically, one y-axis unit is about 20% longer than one x-axis unit.)

Any window can be made square be pressing GRAPH F3 (ZOOM) MORE F2 (ZSQR). To see the effect of a square window, observe the two pairs of graphs below. In each pair, the first graph is on the standard window, and the second is on a square window (after choosing ZOOM:ZSQR). The first pair shows the lines $y = 2x - 3$ and $y = 3 - \frac{1}{2}x$; note that on the square window, these lines look perpendicular (as they should). The second pair shows a circle centered at the origin with a radius of 8. On the standard window, this looks like an oval since the screen is wider than it is tall. (The reason for the gaps in the circle will be addressed in the next section.)

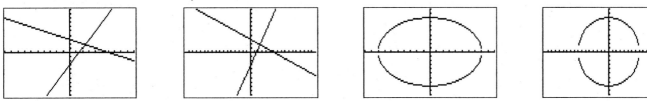

12   Graphing a function

This introductory section only addresses creating graphs in function mode. Procedures for creating parametric and polar graphs are very similar; they are covered beginning on page 109 of this manual, in material related to Chapter 8 of the text. Sequence plotting is covered on page 117 of this manual, in the material related to Section 11.3 from the text.

To see the graph of $y = 2x - 3$, begin by entering the formula into the calculator. This is done by pressing [GRAPH][F1] to access the "y equals" screen of the calculator. Enter the formula as y1 (or any other yn); note that the letter x can be typed by pressing [F1] or [x-VAR] (as well as [2nd][ALPHA][+]). If another y variable has a formula, position the cursor on that line and press either [F4] (DELf—to delete the function) or [F5] (SELCT). The latter has the effect of toggling the "highlighting" for the equals sign "=" for that line (an "unhighlighted" equals sign tells the TI-86 not to graph that formula). In the screen on the right, only y1 will be graphed.

The next step is to choose a viewing window. See the previous section for more details on this. This example uses the standard window ([GRAPH][F3][F4]).

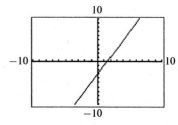

If the graph has not been displayed, press [GRAPH][F5], and the line should be drawn. In order to produce this graph, the TI-86 considers 127 values of x, ranging from xMin to xMax in steps of Δx (assuming that xRes = 1; see below for other possibilities). For each value of x, it computes the corresponding value of y, then plots that point (x, y) and (if the calculator is in Connected [DrawLine] mode) draws a line between this point and the previous one.

If xRes is set to 2, the TI-86 will only compute y for every other x value; that is, it uses a step size of $2\Delta x$. Similarly, if xRes is 3, the step size will be $3\Delta x$, and so on. Setting xRes higher causes graphs to appear faster (since fewer points are plotted), but for some functions, the graph may look "choppy" if xRes is too large, since detail is sacrificed for speed.

Note: If the line does not appear, or the TI-86 reports an error, double-check all the previous steps. Also, check the mode settings (discussed in section 9, page 82).

Once the graph is visible, the window can be changed using [F2] (WINDOW) or [F3] (ZOOM). Pressing [F4] (TRACE) brings up the "trace cursor," and displays the x- and y-coordinates for various points on the line as the [◀] and [▶] keys are pressed. Tracing beyond the left or right columns causes the TI-86 to adjust the values of xMin and xMax and redraw the graph.

To graph the function

$$y = \frac{1}{x - 3},$$

enter that formula into the "y equals" screen (note the use of parentheses). As before, this example uses the standard viewing window.

For this function, the TI-86 produces the graph shown on the right. This illustrates one of the pitfalls of the connect-the-dots method used by the calculator: The nearly-vertical line segment drawn at $x = 3$ *should not be there*, but it is drawn because the calculator connects the points

$$x = 2.85714, \ y = -6.99999 \ \text{and} \ x = 3.01587, \ y = 62.99999.$$

Calculator users must learn to recognize these flaws in calculator-produced graphs.

The graph of a circle centered at the origin with radius 8 (shown on the square window ZOOM:ZSTD - ZOOM:ZSQR) shows another problem that arises from connecting the dots. When $x = -8.093841$, y is undefined, so no point is plotted (that is, there is no point on this circle that has x-coordinate less than -8, or greater than 8). The next point plotted on the upper half of the circle is $x = -7.824046$ and $y = 1.668619$; since no point had been plotted for the previous x-coordinate, this is not connected to anything, so there appears to be a gap between the circle and the x-axis. The calculator is not "smart" enough to know that the graph should extend from -8 to 8.

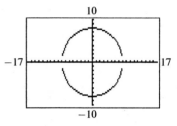

One additional feature of graphing with the TI-86 is that each function can have a "style" assigned to its graph. The symbol to the left of y1, y2, etc. indicates this style, which can be changed by choosing GRAPH:y(x)=:STYLE to cycle through the options. These options are shown on the right (with brief descriptive names); complete details are in the TI-86 manual.

13   Adding programs to the TI-86

The TI-86's capabilities can be extended by downloading or entering programs into the calculator's memory. Instructions for writing a program are beyond the scope of this manual, but programs written by others and downloaded from the Internet (or obtained as printouts) can be transferred to the calculator in one of three ways:

1. If one TI-86 already has a program, it can be transferred to another using the calculator-to-calculator link cable. To do this, first make sure the cable is firmly inserted in both calculators. On the sending calculator, press [2nd][x-VAR] (LINK), then [F1]:[F2] (SEND:PRGM), and then select (by using the [▲] and [▼] keys and [F2]) the program(s) to be transferred. *Before* pressing [F1] (SEND) on the sending calculator, prepare the receiving calculator by pressing [2nd][x-VAR][F2], and *then* press [F1] on the sending calculator.

2. If a computer with the TI-Graph Link is available, and the program file is on that computer (e.g., after having been downloaded from the Internet), the program can be transferred to the calculator using the TI Graph Link software. This transfer is done in a manner similar to the calculator-to-calculator transfer described above; specific instructions can be found in the documentation that accompanies the Graph Link software. (They are not given here because of slight differences between platforms and software versions.)

3. View a listing of the program and type it in manually. (**Note:** Even if the TI-Graph Link cable is not available, the Graph Link software can be used to view program listings on a computer.) While this is the most tedious method, studying programs written by others can be a good way to learn programming. To enter a program, start by choosing [PRGM][F2] (EDIT), then type a name for the new

program (up to eight letters, like "QuadForm" or "Midpoint")—note that the TI-86 is automatically put into ALPHA mode. Then type each command in the program, and press 2nd EXIT (QUIT) to return to the home screen when finished.

To run the program, make sure there is nothing on the current line of the home screen, then press PRGM F1, select the program using one of the keys F1–F5 and MORE (a sample screen is shown; only the first four to six characters of each 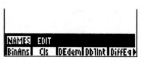 program name are shown), and press ENTER. If the program was entered manually (option 3 above), errors may be reported; in that case, choose GOTO, correct the mistake and try again.

Programs can be found at many places on the Internet, including:

- http://www.awl.com/lhs—the Web site for the text;

- http://www.bluffton.edu/~nesterd—the Web site of the author of this manual;

- http://tifaq.calc.org—A "Frequently Asked Questions" page maintained by Ray Kremer; and

- http://www.ticalc.org.

Examples

Here are the details for using the TI-86 for several of the examples from the textbook. Also given are the keystrokes necessary to produce some of the commands shown in the text's examples. In some cases, some suggestions are made for using the calculator more efficiently.

Throughout this section, it is assumed that the textbook is available for reference. The problems from the text are not restated here, and there are frequent references to the calculator screens shown in the text.

Section R.1   Example 2   (page 4)   Evaluating Exponential Expressions

This example discusses how to evaluate 4^3, $(-6)^2$, -6^2, $4 \cdot 3^2$, and $(4 \cdot 3)^2$.

To evaluate 4^3 with a TI-86, type $\boxed{4}\boxed{\wedge}\boxed{3}\boxed{\text{ENTER}}$; the TI-86 does not have a superscripted 3 for cubing. Only squaring and reciprocating—that is, the powers 2 and -1—can be displayed as superscripts (using $\boxed{x^2}$ and $\boxed{\text{2nd}}\boxed{\text{EE}}$, respectively). All other powers must use the $\boxed{\wedge}$ key. All other computations in this example are straightforward with the TI-86, except for this *caveat*: For $(-6)^2$ and -6^2, one

```
4^3
              64
( -6)²
              36
-6²
             -36
( -6)²■
```

must use the $\boxed{(-)}$ key rather than the $\boxed{-}$ key to enter "negative 6." In the screen shown, the second line was typed as $\boxed{(}\boxed{(-)}\boxed{6}\boxed{)}\boxed{x^2}$, while the fourth line was $\boxed{(}\boxed{-}\boxed{6}\boxed{)}\boxed{x^2}$. When $\boxed{\text{ENTER}}$ is pressed, the fourth line produces a syntax error—the calculator's way of saying that the line makes no sense.

Section R.1   Example 3   (page 5)   Using Order of Operations

Using the calculator for parts (a) and (b) of this example is straightforward; the expressions are entered as printed. For (c) and (d), we have the expressions

$$\frac{4 + 3^2}{6 - 5 \cdot 3} \quad \text{and} \quad \frac{-(-3)^3 + (-5)}{2(-8) - 5(3)}.$$

Entering these on the TI-86 requires us to add some additional parentheses to make sure the correct order of operations is followed.

Proper entry of the expression in (d) is shown on the right, in two different forms. The second illustrates some time-saving that can be done in keying in such expressions: The parentheses around -5 in the numerator were omitted, and the denominator $2(-8) - 5(3)$ was typed in as $\boxed{2}\boxed{\times}\boxed{(-)}\boxed{8}\boxed{-}\boxed{5}\boxed{\times}\boxed{3}$—the parentheses were exchanged for the multiplication symbol. It would be fine to type the

```
( -( -3)^3+( -5))/(2( -8)
-5(3))▶Frac
              -22/31
( -( -3)^3+ -5)/(2* -8-5*
3)▶Frac
              -22/31
■
```

expression unchanged, but the extra parentheses make it somewhat harder to read (and also mean more opportunities to make a mistake).

The screen shown above also illustrates the command ▶Frac at the end of the line. This command (which simply means "display the result of this computation as a fraction, if possible") is available in the MATH:MISC menu ($\boxed{\text{2nd}}\boxed{\times}\boxed{\text{F5}}\boxed{\text{MORE}}\boxed{\text{F1}}$). This is a useful enough command that one may wish to put it in the CUSTOM menu (see page 82).

Section R.2   Example 2   (page 18)   Evaluating Absolute Value

Section R.2   Example 3   (page 18)   Finding Absolute Values of Sums and Differences

The absolute value function abs is found in the MATH:NUM menu (2nd ✕ F1 F5).
See the discussion of typing commands on page 81; the screen on the right illustrates that the TI-86 does not pay attention to upper- and lowercase.

```
abs (-5/8)▶Frac
                  5/8
ABS (-5/8)▶Frac
                  5/8
aBs (-5/8)▶Frac
                  5/8
■
```

Section R.6   Example 4   (page 58)   Using the Definition of $a^{1/n}$

In evaluating these fractional exponents with a calculator, some time can be saved by entering fractions as decimals. The screen on the right performs the computations for (a), (b) and (c) with fewer keystrokes. (Of course, as noted in Section R.7 of the text, $36^{1/2} = \sqrt{36}$, which requires even fewer keystrokes.)

```
36^.5
              6
-100^.5
            -10
625^.25
              5
■
```

Note for (d), the parentheses around -1296 cannot be omitted: The text observes that this is not a real number, but the calculator will display a real result if the parentheses are left out. (See also the next example.) For (e), the decimal equivalent of $1/3$ is $0.\overline{3}$, which can be entered as a sufficiently long string of 3s (at least 12). The last line shows a better way to do this; the TI-86's order of operations

```
-1296^.25
               -6
(-27)^.333333333333
               -3
(-27)^3⁻¹
               -3
■
```

is such that 3^{-1} is evaluated before the other exponentiation. This method would also work for the other computations; e.g., (a) could be entered 3 6 ^ 2 2nd EE.

Section R.6   Example 5   (page 59)   Using the Definition of $a^{m/n}$

For (f), attempting to evaluate $(-4)^{5/2}$ will produce the result shown on the right. This is the TI-86's way of displaying complex numbers (which are discussed in the text beginning in Section 1.3); the result $(0,32)$ would be written as $0 + 32i$ in the format used by the text.

```
(-4)^(5/2)
            (0,32)
■
```

Section R.7   Example 1   (page 65)   Evaluating Roots

Aside from the square root function $\int$ (2nd x^2), the TI-86 has an "x-root" function ($^x\!\int$), found in the MATH:MISC menu (2nd ✕ F5 MORE F4). For example, "3$^x\!\int$ 1000" would compute $\sqrt[3]{1000}$ for part (d). It is worth noting that fourth roots can be typed in more efficiently using two square roots, since $\sqrt[4]{a} = a^{1/4} = (a^{1/2})^{1/2} = \sqrt{a^{1/2}} = \sqrt{\sqrt{a}}$.

Section 1.1   Example 1   (page 87)   Solving a Linear Equation

The TI-86 offers several approaches to solving (or confirming a solution to) an equation. Aside from graphical approaches to solving equations (which are discussed later, on page 98), here are some non-graphical (numerical) approaches: As illustrated on the right, the TI-86's `Solver` function (found in the CATALOG) attempts to find a value of x that makes the given expression equal to 0, given a guess (5, in this case). The solution is stored in the variable x (or whatever variable is used in the equation), but as the screen shows, this solution is not automatically displayed. A colon can be used to place the two lines shown on a single line.

For the equations in this section, the "guess" value does not affect the result, but for equations in later sections, different guesses might produce different results. Full details on how to use this function can be found in the TI-86 manual.

Since it is difficult to access the `Solver` command, it might be a good idea to place `Solver` in the CUSTOM menu (see page 82), or to use the "interactive solver" built-in to the TI-86. This feature is found by pressing 2nd GRAPH.

Solver begins with the first screen below (a), requesting an equation, which must include at least one variable. (The "eqn:" line might not be blank, since Solver remembers the most recent equation entered into it.) The menu at the bottom of the screen lists any user-defined variables in the calculator's memory. The expression for this example is shown in screen (b); use ALPHA STO▸ to type the equals sign. Pressing ENTER or ▼ brings up screen (c). Type the guess (this example uses 5), then press F5 (SOLVE) and the TI-86 seeks a solution near 5, which is reported in screen (d). (Make sure the cursor is on the "x=" line when F5 is pressed.)

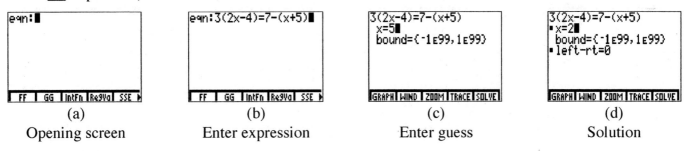

| (a) | (b) | (c) | (d) |
| Opening screen | Enter expression | Enter guess | Solution |

From screen (c) or (d), pressing ▲ returns to screen (b), so that the equation can be edited.

The Solver can also be used with equations containing more than one variable; simply provide values for all but one variable, then place the cursor on the line containing the variable for which a value is needed and press F2.

Note: In this example, we learned how the TI-86 can be used to support an analytic solution. But the TI-86 and any other graphing calculator also can be used for solving problems when an analytic solution is **not** possible—that is, when one cannot solve an equation "algebraically." This is often the case in many "real-life" applications, and is one of the best arguments for the use of graphing calculators.

| Section 1.3 | Example 1 | (page 109) | Writing $\sqrt{-a}$ as $i\sqrt{a}$ |

| Section 1.3 | Example 2 | (page 109) | Finding Products and Quotients Involving Negative Radicands |

| Section 1.3 | Example 3 | (page 110) | Simplifying a Quotient Involving a Negative Radicand |

The TI-86 does these computations almost as shown in the text, except that it reports the results differently. The screen on the right illustrates the output from the computations for parts (b) and (d) of Example 2. The TI-86 uses the format (a, b) for the complex number $a + bi$; whenever the TI-86 does a computation involving square roots of negative numbers, it reports the results in this format *even if the result is real.* Thus $(-7.74596669242, 0)$ represents the real number $-7.74596669242 \approx -2\sqrt{15}$, and $(0, 1.41421356237)$ is $i\sqrt{2}$.

While the calculator always reports complex *results* in this format*, it can recognize *input* typed in using the text's format by first defining a variable i as the complex number $(0, 1) = 0 + 1i$. Shown on the right is a computation using this definition. One could also use I (uppercase), which can be typed with one less keystroke, but i will be used in these examples.

*Results can also be reported in "polar format" by changing the "RectC PolarC" mode setting, but this format is even further removed from the $a + bi$ format used in the text.

| Section 1.3 | Example 4 | (page 110) | Adding and Subtracting Complex Numbers |

| Section 1.3 | Example 5 | (page 111) | Multiplying Complex Numbers |

| Section 1.3 | Example 6 | (page 112) | Simplifying Powers of i |

| Section 1.3 | Example 7 | (page 113) | Dividing Complex Numbers |

Using the variable i defined to be $(0, 1)$ — as was described in the previous example — computations like these can be done in a manner similar to those illustrated in the text's calculator screens. The screens on the right show (in the TI-86's format) the same results as those in the text accompanying Examples 5 and 7.

Section 1.4	Example 5	(page 120)	Using the Quadratic Formula (Real Solutions)
Section 1.4	Example 6	(page 120)	Using the Quadratic Formula (Nonreal Complex Solutions)
Section 1.4	Example 7	(page 121)	Solving a Cubic Equation

The TI-86 can solve quadratic and cubic equations (as well as higher-degree polynomial equations) using its built-in polynomial solver, accessed through [2nd] [PRGM] (POLY). This first prompts the user for the "order" (degree) of the polynomial, meaning the highest power of x. For the quadratic equations of Examples 5 and 6, this should be 2; for Example 7, the order is 3.

Pressing [ENTER] then brings up the screen on the right, requesting the coefficients of the equation. Note that the top line of the screen contains a reminder that the expression must be equal to 0. The menu at the bottom indicates that [F1] will clear the coefficients, while [F5] solves the equation.

Pressing [F5] reports the solutions in much the same way as the program shown in the text (although it does not specify that the roots are real). [F1] allows the user to change the coefficient values (that is, it goes back to the previous screen), and [F2] provides a way to store the coefficients in a variable (as a list).

For Example 6, the TI-86 reports the solutions (using its complex number format) as approximately $0.25 \pm 1.3919i$ — the decimal equivalents of the answers given in the text. Note in the results for Example 7, the real solution -2 is displayed as $(-2, 0) = -2 + 0i$; if any of the solutions are complex, the TI-86 displays all of them in its complex format.

Section 1.5	Example 1	(page 126)	Solving a Problem Involving the Volume of a Box

A *table* can be a useful tool to solve equations like this. To use the table features of the TI-86, begin by entering the formula ($y = 15x^2 - 200x + 500$) on the GRAPH:y(x)= screen, as one would to create a graph. (The highlighted equals signs determine which formulas will be displayed in the table, just as they do for graphs.)

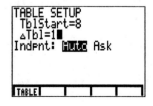

Next, press [TABLE][F2] to access the TABLE SETUP screen. The table will display y values for given values of x. The TblStart value sets the lowest value of x, while ΔTbl determines the "step size" for successive values of x. These two values are only used if the Indpnt option is set to Auto — this means, "automatically generate the values of the independent variable (x)." The effect of setting this option to Ask is illustrated at the end of this example.

When the TABLE SETUP options are set satisfactorily, press [F1] (TABLE) to produce the table. Shown (above, right) is the table generated based on the settings in the above screen; the fact that y is negative for $x = 8$ and $x = 9$ supports the restriction $x > 10$ from Step 3 of the example. By pressing [▼] repeatedly, the x values are increased, and the y values updated. (Pressing [▲] decreases the x values, but clearly that is not appropriate for this problem.) After pressing [▼] ten times, the table looks like the second screen, which shows that y1 equals 1435 when x equals 17.

Extension: Suppose the specifications called for the box to be 1500 cubic inches (instead of 1435). We see from the table above that x must be between 17 and 18 inches. The TI-86's table capabilities provide a convenient way to "zoom in" on the value of x (which could also be found with the Solver, or by other methods).

Since $17 < x < 18$, set TblStart to 17 and ΔTbl to 0.1. This produces the table shown on the right, from which we see that $17.2 < x < 17.3$. Now set TblStart to 17.2 and ΔTbl to 0.01, which reveals that x is between 17.2 and 17.21. This process can be continued to achieve any desired degree of accuracy.

Finally, the screen on the right shows the effect of setting Indpnt to Ask. Initially, the table is blank, but as values of x are entered, the y values are computed. Up to six x values can be entered; if more are desired, the [DEL] key can be used to make room.

Section 1.7 Example 1 (page 147)	Solving a Linear Inequality

Section 1.7 Example 2 (page 148)	Solving a Linear Inequality

Shown is one way to visualize the solution to inequalities like these. The inequality symbols $>$, $<$, $\geq$, $\leq$ are found in the TEST menu ([2nd][2nd][×]). The TI-86 responds with 1 when a statement is true and 0 for false statements. This is why the graph of y1 appears as it does: For values of x less than 4, the inequality is true (and so y1 equals 1), and for $x \geq 4$, the inequality is false (and y1 equals 0). Note that this picture does *not* help one determine what happens when $x = 4$.

Section 1.7   Example 3   (page 149)   Solving a Three-Part Inequality

To see a "picture" of this inequality like the one shown for the previous two examples requires a little additional work. Setting y1=-2<5+3x<20 will *not* work correctly. Instead, one must enter either

   y1=(-2<5+3x)(5+3x<20)   or   y1=(-2<5+3x) and (5+3x<20)

which will produce the desired results: A function that equals 1 between $-\frac{7}{3}$ and 5, is equals 0 elsewhere. ("and" is most easily entered either by selecting it from the CATALOG, or by simply typing it letter-by-letter; note the spaces before and after, typed by pressing [2nd][(-)]).

Section 1.7   Example 5   (page 150)   Solving a Quadratic Inequality

Section 1.7   Example 6   (page 151)   Solving a Quadratic Inequality

Section 1.7   Example 8   (page 154)   Solving a Rational Inequality

Section 1.7   Example 9   (page 155)   Solving a Rational Inequality

The methods described above can also be applied to these inequalities.

Extension: Can the calculator be used to solve the inequality $x^2 + 6x + 9 > 0$? Yes—if it is used carefully. Shown is the graph of the expression $x^2 + 6x + 9 >$ 0. This suggests that the inequality is true for all x; that is, the solution set is $(-\infty, \infty)$.

This conclusion is **not correct**: The graph of $y = x^2 + 6x + 9$ (without "> 0") touches the x-axis at $x = -3$, which means that this must be excluded from the solution set, since "> 0" means the graph must be above (not on) the x-axis. The correct solution set is $(-\infty, -3) \cup (-3, \infty)$.

This example should serve as a warning: Sometimes, the TI-86 will mislead you. When possible, try to confirm the calculator's answers in some way.

Section 1.8   Example 1   (page 161)   Solving Absolute Value Equations

The "solver" features described on page 94 of this manual can be used for these equations, too. Recall that abs is entered as [2nd][×][F1][F5].

Section 2.1   Example 5   (page 186)   Using the Midpoint Formula

The TI-86 can do midpoint computations nicely by putting coordinates in parentheses, as shown on the right. (The TI-86 interprets an ordered pair such as (8,-4) as the complex number $8 - 4i$, but since adding two complex numbers means adding their corresponding parts, the computations are done in the correct way to find the midpoint.)

Section 2.1   Example 10   (page 190)   Graphing a Circle

The text suggests graphing y1=4+∫(36-(x+3)²) and y2=4-∫(36-(x+3)²). Here are three options to speed up entering these formulas:

- After typing the formula in y1, move the cursor to y2 and press 2nd STO► (RCL), then type y1 ENTER (note that F2 will produce the lowercase y). This will "recall" the formula of y1, placing that formula in y2. Now edit this formula, changing the first "+" to a "−."

- After typing the formula in y1, enter y2=8-y1. This produces the desired results, since $8 - y1 = 8 - (4 + \sqrt{36 - (x + 3)^2}) = 8 - 4 - \sqrt{36 - (x + 3)^2} = 4 - \sqrt{36 - (x + 3)^2}$.

- Enter the single formula y1=4+{-1,1}∫(36-(x+3)²). (The curly braces { and } are F1 and F2 in the LIST menu, 2nd −). When a list (like {-1,1}) appears in a formula, it tells the TI-86 to graph this formula several times, using each value in the list.

The window chosen in the text is a square window (see Section 11 of the introduction of this chapter), so that the graph looks like a circle. (On a non-square window, the graph would look like an ellipse—that is, a distorted circle.) Note, however, that on the TI-86, this window is not square. Other square windows would also produce a "true" circle, but some will leave gaps similar to those circles shown in Sections 11 and 12 of the introduction (pages 85–86). Shown is the same circle on the square window produced by "squaring up" the standard window— GRAPH:ZOOM:ZSTD - ZOOM:ZSQR.

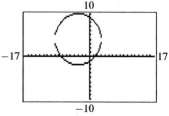

Section 2.2   Example 6   (page 205)   Using Function Notation

Section 2.2   Example 7   (page 205)   Using Function Notation

The TI-86 will do *some* computations in function notation. Simply enter the function in y1 (or any other function). Return to the home screen and enter y(2) to evaluate that function with the input 2. The result shown on the screen agrees with (a) in the text.

   The TI-86 is less helpful if asked to evaluate expressions like those given in Example 6(b) or Example 7. For example, "y1(q)" produces an error message or an unpredictable result (depending on how the variable q is defined), rather than the desired result $-q^2 + 5q - 3$.

Section 2.3   Example 3   (page 215)   Graphing a Vertical Line

The text notes that such a line is not a function; therefore, it cannot be graphed by entering the equation on the GRAPH:y(x)= screen. However, the TI-86 does provide a fairly straightforward method of graphing vertical lines using the Vert command.

From the home screen, type the Vert command one letter at a time, or using the function catalog (see page 82), then type the x-coordinate of the line. When ENTER is pressed, the line will be drawn.

Alternatively, the vertical line can be drawn "interactively" if the VERT command is accessed through the GRAPH:DRAW menu (GRAPH MORE F2 F3). This allows the user to move the cursor (and the vertical line) to the desired position using the ◀ and ▶ keys. Pressing ENTER places the line at that location, then allows more lines to be drawn. (Press GRAPH to finish drawing vertical lines.) Note that since $x = -3$ does not correspond to a column of pixels on the screen (see page 85), the vertical line is actually located at $x \approx -3.0159$, but the appearance on the screen is the same as if it were at $x = -3$.

Section 2.4   Example 5   (page 230)   Finding Equations of Parallel and Perpendicular Lines

In the discussion following this example (on page 231), the text notes that the lines from part (b) do not appear to be perpendicular unless they are plotted on a square window. See Section 11 of the introduction of this chapter (page 85) for more information about square windows.

Section 2.4   Example 6   (page 232)   Finding an Equation of a Line That Models Data

Section 2.4   Example 7   (page 233)   Finding a Linear Equation That Models Data

Aside from the methods described in these two examples, the text refers to the technique of linear regression on page 235. Figure 48 illustrates the steps on a TI-83; here is a more detailed description of the process on a TI-86 (using the data of Example 7).

Given a set of data pairs (x, y), the TI-86 can find various formulas (including linear and quadratic, as well as more complex formulas) that approximate the relationship between x and y. These formulas are called "regression formulas."

The first step in determining the regression formula is to enter the data into the TI-86. This is done by pressing 2nd + F2 (STAT:EDIT), which should produce the screen on the right. If xStat, yStat, and fStat are not on the STAT:EDIT screen, and pressing ◀ and ▶ does not reveal them, they can be restored to this screen by entering the command SetLEdit ("set up the list editor") on the home screen. This command is available by pressing 2nd – F5 MORE MORE MORE F3.

In the STAT:EDIT screen, enter the year values into the first column (xStat) and the percentage of women into the second column (yStat). The third column (fStat) should contain ten "1"s; this tells the TI-86 that each of these (x, y) pairs occurs only once in the data list. If any column already contains data, the DEL key can be used to delete numbers one at a time, or—to delete the whole column at once—press the ▲ key until the cursor is at the top of the column (on xStat, yStat, or fStat) and press CLEAR ENTER. Make sure that all three columns contain the same number of entries.

To do the computation, press EXIT, then 2nd + F1 (STAT:CALC). The bottom of the screen now lists the various options for the type of calculation to be done. We want to do a linear regression, which is F3 (LinR).

Pressing ENTER displays the results of the regression (shown on the right). These numbers agree (after rounding) with those in the text, except that the roles of a and b have been switched; these numbers are for a model of the form y=a+bx, rather than y=ax+b.

Section 2.4   Example 8   (page 235)   Solving an Equation with a Graphing Calculator

The text illustrates a graphical process for solving the equation $-2x - 4(2-x) = 3x + 4$; in this discussion, we will show two graphical methods for solving the equation $\frac{1}{2}x - 6 = \frac{3}{4}x - 9$. (The answer is $x = 12$.)

The first method is the **intersection** method. To begin, set up the TI-86 to graph the left side of the equation as y1, and the right side as y2. **Note:** Putting the fractions in parentheses ensures no mistakes with order of operations. This is not crucial for the TI-86, but is a good practice because some other models give priority to implied multiplication. See section 8 of the introduction, page 82.

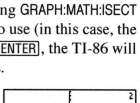

We are looking for an x value that will make the left and right sides of this equation equal to each other, which corresponds to the x-coordinate of the point of intersection of these two graphs.

After selecting a viewing window which shows the point of intersection—in this example, $[-15, 15] \times [-10, 10]$ is a convenient choice—the TI-86 can automatically locate this point using GRAPH:MATH:ISECT (GRAPH MORE F1 MORE F3). Use ▲, ▼ and ENTER to specify which two functions to use (in this case, the only two being displayed), and then use ◄ or ► to specify a guess. After pressing ENTER, the TI-86 will try to find an intersection of the two graphs. The screens below illustrate these steps.

    GRAPH MORE   ENTER (choose y1)   ENTER (choose y2)   ENTER (specify
    F1 MORE F3   guess)

The final result of this process is the screen shown on the right. The x-coordinate of this point of intersection is calculated to 14 digits of accuracy, so if the solution were some less "convenient" number (say, $\sqrt{3}$ or $1/\pi$), we would have an answer that would be accurate enough for nearly any computation.

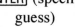

Note: An approximation for the point of intersection can be found simply by moving the TRACE cursor as near the intersection as possible. The amount of error can be minimized by "zooming in" on the graph. This is the only method available for graphing calculators such as the TI-81.

The second graphical approach is to use the x-**intercept method**, which seeks the x-coordinate of the point where a graph crosses the x-axis. Specifically, we want to know where the graph of y1−y2 crosses the x-axis, where y1 and y2 are as defined above. This is because the equation $\frac{1}{2}x - 6 = \frac{3}{4}x - 9$ can only be true when $\frac{1}{2}x - 6 - \left(\frac{3}{4}x - 9\right) = 0$. (This is the approach illustrated in the text for Example 8.)

To find this x-intercept, begin by defining y3=y1-y2 on the GRAPH:y(x)= screen. We could do this by re-typing the formulas entered for y1 and y2, but having typed those formulas once, it is more efficient to do this as shown on the right. The simplest way to type "y1" and "y2" is to use the F2 key to produce "y." Note that y1 and y2 have been "de-selected" so that they will not be graphed (see section 12 of the introduction, page 86).

We must first select a viewing window which shows the x-intercept; we again use $[-15, 15] \times [-10, 10]$. The TI-86 can automatically locate this point with the GRAPH:MATH:ROOT (GRAPH MORE F1 F1) feature ("root" is a synonym for "x-intercept"). The TI-86 prompts for left and right bounds (numbers that are, respectively, less than and greater than the root) and a guess, then attempts to locate the root between the given bounds. (Provided there is only one root between the bounds, and the function is "well-behaved"— meaning it has some nice properties like continuity—the calculator will find it.) The screens below illustrate these steps.

| (move cursor) | (move cursor) | (move cursor) | Here is the result. |
| ENTER | ENTER | ENTER | |

Section 2.5   Example 2   (page 246)   Graphing Piecewise-Defined Functions

The text shows two methods for entering piecewise-defined functions on the TI-86. Recall that the inequality symbols $>$, $<$, $\geq$, $\leq$ are found in the TEST menu (2nd 2). The use of DOT (DrawDot) mode is not crucial to the graphing process, as long as one remembers that vertical line segments connecting the "pieces" of the graph (in this case, at $x = 2$) are not really part of the graph.

The advantage of the method used in (b)—placing the piecewise definition in a single formula—is that y1 will act exactly like the function f. For example, to evaluate $f(5)$ in (a), one would first have to check which formula to use (y1 or y2). To evaluate $f(5)$ in (b), simply enter y1(5). Also, when a single formula is used, TRACE will properly show the behavior of the function as the trace cursor moves left and right.

Extension: Use a similar procedure for more complicated piecewise-defined functions, such as

$$f(x) = \begin{cases} 4 - x^2 & \text{if } x < -1 \\ 2 + x & \text{if } -1 \leq x \leq 4 \\ -2 & \text{if } x > 4 \end{cases}$$

shown here in DOT (DrawDot) mode on the standard viewing window. It does not work to define y1=(4-x²)(x<-1)+(2+x)(-1≤x≤4)+(-2)(x>4). Instead, use

   y1=(4-x²)(x<-1)+(2+x)(-1≤x and x≤4)+(-2)(x>4),   or

   y1=(4-x²)(x<-1)+(2+x)(-1≤x)(x≤4)+(-2)(x>4)

(the "and" in the first formula is most easily entered either by selecting it from the CATALOG, or by simply typing it letter-by-letter; note the spaces before and after, typed by pressing 2nd (-)).

Section 2.5   Example 3   (page 247)   Graphing a Greatest Integer Function

We wish to graph the step function $y = \left[\!\left[\frac{1}{2}x + 1\right]\!\right]$. This is entered on the TI-86 as shown on the right (any one of y1, y2, or y3). int is found in the MATH:NUM menu, $\boxed{\text{2nd}}\boxed{\times}\boxed{\text{F1}}$.

```
Plot1 Plot2 Plot3
\y1 int (x/2+1)
\y2 int ((1/2)x+1)
\y3 int (.5 x+1)
```
```
  x     y    INSf  DELf  SELCT
round iPart fPart  int   abs ▸
```

Section 2.6   Example 1   (page 253)   Stretching or Shrinking a Graph

---

Section 2.6   Example 2   (page 254)   Reflecting a Graph Across an Axis

---

Section 2.6   Example 6   (page 259)   Translating a Graph Vertically

---

Section 2.6   Example 7   (page 260)   Translating a Graph Horizontally

See page 87 for information on setting the thickness of a graph. Note that the symbol next to Y2 in the screen shown in the text indicates that the graph should be thick, as it does (for y2) on the TI-86.

It is possible to distinguish between the two graphs without having them drawn using different styles. When two or more graphs are drawn, the TRACE feature can be used to determine which graphs correspond to which formulas: By pressing $\boxed{\blacktriangle}$ and $\boxed{\blacktriangledown}$, the trace cursor jumps from one graph to another, and the upper right corner displays the number of the current formula. On the right, the trace cursor is on graph 2—that is, the graph of $g(x) = 2|x|$.

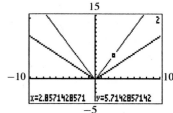

Also note that the TI-86 does not support split-screen mode, which was used to produce the screen shown in the text (with a graph above, and the "y equals" screen below).

Section 2.7   Example 5   (page 272)   Evaluating Composite Functions

The expressions shown in the calculator screens on page 273 will also work on the TI-86's home screen. To type "y" on the home screen, press $\boxed{\text{2nd}}\boxed{\text{ALPHA}}\boxed{0}$. Note that while commands and built-in functions like abs can be typed in in either upper- or lowercase, functions like y1 must be typed with a lowercase y.

Section 3.1   Example 1   (page 295)   Graphing Quadratic Functions

---

Section 3.1   Example 2   (page 297)   Graphing a Parabola by Completing the Square

---

Section 3.1   Example 3   (page 298)   Graphing a Parabola by Completing the Square

The TI-86 can automatically locate the vertex of the parabola (to a reasonable degree of accuracy). We illustrate this procedure for the function in Example 1(c). After defining y1=-(1/2)(x-4)²+3 and choosing a suitable window, go to the GRAPH:MATH menu ($\boxed{\text{MORE}}\boxed{\text{F1}}$), shown on the first screen below. Pressing $\boxed{\text{MORE}}$ again brings up the menu shown in the second screen; choose $\boxed{\text{F4}}$ for an upward-opening parabola, or $\boxed{\text{F5}}$ for a downward-opening parabola (like the one in this example). The TI-86 then prompts for left and right bounds (numbers that are, respectively, less than and greater than the location of the vertex) and a guess, and the TI-86 will try to find the highest (or lowest) point on the graph between the given bounds. (For some functions, it might not always find the correct maximum or minimum, but for parabolas, it should succeed.) The screens below illustrate the procedure.

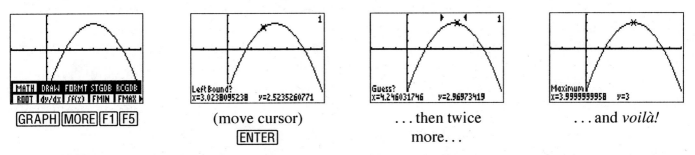

GRAPH MORE F1 F5   (move cursor)   . . . then twice   . . . and *voilà!*
                                ENTER   more. . .

Note that the x-coordinate rounds to 4; the degree of accuracy depends on the guess and the value of `tol` set on the TOLERANCE screen (2nd 3 F4). The results shown arose from `tol=1E-5`.

Section 3.1   Example 6   (page 302)   Modeling the Number of Hospital Outpatient Visits

See page 97 for information about using the TI-86 for regression computations. On the TI-86, a quadratic regression is called a "P2Reg" (polynomial-degree-2 regression.)

Section 3.2   Example 3   (page 317)   Deciding whether a Number is a Zero

The TI-86's "function notation" evaluation method (page 96 of this manual) can also be used to check for zeros: In the screen on the right, y1, y2, and y3 have been defined (respectively) as the functions in (a), (b), and (c). While the "function notation" evaluation method fails for complex numbers—y3(1+2i) or y3(1,2) results in an error—one can evaluate y3 at $1 + 2i$ by first storing that value in x, then requesting the value of y3 (with no parentheses, which means "evaluate using the current value of x"). The screen on the right shows the output of this sequence of commands. This screen assumes that i has been defined as (0, 1), as described on page 92; the command (1,2)→x:y3 would also work.

Section 3.3   Example 6   (page 327)   Finding All Zeros of a Polynomial Given One Zero

Section 3.4   Example 7   (page 340)   Approximating Real Zeros of a Polynomial Function

The TI-86's POLY feature (described on page 93) can determine *all* the zeros— not just the real zeros. The result of using this feature is shown on the right for Example 6, using the TI-86's complex number format.

Section 3.5   Example 2   (page 352)   Graphing a Rational Function

Note that this function is entered as y1=2/(1+x), **not** y1=2/1+x.

The issue of incorrectly drawn asymptotes is also addressed in Section 12 of the introduction to this chapter (page 86). Changing the window to xMin $= -5$ and xMax $= 3$ (or any choice of xMin and xMax which has -1 halfway between them) eliminates this vertical line because it forces the TI-86 to attempt to evaluate the function at $x = -1$. Since f is not defined at -1, it cannot plot a point there, and as a result, it does not attempt to connect the dots across the "break" in the graph.

Section 4.1   Example 7   (page 396)   Finding the Inverse of a Function with a Restricted Domain

Note that Figure 10 shows a square viewing window (see page 85); the mirror-image property of the inverse function would not be as clear on a non-square window. Note also that although this window is square on a TI-83, it is not quite square on a TI-86.

Section 4.2   Example 11   (page 412)   Using Data to Model Exponential Growth

See page 97 for information about using the TI-86 for regression computations.

Section 4.4   Example 1   (page 433)   Finding pH

For (a), the text shows -log(2.5*10^(-4)), but this could also be entered as shown on the first line of the screen on the right, since "E" (produced with [EE]) and "*10^" are nearly equivalent. The two are not completely interchangeable, however; in particular, in part (b), "10^" **cannot** be replaced with "E", because "E" is only valid when followed by an *integer*. That is, E-7 produces the same result as 10^-7, but the last line shown on the screen produces a syntax error.

```
-log (2.5E-4)
              3.60205999133
E-7
                        1E-7
E-7.1█
```

(Incidentally, "10^" is [2nd][LOG], but [1][0][^] produces the same results.)

Section 4.5   Example 8   (page 448)   Modeling Coal Consumption in the U.S.

The modeling function given in the text was found using a regression procedure (LnR, or logarithmic regression) similar to that described on page 97.

Section 5.1   Example 2   (page 476)   Calculating with Degrees, Minutes, and Seconds

---

Section 5.1   Example 3   (page 476)   Converting between Decimal Degrees
and Degrees, Minutes, and Seconds

See section 9 of this chapter's introduction (page 82) for information about selecting Degree mode. The alternative to putting the calculator in Degree mode is to use the degree symbol following each angle measure.

The MATH:ANGLE menu ([2nd][×][F3]) is shown on the right. It includes the degrees and minutes symbols, and the ▸DMS operator (which causes an angle to be displayed in degrees, minutes, and seconds, rather than as a decimal).

Entering angles on a TI-86, however, is different than on a TI-83 (which was used to create the screens shown in the text.) The degree and seconds symbols (° and ") are not used; the minutes symbol is used for all three positions, as in the screen on the right. (The results of the computations are displayed with the "usual" symbols.)

The screen on the right shows the proper way to enter the angles from Example 3 for computation on the TI-86.

Section 5.2   Example 4   (page 484)   Finding Function Values of Quadrantal Angles

The alternative to putting the calculator in Degree mode is to use the degree symbol ([2nd][×][F3][F1]) following each angle measure; e.g., enter sin 90° rather than just sin 90. (However, see the comment in the next example.)

Since the cotangent, secant, and cosecant functions are the reciprocals of the tangent, cosine, and sine, they can be entered as (e.g.) 1/sin 90. Note, though, that this will not properly compute cot 90°, since 1/tan 90 produces a domain error. Entering $\cot x$ as $\cos x / \sin x$ will produce the correct result at 90°.

One might guess that the other three trigonometric functions are accessed with [2nd] followed by [SIN], [COS], or [TAN] (which produce, e.g., sin^{-1}). This is **not** what these functions do; in this case, the exponent -1 does not mean "reciprocal," but instead indicates that these are inverse functions (which are discussed in Sections 5.3 and 7.5 of the text). The text comments on this distinction at th bottom of page 485.

Section 5.3   Example 6   (page 500)   Finding Function Values with a Calculator

Recall that the TI-86 uses a slightly different format for entering angles in degrees and minutes, as illustrated on the right. This screen also shows how computations like the secant in part (b) can be entered on a single line. These computations were done in Degree mode.

The screen on the right (with computations done in Radian mode) illustrates a somewhat unexpected behavior: Even if an angle is entered in DMS format, the TI-86 assumes that the angle is in radians. In order to remedy this, either put the calculator in Degree mode, or use the degree symbol ([2nd][×][F3][F1]) as was done in the second entry.

Section 5.3   Example 7   (page 500)   Using an Inverse Trigonometric Function to Find an Angle

---

Section 5.3   Example 8   (page 501)   Finding Angle Measures

The sin^{-1} ("inverse sine," or "arcsine") function is [2nd][SIN], while cos^{-1} is [2nd] [COS]. The computations shown in Figures 34 and 36 in the text were done in Degree mode; the screen on the right shows the result for Example 7 when done in Radian mode. Note that in the second entry, an attempt was made to get the TI-86 to report the result in degrees (by placing the degree symbol at the end of the entry), but this does not have the desired result.

Section 5.4   Example 1   (page 510)   Solving a Right Triangle Given an Angle and a Side

---

Section 5.4   Example 2   (page 511)   Solving a Right Triangle Given Two Sides

For problems like these, the Ans variable can be used to avoid loss of accuracy from rounding off intermediate results. Shown are computations for Example 1. (Be sure the TI-86 is in Degree mode. Also, recall that the arcsine (or inverse sine) function is 2nd SIN — *not* SIN 2nd EE.)

```
12.7 sin 34'30'
              7.19335920895
√(12.7²-Ans²)
              10.4664025955
sin⁻¹ (Ans/12.7)▶DMS
              55°30'0"
■
```

Section 5.4   Example 7   (page 514)   Solving a Problem Involving Angles of Elevation

The TI-86's GRAPH:MATH:ISECT (GRAPH MORE F1 MORE F3) feature will automatically locate the intersection of two graphs. Use ▲, ▼ and ENTER to specify which two functions to use (in this case, the only two being displayed), and then use ◄ or ► to specify a guess. After pressing ENTER, the TI-86 will try to find an intersection of the two graphs. The screens below illustrate these steps; the final result is the screen shown as Figure 51 of the text.

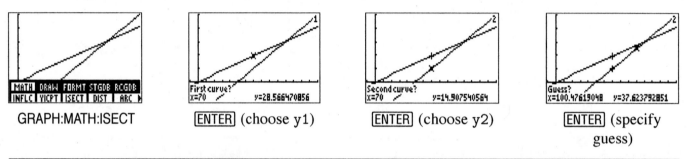

GRAPH:MATH:ISECT   ENTER (choose y1)   ENTER (choose y2)   ENTER (specify guess)

Section 6.1   Example 1   (page 535)   Converting Degrees to Radians

The number π is available as 2nd ^, and the degree symbol is 2nd × F3 F1. With the calculator in Radian mode (see page 82), entering 45° causes the TI-86 to automatically convert to radians.

A useful technique to aid in recognizing when an angle is a multiple of π is to divide the result by π. This approach is illustrated in the screen on the right, showing that 45° is $\pi/4$ radians, and 30° is $\pi/6$ radians. This screen also makes use of the ▶Frac command from the MATH:MISC menu (2nd × F5 MORE F1), which simply means "display the result of this computation as a fraction, if possible."

```
45°
           .785398163397
Ans/π▶Frac
                    1/4
30°/π▶Frac
                    1/6
■
```

This is a useful enough command that one may wish to put it in the CUSTOM menu (see page 82).

An alternative to using the degree symbol is to store $\pi/180$ in the calculator variable D (see page 82). Then typing, for example, 45D ENTER will multiply 45 by $\pi/180$. This approach will work regardless of whether the calculator is in Degree or Radian mode. (A value stored in a variable will remain there until it is replaced by a new value.)

```
π/180→D
           .01745329252
45D
           .785398163397
249.8D
           4.35983247148
■
```

Section 6.1   Example 2   (page 535)   Converting Radians to Degrees

With the TI-86 in Degree mode (see page 82), the radian symbol (a superscripted r), produced with 2nd × F3 F2, will automatically change a radian angle measurement to degrees.

Alternatively, with the value $180/\pi$ stored in the calculator variable R (see page 82), typing $(9\pi/4)$R [ENTER] will convert from radians to degrees regardless of whether the calculator is in Degree or Radian mode. (The same result can be achieved by *dividing by* the calculator variable D as defined in the previous example.)

```
180/π→R
            57.2957795131
(9π/4)R
                      405
4.25R
            243.507062931
■
```

Section 6.2   Example 4   (page 549)   Finding a Number Given Its Circular Function Value

The arccosine (or inverse cosine) function is [2nd][COS] —*not* [COS][2nd][EE]. Likewise, $\tan^{-1}$ is [2nd][TAN].

Section 6.3   Example 1   (page 559)   Graphing $y = a\sin x$

Note that the TI-86 must be in Radian mode in order to produce the desired graph. See page 87 for information on setting the thickness of a graph.

The graphs in the text are shown in the "trig viewing window," described on the top of page 558. The TI-86's default trig window (selected with [GRAPH][F3][MORE][F3]) is slightly wider than that shown in the text; it shows x from -2.625π to 2.625π. (If the TI-86 is in Degree mode, xMin and xMax will be ±472.5 instead of $\pm2.625\pi$.) The graph below is shown using the text's trig window, rather than the TI-86's.

It is possible to distinguish between the two graphs without having them drawn using different styles by using the TRACE ([GRAPH][F4]) feature. On the right, the trace cursor is on graph 2—that is, the graph of $y_2 = \sin x$. This approach is discussed on page 100 of this manual.

Section 6.3   Example 8   (page 566)   Modeling Temperature with a Sine Function

The "sine regression" illustrated at the end of this example is a built-in feature of the TI-86 (found in the STAT:CALC menu, [2nd][+][F1][MORE][F2]). See page 97 for information about using the TI-86 for regression computations.

Section 6.4   Example 1   (page 578)   Graphing $y = a\sec bx$

Section 6.4   Example 2   (page 579)   Graphing $y = a\csc(x - d)$

See section 9 of the introduction (page 82) for information about DrawLine versus Dot (DrawDot) mode. The function in Example 1 can be entered as y1=2cos (x/2)$^{-1}$ (or as shown in the text). The function in Example 2 can be entered as y1=(3/2)(1/sin (x-π/2)) or y1=3/(2sin (x-π/2)). A reminder: sin^{-1} ([2nd][SIN]) is *not* the cosecant function.

Section 7.1   Example 3   (page 609)   Rewriting an Expression in Terms of Sine and Cosine

The top screen on the right shows how these expressions are entered on the "y equals" screen. As an alternative to graphing these two functions, the TI-86's table feature (see page 93 of this manual) can be used: If the *y* values are the same for a reasonably large sample of *x* values, one can be fairly sure (though not certain) that the two expressions are equal. To make this approach more reliable, be sure to choose *x* values that are not, for example, all multiples of π.

Section 7.3   Example 1   (page 622)   Finding Exact Cosine Function Values

Section 7.3   Example 4   (page 626)   Finding Exact Sine and Tangent Function Values

The TI-86 can graphically and numerically support exact value computations such as $\cos 15° = \frac{\sqrt{6}+\sqrt{2}}{4}$. Starting with a graph of y1=cos x, the TI-86 makes it possible to evaluate y1 (or any function) for any value of *x* between xMin and xMax using the TI-86's GRAPH:EVAL (GRAPH MORE MORE F1) option. GRAPH:EVAL prompts for a value of *x*, which can be either a number like 15 or expression (like $1/\pi$ or $\sqrt{2}$). Pressing ENTER causes the cursor to jump to that *x*-coordinate.

Note that Example 8 in Section 7.4 (page 639) shows that $\cos 15°$ can also be written as $\frac{\sqrt{2+\sqrt{3}}}{2}$.

Section 7.5   Example 1   (page 646)   Finding Inverse Sine Values

Section 7.5   Example 2   (page 646)   Finding Inverse Cosine Values

Of course, it is not necessary to graph $y = \sin^{-1} x$ to find these values; one can simply enter, e.g., sin⁻¹ (1/2) on the home screen. The first entry of the screen on the right shows what happens when the calculator is in Degree mode; note that the result is not in $[-\pi/2, \pi/2]$. With the calculator in Radian mode, results similar to those in the text are found, and the method employed on page 104 of this manual (in the discussion of text Example 1 from Section 6.1) confirms that these values are $\pi/6$ and $3\pi/4$.

Note that the TI-86 does *not* give an error for the input sin⁻¹ -2, but instead gives a complex result: $-\pi/2 + i \ln(2 + \sqrt{3})$. The reason that this is technically a correct result is beyond the scope of the textbook; TI-86 owners should recognize that a complex answer is not appropriate for this problem, and so should ignore this result.

Section 7.5   Example 4   (page 651)   Finding Inverse Function Values with a Calculator

Note that the answer given for (c), 109.499054°, overrepresents the accuracy of that value. A typical rule for doing computations involving decimal values (like -0.3541) is to report only as many digits in the result as were present in the original number—in this case, four. This means the reported answer should be "about 109.5°," and in fact, any angle θ between about 109.496° and 109.501° has a cotangent which rounds to -0.3541.

Section 7.6   Example 9   (page 663)   Describing a Musical Tone from a Graph

Section 7.6   Example 10   (page 664)   Analyzing Pressures of Upper Harmonics

Note that the calculator screens shown in Figures 27–30 illustrate the importance of choosing a "good" viewing window. If we choose the wrong vertical scale (yMin and yMax), we might not be able to see the graph at all—it might be squashed against the x-axis. If we make the window too wide—that is, if xMax minus xMin is too large—we might see the "wrong" picture, like the one on the right (for Example 10): We seem to see six periods in this view, when in fact there are 44. Each of the six "pseudo-cycles" is made of parts of seven or eight full periods.

This observation—that a periodic function, viewed at fixed intervals, can appear to be a *different* periodic function—is the same effect that causes wagon wheels to appear to run backwards in old movies.

Section 8.3   Example 1   (page 716)   Finding Magnitude and Direction Angle

Section 8.3   Example 2   (page 716)   Finding Horizontal and Vertical Components

The TI-86 does not have the conversion functions shown in Figures 26 and 28, but can do the desired conversions in a manner that is perhaps even more convenient. The TI-86 recognizes vectors entered in either of two formats:

[*horizontal component , vertical component*]   or   [*magnitude ∠ angle*]

(The square brackets are 2nd [( ] and 2nd [ )], and "∠" is 2nd [,].) Regardless of how the vector is entered, the TI-86 displays it according to the R̲e̲c̲t̲V̲ ̲C̲y̲l̲V̲ ̲S̲p̲h̲e̲r̲e̲V̲ mode setting (see page 82); specifically, it displays the vector in component form in RectV mode, and in magnitude/angle form for either of the other two modes.

For Example 1, then, either put the TI-86 in CylV or SphereV mode, or (perhaps more conveniently), use the ▸Pol command (2nd 8 F4 F3), as the screen on the right illustrates. This causes a vector to be displayed in magnitude/direction angle format regardless of the mode setting. On the fourth line, we see the results of pressing ▸ to see all the digits of the angle. (With the TI-86 in Degree mode, the angle returned is in degrees.)

For Example 2, both the horizontal and vertical components can be found at once, as the screen on the right shows. (The vertical component is too long to fit on the screen, but the other digits can be seen by pressing ▶. Note that the screen shown in the text was created with the calculator set to display only one digit after the decimal.) These computations were done with the TI-86 in Degree mode, so it was not necessary to include the degree symbol on the angle. The third entry shown uses the ▶Rec command, which forces the vector to be displayed in component form regardless of the mode setting. (It was unnecessary in this case, because the TI-86 with in RectV mode.)

Section 8.3   Example 3   (page 717)   Writing Vectors in the Form ⟨*a*, *b*⟩

Note how easily these conversions are done in the TI-86's polar vector format. (The TI-86 was in Degree mode.)

Section 8.3   Example 5   (page 718)   Performing Vector Operations

Section 8.3   Example 6   (page 719)   Finding the Dot Product

Using the TI-86's vector notation, the vectors can be stored in calculator variables (see page 82) which can then be used to do the desired operations. Shown are the commands to compute 5(c): 4**u** − 3**v**, and 6(a): ⟨2, 3⟩ · ⟨4, −1⟩ (the dot command is 2nd 8 F3 F4).

Section 8.5   Example 2   (page 734)   Converting from Trigonometric Form to Rectangular Form

Complex numbers can be entered in trigonometric form in a manner similar to the polar format for vectors (see page 107); the screen on the right illustrates how to quickly convert from the TI-86's trigonometric form to its rectangular form (assuming the calculator is in RectC mode; see page 82). "∠" is 2nd ,.

Section 8.5   Example 3   (page 734)   Converting from Rectangular Form to Trigonometric Form

Although the TI-86 does not have the conversion functions shown on page 735, the same thing can be accomplished with the abs and angle commands, found in the TI-86's CPLX menu (2nd 9), and shown on page 737 of the text. On the screen on the right, note that if one makes use of the variable i defined as (0, 1), the angle and abs functions require parentheses; the third output is incorrect because it first computes the "angle" of the real number $-\sqrt{3}$ (which is π) and then adds this to i.

More convenient is the TI-86's ▶Pol command, found by pressing MORE in the CPLX menu. (This command is also found in the VECTR:OPS menu.) This gives both the magnitude and angle at the same time.

Section 8.5   Example 4   (page 735)

Converting Between Trigonometric and Rectangular Forms
Using Calculator Approximations

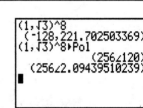

Aside from entering the expression in (a) as it is shown in the text (using the cos and sin functions), one can use the TI-86's polar format $(r \angle \theta)$, but be sure to either put the TI-86 in the correct mode (Degree or Radian) or use the degrees or radians symbol from the MATH:ANGLE menu. Both computations on the right were done in Radian mode, and the first result is incorrect.

Section 8.6   Example 1   (page 743)

Finding a Power of a Complex Number

The screen on the right shows several options for computing $(1 + i\sqrt{3})^8$ with the TI-86. The first is fairly straightforward, but the reported result shows the complex part of the answer ($128i\sqrt{3}$) given in decimal form. For an "exact" answer, the TI-86's polar format can be used. The TI-86 was in Degree mode for the first of the two polar-format answers, and in Radian mode for the second.

Section 8.6   Example 4   (page 746)

Solving an Equation by Finding Complex Roots

The TI-86's POLY polynomial solver (see page 93) can be used to see the pattern of these roots, if the calculator is in PolarC and Degree modes. The two negative angles shown in the second screen are coterminal with the angles $216°$ and $288°$ given in the text.

Section 8.7   Example 3   (page 751)

Examining Polar and Rectangular Equations
of Lines and Circles

Section 8.7   Example 4   (page 753)

Graphing a Polar Equation (Cardioid)

Section 8.7   Example 5   (page 753)

Graphing a Polar Equation (Rose)

Section 8.7   Example 6   (page 754)

Graphing a Polar Equation (Lemniscate)

To produce these polar graphs, the TI-86 should be set to Degree and Polar modes (see the screen on the right). In this mode, [GRAPH][F1] allows entry of polar equations (r as a function of θ). One could also use Radian mode, adjusting the values of θMin, θMax, and θStep accordingly (e.g., use 0, 2π, and $\pi/30$ instead of 0, 360, and 5).

For the cardioid, rose, and lemniscate, the window settings shown in the text show these graphs on "square" windows (see section 11 of the introduction, page 85), so one can see how their proportions compare to those of a circle. Note, however, that on the TI-86, these window are not square; the ZOOM:ZSQR option can be used to adjust the window dimensions to make it square.

For the cardioid, the value of θStep does not need to be 5, although that choice works well for this graph. Too large a choice of θStep produces a graph with lots of sharp "corners," like the one shown on the right (drawn with θStep=30). Setting θStep too small, on the other hand, produces a smooth graph, but it is drawn very slowly. Sometimes it may be necessary to try different values of θStep to choose a good one.

The lemniscate can be drawn by setting θMin=0 and θMax=180, or θMin=-45 and θMax=45. In fact, with θ ranging from -45 to 225, the graph of r1=$\int$cos (2θ) (alone) will produce the entire lemniscate. (θStep should be about 5.)

The rose can be produced by setting θMin=0 and θMax=360, or using any $360°$-range of θ values (with θStep about 5).

Section 8.7   Example 7   (page 755)   Graphing a Polar Equation (Spiral of Archimedes)

To produce this graph on the viewing window shown in the text, the TI-86 must be in Radian mode. (In Degree mode, it produces the same shape, but magnified by a factor of $180/\pi$ — meaning that the viewing window needs to be larger by that same factor.)

Section 8.8   Example 1   (page 761)   Graphing a Plane Curve Defined Parametrically

Place the TI-86 in Parametric mode, as the screen on the right shows. In this mode, GRAPH F1 allows entry of pairs of parametric equations (x and y as functions of t). No graph is produced unless both functions in the pair are entered and selected (that is, both equals signs are highlighted).

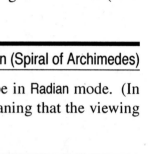

The value of tStep does not need to be 0.05, although that choice works well for this graph. Too large a choice of tStep produces a less-smooth graph, like the one shown on the right (drawn with tStep=1). Setting tStep too small, on the other hand, produces a smooth graph, but it is drawn very slowly. Sometimes it may be necessary to try different values of tStep to choose a good one.

Section 8.8   Example 3   (page 762)   Graphing a Plane Curve Defined Parametrically

This curve can be graphed in Degree mode with tMin=0 and tMax=360, or in Radian mode with tMax=2π. In order to see the proportions of this ellipse, it might be good to graph it on a square window. This can be done most easily with the ZOOM:ZSQR option (GRAPH F3 MORE F2). On a TI-86, initially with the window settings shown in the text, this would result in the window $[-6.8, 6.8] \times [-4, 4]$.

Section 8.8   Example 5   (page 763)   Graphing a Cycloid

The TI-86 *must* be in Radian mode in order to produce this graph.

Section 8.8   Example 6   (page 764)   Simulating Motion with Parametric Equations

Section 8.8   Example 8   (page 765)   Analyzing the Path of a Projectile

Parametric mode is particularly nice for analyzing motion, because one can picture the motion by watching the calculator create the graph, or by using TRACE ([GRAPH][F4]) and watching the motion of the trace cursor. (When tracing in parametric mode, the ▶ and ◀ keys increase and decrease the value of t, and the trace cursor shows the location (x, y) at time t.) Figure 80 illustrates tracing on the projectile path in Example 8. Note that the value of t changes by $\pm$tStep each time ▶ or ◀ is pressed, so obviously the choice of tStep affects which points can be traced.

The TI-86's graph styles (see page 87) can be useful, too. The screen on the right shows the three paths for Example 6 being plotted in "ball path" style.

Section 9.1   Example 1   (page 785)   Solving a System by Substitution

Section 9.1   Example 4   (page 787)   Solving a System with Infinitely Many Solutions

Section 9.1   Example 6   (page 790)   Solving a System of Three Equations with Three Variables

The TI-86's built-in SIMULT feature can be used to solve linear systems with up to 30 unknowns. Pressing [2nd] [TABLE] causes the TI-86 to prompt for the number of equations, after which it prompts for the coefficients, one equation at a time. The screens below show the first and third equations being entered; the arrow keys (or [F1] and [F2]) allow the user to move from one coefficient to another. When all the constants have been entered, pressing [F5] solves for the three unknowns (which the TI-86 calls x_1, x_2, and x_3, rather than x, y, and z).

For systems with no solutions, or infinitely many solutions (as in Example 4), the TI-86 gives a SINGULAR MAT error ("MAT" stands for "matrix"; these are discussed in Section 9.2 of the text).

`SIMULT`
`Number=3█`
	`a₁,₁X₁…a₁,₃X₃=b₁`
	`a₁,₁=3`
	`a₁,₂=9`
	`a₁,₃=6`
	`b₁=3█`
	
	`PREV  NEXT  CLRq        SOLVE`
		`a₃,₁X₁…a₃,₃X₃=b₃`
		`a₃,₁=1`
		`a₃,₂=1`
		`a₃,₃=1`
		`b₃=2█`
		
		`PREV  NEXT  CLRq        SOLVE`
			`x₁=2`
			`x₂=⁻1`
			`x₃=1`
			
			`COEFS  STOa  STOb  STOx`

[2nd][TABLE]...	enter coefficients...	Press [F5] when done...	results

Section 9.1   Example 8   (page 792)   Using Curve Fitting to Find an Equation Through Three Points

Note that the equation found in this example by algebraic methods can also be found very quickly on the TI-86 by performing a quadratic regression (P2Reg—see page 97) on the three given points. In the screen shown, PRegC is the list of "polynomial regression coefficients." These agree with the coefficients found in the text.

Section 9.2   Example 1   (page 802)   Using the Gauss-Jordan Method

Section 9.2   Example 2   (page 804)   Using the Gauss-Jordan Method

The menu shown in the text (Figure 7) is from a TI-83. The TI-86 has the four matrix row operations, but they are located in the MATRX:OPS menu (not MATRX:MATH), and the names are slightly different. The screen on the right shows this menu (visible after pressing 2nd 7 F4 MORE).

Before describing these operations, a few words about entering matrices into the TI-86: The matrix in the text has the name " [A]." On the TI-82 and TI-83, all matrices have names of the form [*letter*]; on the TI-86, matrices can have any variable name. (In fact, variable names *cannot* include the bracket characters on the TI-86.)

To change the entries in a matrix (e.g., to enter the augmented matrix for this example), either store the matrix using a home screen command (similar to the form used in the screen above), or use the MATRX:EDIT feature, then choose the name of a matrix (or type a name for a new matrix), specify the number of rows and columns, and type in the entries. The screen on the right shows the "edit" view of the matrix MAT, entered above.

The formats for the matrix row-operation commands are:

- rSwap(*matrix*,*A*,*B*) produces a new matrix that has row *A* and row *B* swapped.

- rAdd(*matrix*,*A*,*B*) produces a new matrix with row *A* added to row *B*.

- multR(*number*,*matrix*,*A*) produces a new matrix with row *A* multiplied by *number*.

- mRAdd(*number*,*matrix*,*A*,*B*) produces a new matrix with row *A* multiplied by *number* and added to row *B* (row *A* is unchanged).

Shown below are examples of each of these operations on the matrix $\text{MAT} = \begin{bmatrix} 1 & 4 & 7 \\ 2 & 5 & 8 \\ 3 & 6 & 9 \end{bmatrix}$.

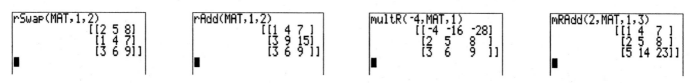

Keep in mind that these row operations leave the matrix MAT untouched. To perform a sequence of row operations, each result must either be stored in a matrix, or use the result variable Ans as the matrix. For example, with MAT equal to the augmented matrix for the system given in this example, the following screens illustrate the initial steps in the Gauss-Jordan method. Note the use of Ans in the last two screens.

As we see in Figure 7(d), the rref command ([2nd][7][F4][F5]) will do all the necessary row operations at once, making these individual steps seem tedious. On the TI-86, the parentheses are not needed, so the necessary command is rref MAT.

Section 9.3   Example 1   (page 813)   Evaluating a 2×2 Determinant

---

Section 9.3   Example 3   (page 816)   Evaluating a 3×3 Determinant

On a TI-86, the parentheses around the matrix name are not needed. The function "det" is available in the MATRX:MATH menu ([2nd][7][F3][F1]). Shown on the right is the TI-86 version of the screen in the text.

```
MAT
                    [[-3  4]
                     [6   8]]
det MAT
                          -48
∎
```

The determinant of a 3×3—or larger—matrix is as easy to find with a calculator as that of a 2×2 matrix. (At least, it is as easy for the user; the calculator is doing all the work!) Note, however, that trying to find the determinant of a non-square matrix (for example, a 3×4 matrix) results in a DIMENSION error.

Section 9.5   Example 2   (page 832)   Solving a Nonlinear System by Elimination

See the discussion of Example 10 from Section 2.1 on page 96 of this manual for tips on entering formulas like these.

The text shows the intersections as found by the procedure built in to the calculator (described on page 98 of this manual, called "ISECT" on the TI-86). However, that is somewhat misleading; for these equations, the TI-86 can only find these intersections if the "guesses" supplied by the user are the exact x coordinates of the intersections (that is, -2 and 2). This is because the two circle equations are only valid for $-2 \le x \le 2$, while the hyperbola equations are only valid for $x \le -2$ and $x \ge 2$. Since only ± 2 fall in both of these domains, any guess other than these two values results in a BAD GUESS error.

Section 9.6   Example 1   (page 843)   Graphing a Linear Inequality

With the TI-86, there are two ways to shade above or below a function. The simpler way is to use the "shade above" graph style (see page 87). The screen on the right shows the "shade above" symbol next to y1, which produces the graph shown in the text.

```
Plot1 Plot2 Plot3
▼y1■-(1/4)x+1∎
```

The other way to shade is the Shade(command, accessed in the GRAPH:DRAW menu ([GRAPH][MORE][F2][F1]). The format is

Shade(*lower*,*upper*,*min X*,*max X*,*pattern*,*resolution*)

Here *lower* and *upper* are the functions between which the TI-86 will draw the shading (above *lower* and below *upper*). The last four options can be omitted. *min X* and *max X* specify the starting and ending x values for the shading. If omitted, the TI-86 uses xMin and xMax.

The last two options specify how the shading should look. *pattern* determines the direction of the shading: 1 (vertical—the default), 2 (horizontal), 3 (negative-slope 45°—that is, upper left to lower right), or 4 (positive-slope 45°—that is, lower left to upper right). *resolution* is a positive integer (1,2,3,...) which specifies how dense the shading should be (1 = shade every column of pixels, 2 = shade every other column, 3 = shade every third column, etc.). If omitted, the TI-86 shades every column; i.e., it uses *resolution* = 1.

To produce a graph like the one accompanying Example 1 in the text, the appropriate command (typed on the home screen) would be something like

    Shade(-(1/4)x+1,10,-2,6,1,2).

The use of 10 for the *upper* function simply tells the TI-86 to shade up as high as necessary; this could be replaced by any number greater than 4 (the value of yMax for the viewing window shown). Also, if the function y1 had previously been defined as -(1/4)x+1, this command could be shortened to Shade(y1,10,-2,6,1,2).

One more useful piece of information: Suppose one makes a mistake in typing the Shade(command (e.g., switching *upper* and *lower*, or using the wrong value of *resolution*), resulting in the wrong shading. The screen on the right, for example, arose from typing Shade(-(1/4)x+1,1,-2,6,1,1). In order to achieve the desired results, the mistake must be erased using the CLDRW (clear drawing) command, found in the GRAPH:DRAW menu (GRAPH MORE F2 MORE MORE F1). Then—perhaps using deep recall (see page 81)—correct the mistake in the Shade(command and try again.

Section 9.6   Example 2   (page 844)   Graphing Systems of Inequalities

The easiest way to produce (essentially) the same graph as that shown in the text is to use the "shade above" graph style (see page 87). The screen on the right (above) shows the "shade above" symbol next to y1 and y2, with the results shown on the graph below. When more than one function is graphed with shading, the TI-86 rotates through the four shading patterns (see page 113); that is, it graphs the first with vertical shading, the second with horizontal, and so on. All shading is done with a resolution of 2 (every other pixel).

The Shade command can be used to produce this from the home screen. If y1=(6-x)/2 and y2=x²/2, the commands at right produce the graph shown in the text.

A nicer picture can be created, with a little more work, by making the observation that if y is greater than both $x^2/2$ and $(6-x)/2$, then for any x, y must be greater than the larger of these two expressions. The TI-86 provides a convenient way to find the larger of two numbers with the max(function, located in the LIST:OPS menu (2nd - F5 F5). Then max(y1,y2) will return the larger of y1 and y2, and the "y equals" screen entries shown on the right (above) will produce the graph shown below it. (Note the graph style settings: y1 and y2 display as solid curves, while y3 has the "shade above" style.) The home-screen command Shade(max(y1,y2),11,-10,10,1,2) would produce similar results.

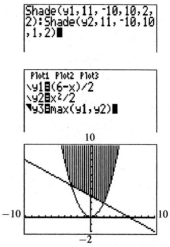

Extension: The table below shows how (using graph styles or home-screen commands) to shade regions that arise from variations on the inequalities in this example, assuming that y1=(6-x)/2 and y2=x²/2. (The results of these commands are not shown here.)

For the system. . .	or equivalently. . .	the command would be. . .
$x < 6 - 2y$ $x^2 < 2y$	$y < (6-x)/2$ $y > x^2/2$	shade below y1 and above y2, or enter Shade(y2,y1,-10,10,1,2)
$x > 6 - 2y$ $x^2 > 2y$	$y > (6-x)/2$ $y < x^2/2$	shade above y1 and below y2, or enter Shade(y1,y2,-10,10,1,2)
$x < 6 - 2y$ $x^2 > 2y$	$y < (6-x)/2$ $y < x^2/2$	shade below y1 and below y2, or enter Shade(-10,min(y1,y2),-10,10,1,2)

Section 9.7   Example 2   (page 854)   Adding Matrices

Section 9.7   Example 3   (page 855)   Subtracting Matrices

Section 9.7   Example 4   (page 856)   Multiplying Matrices by Scalars

---

Section 9.7   Example 6   (page 859)   Multiplying Matrices

See page 112 for information about matrices on the TI-86.

Section 9.8   Example 1   (page 868)   Verifying the Identity Property of I_3

On the TI-86, the function to produce identity matrices is `ident`, which does not require parentheses, and is located in the MATRX:OPS menu ([2nd][7][F4][F3]). The screen on the right shows the 3 × 3 identity matrix.

```
ident 3
          [[1 0 0]
           [0 1 0]
           [0 0 1]]
■
```

Section 9.8   Example 2   (page 870)   Finding the Inverse of a 3×3 Matrix

---

Section 9.8   Example 3   (page 872)   Identifying a Matrix with No Inverse

An inverse matrix is found using [2nd][EE] — the same method used to find the inverse of a real number. For example, to find the inverse of matrix MAT, type MAT (or choose that name from the MATRX:NAMES menu) then press [2nd][EE][ENTER]. An error will occur if the matrix is not square, or if it is a singular matrix (as in Example 3).

Section 10.1	Example 1	(page 893)	Graphing a Parabola with Horizontal Axis

Section 10.1	Example 2	(page 894)	Graphing a Parabola with Horizontal Axis

Section 10.2	Example 1	(page 904)	Graphing Ellipses Centered at the Origin

Section 10.3	Example 1	(page 914)	Using Asymptotes to Graph a Hyperbola

See the discussion of Example 10 from Section 2.1 on page 96 of this manual for tips on entering formulas like these.

When entering these formulas, make sure to use enough parentheses, so that operations are performed in the correct order; e.g., for Example 2 of Section 10.1, the formula in y1 should look like this:

$$y1=-1.5+\int((x-.5)/2)$$

Also, when looking at a calculator graph like the one shown in Figure 18 (page 595), keep in mind that the apparent gap between this graph and the x-axis is not really there; it is a flaw that arises from the calculator's method of plotting functions (see discussion on page 87 of this manual).

Section 11.1	Example 3	(page 939)	Modeling Insect Population Growth

One way to produce this sequence (and similar recursively defined sequences) is with the Ans variable, as shown on the right. (After pressing [1][ENTER], then typing the next line and pressing [ENTER], we simply press [ENTER] over and over to generate successive terms in the sequence.)

Figure 4 of the text shows a table of sequence terms, while Figure 5(b) shows a plot of the terms. While the TI-86 can generate tables for functions, it does not have the TI-83's "sequence mode," which was used to create these screens. See the discussion of Example 7 from Section 11.3 (below) for information on creating a plot like Figure 5(b), but note that on the TI-86, recursive sequences are tedious to plot. (Non-recursive sequences are a bit easier.)

Section 11.1	Example 4	(page 941)	Using Summation Notation

Section 11.2	Example 9	(page 953)	Using Summation Notation

The seq(command can be found in the LIST:OPS menu ([2nd][-][F5][MORE][F3]). Given a formula a_n for the nth term in a sequence, the command

seq(*formula*, *variable*, *start*, *end*, *step*)

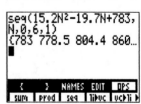

produces the list $\{a_{start}, a_{start+step}, \ldots, a_{end}\}$. If *step* is omitted, a value of 1 is assumed. The size of the resulting list can have no more than 2800 items (or fewer, as available memory allows).

Note that *variable* can be any letter (or letters)—K and I are used in the text, but x is more convenient (since it can be typed with x-VAR).

The sum command can be found in the LIST:OPS menu (2nd – F5 MORE F1). On the TI-86, the parentheses are not required. sum can be applied to any list—either to a list variable (called "list" in the example screen on the right), or directly to a list created with the seq(command.

Note: On the TI-86, list variables can be given any kind of legal variable name (see page 82).

Section 11.3   Example 7   (page 960)   Summing the Terms of an Infinite Geometric Series

To produce the plot from Figure 10 on the TI-86, begin by storing values in the lists xStat and yStat as shown on the right, so that xStat contains values of *n*, and yStat contains the corresponding values of S_n. (The slightly shorter command $(1-(1/3)^{\text{xStat}})/(2/3) \to$ yStat has the same effect as the second command shown.) This step is tedious for recursively defined sequences, but fairly simple in this case.

Next press 2nd + F3 to bring up the STAT:PLOT menu, shown on the right. Select Plot1 by pressing F1 (or choose one of the other two plots).

Make the settings shown on the screen on the right. For Type, choose F1 (SCAT) for a scatterplot.

Set up the viewing window (GRAPH:WINDOW) to match that shown in the text. Also, check that nothing else will be plotted: Press GRAPH F1 and make sure that all the equals signs are not highlighted, and that only Plot1 is highlighted. If Plot2 or Plot3 is on, use the arrow keys to move the cursor up to that plot, then press F5 (SELCT). Finally, press GRAPH F5 to produce the graph.

Note: When finished with a statistics plot like this one, it is a good idea to turn it off so that the TI-86 will not attempt to display it the next time GRAPH is pushed. This can be done using the SELCT option on the GRAPH:y(x)= screen, or by executing the PlOff command, by pressing 2nd + F3 F5 ENTER.

Section 11.4   Example 1   (page 971)   Evaluating Binomial Coefficients

---

Section 11.6   Example 4   (page 984)   Using the Permutations Formula

The nCr and nPr commands are found in the MATH:PROB menu ([2nd][×][F2]). (Also located in that menu is the factorial operator "!.")

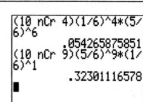

Section 11.7   Example 6   (page 999)   Finding Probabilities in a Binomial Experiment

The TI-86 does not have statistical distribution functions like binompdf. The computations shown in this example must be done by manually entering the entire binomial probability formula (or by obtaining a program to automate such computations.)

Introduction

The information in this section is essentially a summary of material that can be found in the TI-89 manual. Consult that manual for more details.

Owners of a TI-92 will find that most of this material applies to that calculator as well.

1   Power

To power up the calculator, simply press the ON key. The screen displayed at this point depends on how the TI-89 was last used. It may show the "home screen"—a menu (the toolbar) across the top, the results of previous computations (if any) in the middle (the history area), a line for new entries (which may be blank, or may show the previous entry), and a status line at the bottom. An example of this home screen is shown on the right.

The TI-89 may show some other screen—perhaps a graph, an error message, a menu, or something else. If so, one can return to the home screen by pressing either the HOME key (from a graph), or the ESC key (from an error message), or 2nd ESC (from a menu). Note that the "second function" of ESC —written in yellow type above the key—is "QUIT."

If the screen is blank, or is too dark to read, one may need to adjust the contrast (see the next section).

To turn the calculator off, press 2nd ON (OFF), in which case the TI-89 will start up at the home screen next time. This will not work if an error message is displayed. Pressing ◆ ON will also turn the TI-89 off, but when ON is next pressed, the screen will show exactly what it showed before. The calculator will automatically shut off if no keys are pressed for several minutes, in which case it will behave as if ◆ ON had been pressed.

2   Adjusting screen contrast

If the screen is too dark (all black), decrease the contrast by pressing and holding ◆ and ─. If the screen is too light, increase the contrast by pressing and holding ◆ and +. If the screen never becomes dark enough to see, the batteries should be replaced.

3   Replacing batteries

To replace the four AAA batteries, first turn the calculator off ([2nd][ON]), then remove the back cover, remove and replace each battery, replace the back cover, then turn the calculator on again. (After replacing batteries, one may need to adjust the contrast down as described above.) Note: The status line at the bottom of the home screen should display BATT when the batteries are getting low.

4   Basic operations

Simple computations are entered in essentially the same way they would be written. For example, to compute $2 + 17 \times 5$, press [2][+][1][7][×][5][ENTER] (the [ENTER] key tells the calculator to act on what has been typed). Standard order of operations (including parentheses) is followed. Note that the entry and the result (87) are displayed in the last line of the history area, and the entry is also displayed (and highlighted) in the entry line. If any new text is typed, this highlighted text will be deleted.

The result of the most recently entered expression is stored in ans(1), which is typed by pressing [2nd][(-)] (the word "ANS" appears in yellow above this key). For example, [5][+][2nd][(-)][ENTER] will add 5 to the result of the previous computation. Note that in the history area, "ans(1)" has been replaced by "87."

After pressing [ENTER], the TI-89 automatically produces ans(1) if the first key pressed is one which requires a number before it; the most common of these are [+], [-], [×], [÷], [^], and [STO▶]. For example, [+][5][ENTER] would accomplish the same thing as the keystrokes above (that is, it adds 5 to the previous result). Again, note that the history area shows the value of ans(1) rather than the text "ans(1)."

Although the previously entered expression disappears from the entry line if anything is typed, that expression can be re-evaluated by simply pressing [ENTER]. This can be especially useful in conjunction with ans(1).

Several expressions can be evaluated together by separating them with colons ([2nd][4]). When [ENTER] is pressed, the result of the *last* computation is displayed. (The other results are lost. An example showing how this can be used is shown later.)

5   Cursors

When typing, the appearance of the cursor and the status line indicates the behavior of the next keypress.

The cursor appears as either a flashing vertical line (the default) or a flashing solid block. The vertical line indicates that subsequent keypresses will be *inserted* at the current cursor location. The block cursor indicates that subsequent keypresses will *overwrite* the character(s) to the right of the cursor. (Of course, if the cursor is located at the right end of the entry line text, these two behaviors are equivalent.) To switch between between these two modes of operation, press 2nd ← (INS).

By default, most keys produce the character shown on the key itself. The four modifier keys 2nd, ♦, ↑, and alpha change this. Pressing any one of these keys causes a corresponding indicator to appear in the status line, and the next keypress will then do something different from its primary function. Pressing 2nd or ♦ causes the next keypress to produce the results—the character or operation—indicated by (respectively) the yellow or green text above that key. If 2nd or ♦ is pressed by mistake, pressing it a second time will undo that modifier.

For 2nd, that makes each key's function fairly clear, but many of the keys have no green text above them, leading one to think that the ♦ modifier would accomplish nothing with that key. In fact, nearly every key does something in response to the ♦ key. For an easy way to see the ♦ functions of the lower half of the keypad, press ♦ EE, which produces the display on the right. (Note that the letter associated with EE is "K"—think "K" for "keys.") For example, ♦ followed by =,), ÷, ×, STO▶, 0, or . produces the character shown. ♦ (followed by any letter produces the Greek equivalent of that letter (or as near an equivalent as there is); e.g., ♦ (Z produces ζ ("zeta"). ♦ | allows one to change the number of previous entries saved in the history area. The other ♦ functions are beyond the scope of this manual.

Pressing alpha means that the next keypress will produce the (lowercase) letter or other character printed in purple above that key (if any). alpha has no effect on (and is not needed for) X, Y, Z, and T. Following that letter, subsequent keypresses will produce their primary functions (i.e., not letters). To produce an uppercase letter, press alpha ↑ followed by a letter key. (alpha is not needed for X, Y, Z, and T.)

The TI-89 can be "locked" into (lowercase) alphabetic mode by pressing 2nd alpha (or alpha alpha). From then on, each key produces its letter. This continues until alpha is pressed again, which takes the TI-89 out of alphabetic mode.

To lock the TI-89 in uppercase alphabetic mode, press ↑ alpha. As before, pressing alpha again takes the TI-89 out of alphabetic mode.

6   Accessing previous entries ("deep recall")

By repeatedly pressing 2nd ENTER (ENTRY), previously typed expressions can be retrieved for editing and re-evaluation. Pressing 2nd ENTER once recalls the most recent entry; pressing 2nd ENTER again brings up the second most recent, etc.

More conveniently, pressing ⊙ and ⊙ allows one to select previous entries and results from the history area; simply highlight the desired expression and press ENTER. For example, pressing ⊙⊙ENTER would copy the previous entry to the new-entry line, while ⊙⊙⊙ENTER would copy the second-previous *result*.

Once an expression is on the new-entry line at the bottom of the home screen, it can be edited in various ways. Text can be deleted (using ← to delete the character before the cursor, or ♦ ← to delete the character after the cursor). New text can be inserted (see the previous section). One can even highlight text by pressing and holding ↑ together with an arrow key, then cut (♦ 2nd) or copy (♦ ↑) it to a "clipboard," so that it can be pasted (♦ ESC) somewhere else in the expression.

7   Menus

Certain keys and key combinations bring up a menu in a window with a variety of options. Shown is the menu produced by pressing ⎡F2⎤ (Algebra) from the home screen. The arrow next to "8" means that there are more options available (which can be seen by pressing ⊙ or ⊙). To select one of these options (and paste the corresponding command on the entry line), simply press the number (or letter) next to the option. Alternatively, use ⊙ and ⊙ to highlight the desired option and press ⎡ENTER⎤.

⎡2nd⎤⎡5⎤ brings up the MATH menu shown in the first screen on the right. For each of these menu options, the triangle ("▶") on the right side indicates that selecting that option brings up a sub-menu. Shown on the far right is the List sub-menu (option 3 of the MATH menu). Note that the status line contains a reminder of how to use these menus; ⎡ESC⎤ can be used to exit from one level of a menu (and ⎡2nd⎤⎡ESC⎤ would remove all menus and return to the home screen).

The various commands in these menus are too numerous to be listed here. They will be mentioned as needed in the examples.

One last comment is worthwhile, however. Some functions that may be used frequently are buried several levels deep in the menus, and may take many keystrokes to access. Worse, the location of the function might be forgotten (is it in the Algebra or MATH:Number menu?), necessitating a search through the menus. It is useful to remember three things:

- Any command can be typed one letter at a time, in either upper- or lowercase; e.g., ⎡↑⎤⎡ALPHA⎤⎡=⎤⎡(⎤ ⎡3⎤⎡ALPHA⎤⎡(⎤ will type the letters "ABS(", which has the same effect as ⎡2nd⎤⎡5⎤⎡1⎤⎡2⎤.

- Any command can be found in the ⎡CATALOG⎤ menu. Since the commands appear in alphabetical order, it may take some time to locate the desired function. Pressing any letter key (it is not necessary to press ⎡alpha⎤ first) brings up commands starting with that letter ; e.g., pressing ⎡9⎤ brings up the list on the right, while pressing ⎡–⎤ shows commands starting with "O."

- An alternate home-screen menu bar can be found by pressing ⎡2nd⎤ ⎡HOME⎤ (CUSTOM). Pressing ⎡2nd⎤⎡HOME⎤ again toggles back to the "standard" home-screen menu bar. It is possible to change the commands listed in this CUSTOM menu, but the process is somewhat tedious. Full details can be found in the TI-89 manual, but as an example: The command

```
Custom:Title "Fns":Item "abs(":Item "log(":Item "ln(":EndCustm
```

would result in a CUSTOM menu bar for which ⎡F1⎤ would produce the menu shown on the right.

8   Variables

The letters A through Z (upper- or lowercase), and also sequences of letters (like "High" or "count") can be used as variables (or "memory") to store numerical values. To store a value, type the number (or an expression) followed by [STO▶], then a letter or letters (pressing [alpha] if necessary), then [ENTER]. That variable name can then be used in the same way as a number, as demonstrated at right. These variable names are *not* case-sensitive, so "A" is the same as "a," and "CoUnT" is the same as "count."

Note: The TI-89 interprets 2a as "2 times a"—the "∗" symbol is not required (this is consistent with how we interpret mathematical notation). As for order of operations, this kind of multiplication is treated the same as "∗" multiplication (see the screen above).

If a variable is used for which no value has been assigned, it is treated as an unknown value, and expressions involving it remain unevaluated. In the screen on the right, the variable x has no assigned value. Any variable's assigned value can be erased ("forgotten") by issuing the command DelVar ([F4][4] from the home screen menubar) followed by the variable name. All one-letter variables can be cleared by choosing [2nd][F1] (Clean Up) [1], or using the NewProb command ([2nd][F1][2]), which also clears the history area.

9   Setting the modes

By pressing [MODE], one can change many aspects of how the calculator behaves. For most of the examples in this manual, the MODE settings will be as shown on the three screens below (although in some cases the settings are not crucial). Some (not all) of these options are described below; consult the TI-89 manual for more details. Changes in the settings are made using the arrows keys and [ENTER].

The Graph setting can be either FUNCTION, PARAMETRIC, POLAR, SEQUENCE, 3D, or DIFF EQUATIONS. Only the first four of these modes are used for this manual. This setting determines whether formulas to be graphed are functions (*y* as a function of *x*), parametric equations (*x* and *y* as functions of *t*), polar equations (*r* as a function of *θ*), or sequences (*u* as a function of *n*). (The current value of this setting is indicated in the status line at the bottom of the calculator screen—FUNC, PAR, etc.)

The Display Digits setting can be FLOAT, FIX *n*, or FLOAT *n*, where *n* is an integer from 1 to 12. This specifies how numbers should be displayed: FLOAT means that the TI-89 should display all non-zero digits (up to a maximum of 12), while (e.g.) FLOAT 4 means that a total of 4 digits will be displayed. Meanwhile, FIX 4 means that the TI-89 will attempt to display 4 digits beyond the decimal point.

Angle can be either RADIAN or DEGREE, indicating whether angle measurements should be assumed to be in radians or degrees. (A right angle measures $\frac{\pi}{2}$ radians, which is equivalent to 90°.) Most of the examples in the text include reminders to set the calculator in the appropriate mode, in cases where this is important. The current value of this setting is indicated in the status line at the bottom of the calculator screen—RAD or DEG.)

The Exponential Format setting is either NORMAL, SCIENTIFIC, or ENGINEER-ING; this specifies how numbers should be displayed. The screen on the right shows the number "12345." displayed in each of these modes: NORMAL mode displays numbers in the range ±999, 999, 999, 999 with no exponents, SCI-ENTIFIC mode displays all numbers in scientific notation, and ENGINEERING mode uses only exponents that are multiples of 3. Note: "E" is short for "times 10 to the power," so 1.2345E4 = 1.2345 × 10^4 = 1.2345 × 10000 = 12345.

The Complex Format is either REAL, RECTANGULAR, or POLAR, and specifies the display mode for complex numbers. REAL means that the TI-89 will produce an error if an expression requires the computation of (e.g.) a square root of a negative number, and the other two settings determine whether complex results should be displayed in rectangular or polar format. The TI-89's rectangular format is the $a + bi$ format used by the text (beginning in Section 1.3); polar format is not discussed in this text, but is closely related to trigonometric format (see page 152 of this manual).

The Vector Format setting (RECTANGULAR, CYLINDRICAL, or SPHERICAL) indicates the default display format for vectors (see page 151 of this manual).

Pretty Print (ON or OFF) determines how expressions (input and output) should be displayed. The first two entries on the right were performed with Pretty Print on, and the other two were done with Pretty Print off.

The Exact/Approx setting (AUTO, EXACT, or APPROXIMATE) determines whether results should be considered to be exact or approximate. EXACT means that all decimals are converted to fractions; e.g., .9 is displayed as 9/10, and ∫(2.5) is $\sqrt{10}/2$. APPROXIMATE means that everything is converted to decimal form; for example, ∫(2.5) produces 1.5811.... With the AUTO setting, the TI-89 decides whether to display a result as exact or approximate based on whether there is a decimal point in the entry—for example, ∫(5/2) yields $\sqrt{10}/2$, while ∫(2.5) yields 1.5811.... **Note:** Regardless of this setting, pressing ◆ENTER instead of ENTER to process an entry will cause the TI-89 to show a decimal (approximate) result. (The current value of this setting is indicated in the status line at the bottom of the calculator screen—AUTO, EXACT, or APPROX.)

The other mode settings deal with issues that are beyond the scope of the textbook, and are not discussed here.

10   Setting the graph window

Pressing ◆ F2 brings up the WINDOW settings. The exact contents of the WINDOW menu vary depending on the Graph mode setting; below are six examples showing this menu in each possible Graph modes. (The last two are not used in this manual, but are shown here for reference.)

Function mode   Parametric mode   Polar mode

Sequence mode   3D mode   Diff Equations mode

All these menus include the values `xmin`, `xmax`, `xscl`, `ymin`, `ymax`, and `yscl`. When ◆ F3 (GRAPH) is pressed, the TI-89 will show a portion of the Cartesian (x-y) plane determined by these values. In function mode, this menu also includes `xres`, the behavior of which is described in section 12 of this manual (page 127). The other settings in this screen allow specification of the smallest, largest, and step values of t (for parametric mode) or θ (for polar mode), or initial conditions for sequence mode.

With settings as in the "Function mode" screen shown above, the TI-89 would display the screen at right: x values from -7.9 to 7.9 (that is, from `xmin` to `xmax`), and y values between -3.8 to 3.8 (`ymin` to `ymax`). Since `xscl` = `yscl` = 1, the TI-89 places tick marks on both axes every 1 unit; thus the x-axis ticks are at -7, -6, ..., 6, and 7, and the y-axis ticks fall on the integers from -3 to 3. This window is called the "decimal" window, and is most quickly set by pressing ◆ F2 F2 4 (Zoom:ZoomDec).

Below are three more sets of window settings, and the graph screens they produce. Note that the first graph on the left has tick marks every 10 units on both axes. The second window is called the "standard" viewing

window, and is most quickly set by pressing ⬥ F2 F2 6 (Zoom:ZoomStd). The setting $\texttt{yscl} = 0$ in the final graph means that no tick marks are placed on the y-axis.

11   The graph screen

The TI-89's graph screen—that is, the portion of the screen used to display graphs, below the menu bar and above the status line—is made up of an array of rectangular dots (pixels) with 77 rows and 159 columns. All the pixels in the leftmost column have x-coordinate $\texttt{xmin}$, while those in the rightmost column have x-coordinate $\texttt{xmax}$. The x-coordinate changes steadily across the screen from left to right, which means that the coordinate for the nth column (counting the leftmost column as column 0) must be $\texttt{xmin} + n\Delta x$, where $\Delta x = (\texttt{xmax} - \texttt{xmin})/158$. Similarly, the nth row of the screen (counting up from the bottom row, which is row 0) has y-coordinate $\texttt{ymin} + n\Delta y$, where $\Delta y = (\texttt{ymax} - \texttt{ymin})/76$.

It is not necessary to memorize the formulas for Δx and Δy. Should they be needed, they can be determined by pressing ⬥ F3 (GRAPH) and then the arrow keys. When pressing ⓟ or ⓠ successively, the displayed x-coordinate changes by Δx; meanwhile, when pressing ⓢ or ⓣ, the y-coordinate changes by Δy. Alternatively, the values can be found by typing "Δx" and "Δy" on the home screen; this is most easily done by pressing 2nd + 1 5 to access the CHAR:Greek menu and type the "Δ" character, then press X or Y. This produces results like those shown on the right; the values of Δx and Δy there are those for the standard viewing window.

In the decimal window $\texttt{xmin} = -7.9$, $\texttt{xmax} = 7.9$, $\texttt{ymin} = -3.8$, $\texttt{ymax} = 3.8$, note that $\Delta x = 0.1$ and $\Delta y = 0.1$. Thus, the individual pixels on the screen represent x-coordinates $-7.9, -7.8, -7.7, \ldots, 7.7, 7.8, 7.9$ and y-coordinates $-3.8, -3.7, -3.6, \ldots, 3.6, 3.7, 3.8$. This is where the decimal window gets its name.

Windows for which $\Delta x = \Delta y$, such as the decimal window, are called square windows. Since there are just over twice as many columns as rows on the graph screen, this means that square windows should have $\texttt{xmax} - \texttt{xmin}$ just over twice as big as $\texttt{ymax} - \texttt{ymin}$. Any window can be made square be pressing ⬥ F2 F2 5 (Zoom:ZoomSqr). To see the effect of a square window, observe the two pairs of graphs below. In each pair, the first graph is on the standard window, and the second is on a square window (after pressing ⬥ F2 F2 5). (This changes $\texttt{xmin}$ and $\texttt{xmax}$ to about -20.8 and 20.8, respectively, while $\texttt{ymin}$ and $\texttt{ymax}$ remain unchanged at -10 and 10.) The first pair shows the line $y = x$; on the square window, this line (correctly) appears to make a $45°$ angle with the x- and y-axes. The second pair shows the lines $y = 2x - 3$

and $y = 3 - \frac{1}{2}x$; note that on the square window, these lines look perpendicular (as they should). Finally, the last pair shows a circle centered at the origin with a radius of 8. On the standard window, this looks like an oval since the screen is wider than it is tall. (The reason for the gaps in the circle will be addressed in the next section.)

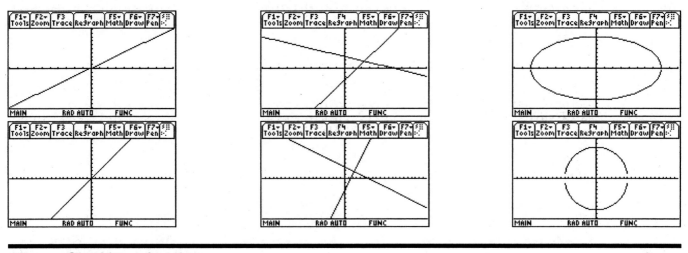

12   Graphing a function

This introductory section only addresses creating graphs in function mode. Procedures for creating parametric and polar graphs are very similar; they are covered beginning on page 154 of this manual, in material related to Chapter 8 of the text. Sequence plotting is covered on page 162 of this manual, in the material related to Section 11.3 from the text.

To see the graph of $y = 2x - 3$, begin by entering the formula into the calculator. This is done by pressing ◆F1 to access the "y equals" screen of the calculator. Enter the formula as y1 (or any other yn). (If y1 already has a formula, press ENTER, F3, or CLEAR first, then type the new formula.) If another y variable has a formula, position the cursor on that line and press either CLEAR (to delete the formula) or F4. The latter has the effect of toggling the check mark for that line; which tells the TI-89 whether or not to graph that formula. In the screen on the right, only y1 will be graphed.

The next step is to choose a viewing window. See the previous section for more details on this. This example uses the standard window (F2 6).

If the graph has not been displayed, press ◆F3, and the line should be drawn. In order to produce this graph, the TI-89 considers 159 values of x, ranging from xmin to xmax in steps of Δx (assuming that xres = 1; see below for other possibilities). For each value of x, it computes the corresponding value of y, then plots that point (x, y) and draws a line between this point and the previous one. (See also the information about graph styles later in this section.)

If xres is set to 2, the TI-89 will only compute y for every other x value; that is, it uses a step size of $2\Delta x$. Similarly, if xres is 3, the step size will be $3\Delta x$, and so on. Setting xres higher causes graphs to appear faster (since fewer points are plotted), but for some functions, the graph may look "choppy" if xres is too large, since detail is sacrificed for speed.

Note: If the line does not appear, or the TI-89 reports an error, double-check all the previous steps. Also, check the mode settings (discussed in section 9, page 123).

Once the graph is visible, the window can be changed using ◆ F2 (WIN-DOW) or F2 (Zoom). Pressing F3 (TRACE) brings up the "trace cursor," and displays the x- and y-coordinates for various points on the line as the ◁ and ▷ keys are pressed. (These variables—xc and yc—can also be referenced from the home screen; that is, typing xc ENTER on the home screen would show the value 2.40506. . . .) Tracing beyond the left or right columns causes the TI-89 to adjust the values of xmin and xmax and redraw the graph.

To graph the function

$$y = \frac{1}{x - 3},$$

enter that formula into the "y equals" screen (note the use of parentheses on the entry line). As before, this example uses the standard viewing window.

For this function, the TI-89 produces the graph shown on the right. This illustrates one of the pitfalls of the connect-the-dots method used by the calculator: The nearly-vertical line segment drawn at $x = 3$ *should not be there*, but it is drawn because the calculator connects the points

$$x \approx 2.911, \, y \approx -11.286 \text{ and } x \approx 3.165, \, y \approx 6.077.$$

Calculator users must learn to recognize these flaws in calculator-produced graphs.

The graph of a circle centered at the origin with radius 8 (shown on a square window, with xres = 1) shows another problem that arises from connecting the dots. When $x = -8.157895$, y is undefined, so no point is plotted (that is, there is no point on this circle that has x-coordinate less than -8, or greater than 8). The next point plotted on the upper half of the circle is $x = -7.894737$ and $y = 1.2934953$; since no point had been plotted for the previous x-coordinate, this is not connected to anything, so there appears to be a gap between the circle and the x-axis. The calculator is not "smart" enough to know that the graph should extend from -8 to 8.

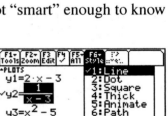

One additional feature of graphing with the TI-89 is that each function can have a "style" assigned to its graph. To see this style, go to the "y equals" screen and press 2nd F1 (Style); the check mark indicates which style applies to the current function. These options are shown on the right; "Line," the default, means that the calculator should draw lines between the plotted points. Complete details are in the TI-89 manual.

13   Adding programs to the TI-89

The TI-89's capabilities can be extended by downloading or entering programs into the calculator's memory. Instructions for writing a program are beyond the scope of this manual, but programs written by others and downloaded from the Internet (or obtained as printouts) can be transferred to the calculator in one of three ways:

1. If one TI-89 already has a program, it can be transferred to another using the calculator-to-calculator link cable. To do this, first make sure the cable is firmly inserted in both calculators. On both calculators, press [2nd][−] (VAR-LINK). On the sending calculator, use the arrow keys and [F4] to place check marks next to the programs to be transferred. On the receiving calculator, press [F3][2] (Link:Receive), then on the sending calculator, press [F3][1] (Link:Send to TI-89/TI-92 Plus).

2. If a computer with the TI-Graph Link is available, and the program file is on that computer (e.g., after having been downloaded from the Internet), the program can be transferred to the calculator using the TI Graph Link software. This transfer is done in a manner similar to the calculator-to-calculator transfer described above; specific instructions can be found in the documentation that accompanies the Graph Link software. (They are not given here because of slight differences between platforms and software versions.)

3. View a listing of the program and type it in manually. (**Note:** Even if the TI-Graph Link cable is not available, the Graph Link software can be used to view program listings on a computer.) While this is the most tedious method, studying programs written by others can be a good way to learn programming. To enter a program, start by choosing [APPS][7][3] (Program Editor:New), then specify whether this is a program or a function, and give it a name (up to eight characters, like "quadform" or "midpoint")—note that the TI-89 is automatically put into alpha mode while typing this name. Then press [ENTER] (OK), enter the commands in the program or function, and press [2nd][ESC] (QUIT) to return to the home screen when finished.

To run the program, make sure there is nothing on the current line of the home screen, then type the name of the program or function (this name is not case sensitive). Follow this with a set of parentheses, containing any required arguments, then press [ENTER]. If the program was entered manually (option 3 above), errors may be reported; in that case, press [ENTER] (GOTO), correct the mistake and try again.

Programs can be found at many places on the Internet, including:

- http://www.awl.com/lhs—the Web site for the text;

- http://www.bluffton.edu/~nesterd—the Web site of the author of this manual;

- http://tifaq.calc.org—a "Frequently Asked Questions" page maintained by Ray Kremer; and

- http://www.ticalc.org.

Examples

Here are the details for using the TI-89 for several of the examples from the textbook. Also given are the keystrokes necessary to produce some of the commands shown in the text's examples. In some cases, some suggestions are made for using the calculator more efficiently.

Throughout this section, it is assumed that the textbook is available for reference. The problems from the text are not restated here, and there are frequent references to the calculator screens shown in the text.

Section R.1   Example 2   (page 4)   Evaluating Exponential Expressions

This example discusses how to evaluate 4^3, $(-6)^2$, -6^2, $4 \cdot 3^2$, and $(4 \cdot 3)^2$.

To evaluate 4^3 with a TI-89, type $\boxed{4}\boxed{\wedge}\boxed{3}\boxed{\text{ENTER}}$. While all exponents are entered with the $\boxed{\wedge}$ key, note that they are displayed in the history area as superscripts. All other computations in this example are straightforward with the TI-89, except for this *caveat*: For $(-6)^2$ and -6^2, one must use the $\boxed{(-)}$ key rather than the $\boxed{-}$ key to enter "negative 6." In the screen shown, the second entry in the history area was typed as $\boxed{(}\boxed{(-)}\boxed{6}\boxed{)}\boxed{\wedge}\boxed{2}$, while the entry at the bottom was typed as $\boxed{(}\boxed{-}\boxed{6}\boxed{)}\boxed{\wedge}\boxed{2}$. When $\boxed{\text{ENTER}}$ is pressed, this entry produces a syntax error—the calculator's way of saying that the line makes no sense.

Section R.1   Example 3   (page 5)   Using Order of Operations

Using the calculator for parts (a) and (b) of this example is straightforward; the expressions are entered as printed. For (c) and (d), we have the expressions

$$\frac{4+3^2}{6-5 \cdot 3} \quad \text{and} \quad \frac{-(-3)^3 + (-5)}{2(-8) - 5(3)}.$$

Entering these on the TI-89 requires us to add some additional parentheses to make sure the correct order of operations is followed.

The history area on the right shows the results for (c) and (d). The entry for (c) looks the same as the printed appearance in the text, but note that it was entered as $(4+3^2)/(6-5*3)$. For (d), note the expression was entered nearly the same as it was printed, except for the addition of parentheses around the numerator and denominator (see the entry line of the screen), but in the history area, the TI-89 has dropped the unnecessary parentheses around -5 in the numerator, while in the denominator, the parentheses were exchanged for the multiplication symbol.

The entry line on the right shows a quicker way of entering the expression for (d), based on the TI-89's modification of the original entry. The extra parentheses in the original make it somewhat harder to read (and also mean more opportunities to make a mistake).

Section R.2   Example 2   (page 18)   Evaluating Absolute Value

---

Section R.2   Example 3   (page 18)   Finding Absolute Values of Sums and Differences

The `abs(` function of the TI-89 is in the MATH:Number menu (2nd 5 1 2).
Note that while this function is entered as `abs(`, it is displayed in the history
area using the "bar" notation.

Section R.6   Example 4   (page 58)   Using the Definition of $a^{1/n}$

In evaluating these fractional exponents with a calculator, be sure to put
parentheses around the fractions. Note for (d), where the text notes that
$(-1296)^{1/4}$ is not a real number, the TI-89 gives a complex result if the
complex format setting (see page 124) is something other than REAL.

In fact, if the complex format setting is RECTANGULAR or POLAR, the TI-89 is a
bit too clever to be useful! Observe the results reported for (e) and (f) in the
screen shown here. These *are* correct, in a way; for example, the cube of
$\frac{3}{2} + \frac{3\sqrt{3}}{2}i$ really is -27, but they are not the results that we are looking for.

If we set the complex format to REAL, we get the desired results.

Section R.6   Example 5   (page 59)   Using the Definition of $a^{m/n}$

For (f), attempting to evaluate $(-4)^{5/2}$ will produce either a complex result
or the error message shown, depending on the complex format setting (see
the previous example).

Section R.7   Example 1   (page 65)   Evaluating Roots

Aside from the square root function ∫ (2nd ×), the TI-89 has no other root functions, so expressions like
those in this example must be entered in exponential form.

Section R.7   Example 5   (page 68)   Using the Rules for Radicals to Simplify Radical Expressions

If the TI-89 is in AUTOMATIC or EXACT mode (see page 124), it can simplify many such expressions. Here are the TI-89's results for (a), (c), and (d).

Section 1.1   Example 1   (page 87)   Solving a Linear Equation

The TI-89 offers several approaches to solving (or confirming a solution to) an equation. Aside from graphical approaches to solving equations (which are discussed later, on page 139), here are some non-graphical (numerical) approaches: As illustrated on the right, the TI-89's solve and nSolve functions attempt to find solutions to an equation, while the zeros function attempts to find the zeros of an expression. Full details on how to use these functions (all of which are found in the Algebra menu) can be found in the TI-89 manual.

Additionally, the TI-89 includes an "interactive solver," accessed with APPS 9. This prompts for the equation to be solved, then allows the user to enter a guess for the solution (or a range or numbers between which a solution should be sought). To solve the equation, place the cursor on the line beginning with x= and press F2 (Solve).

Enter equation	Specify guess, or press F2	Here is the solution.

The solver can also be used with equations containing more than one variable; simply provide values for all but one variable, then place the cursor on the line containing the variable for which a value is needed and press F2.

Note: In this example, we learned three methods by which the TI-89 can be used to support an analytic solution. But the TI-89 and any other graphing calculator also can be used for solving problems when an analytic solution is **not** possible—that is, when one cannot solve an equation "algebraically." This is often the case in many "real-life" applications, and is one of the best arguments for the use of graphing calculators.

Section 1.3	Example 1	(page 109)	Writing $\sqrt{-a}$ as $i\sqrt{a}$
Section 1.3	Example 2	(page 109)	Finding Products and Quotients Involving Negative Radicands
Section 1.3	Example 3	(page 110)	Simplifying a Quotient Involving a Negative Radicand

Note that the TI-89's Complex Format mode should be RECTANGULAR (see page 124). The screen on the right shows results from performing some computations in REAL mode; note that this *will* work for (a), (b), and (c) in Example 2, for which the final result is a real number, but an error occurs if the result is complex.

The screen on the right (also produced in REAL mode) illustrates an exception to this rule: A complex result produces no error in REAL mode if the entered expression included the character "ι" ([2nd][CATALOG] — this is different from the "regular" lowercase i, [alpha][9]).

Section 1.3	Example 4	(page 110)	Adding and Subtracting Complex Numbers
Section 1.3	Example 5	(page 111)	Multiplying Complex Numbers
Section 1.3	Example 6	(page 112)	Simplifying Powers of i
Section 1.3	Example 7	(page 113)	Dividing Complex Numbers

Use [2nd][CATALOG] for the "ι" character. Note that the TI-89's Complex Format mode should be REAL or RECTANGULAR (see page 124) to produce output similar to that shown in the text. The command ▸Frac ("to fraction"), shown in the screen accompanying Example 7, is not necessary (nor is it available) on a TI-89; provided it is set to either EXACT or AUTO mode, results will be displayed as exact fractions.

Section 1.4	Example 5	(page 120)	Using the Quadratic Formula (Real Solutions)
Section 1.4	Example 6	(page 120)	Using the Quadratic Formula (Nonreal Complex Solutions)
Section 1.4	Example 7	(page 121)	Solving a Cubic Equation

The solve and zeros functions, previously described on page 132, can be used for many types of equations, including quadratics and cubics like these. For equations with complex solutions, use cSolve or cZeros rather than solve and zeros.

Section 1.5   Example 1   (page 126)   Solving a Problem Involving the Volume of a Box

A *table* can be a useful tool to solve equations like this. To use the table features of the TI-89, begin by entering the formula ($y = 15x^2 - 200x + 500$) on the Y= screen, as one would to create a graph. (The check marks determine which formulas will be displayed in the table, just as they do for graphs.)

Next, press ◆F4 to access the Table Setup screen. The table will display y values for given values of x. The tblStart value sets the lowest value of x, while Δtbl determines the "step size" for successive values of x. These two values are only used if the Independent option is set to AUTO—this means, "automatically generate the values of the independent variable (x)." The effect of setting this option to ASK is illustrated at the end of this example.

When the Table Setup options are set satisfactorily, press ENTER then ◆F5 to produce the table. The first screen on the right is the table generated based on the settings in the above screen; the fact that y is negative for $x = 8$ and $x = 9$ supports the restriction $x > 10$ from Step 3 of the example. By pressing ⊙ repeatedly, the x values are increased, and the y values updated. (Pressing ⊙ decreases the x values, but clearly that is not appropriate for this problem.) After pressing ⊙ several times, the table looks like the second screen, which shows that y1 equals 1435 when x equals 17.

Extension: Suppose the specifications called for the box to be 1500 cubic inches (instead of 1435). We see from the table above that x must be between 17 and 18 inches. The TI-89's table capabilities provide a convenient way to "zoom in" on the value of x (which could also be found with the solve feature, or by other methods).

Since $17 < x < 18$, set tblStart to 17 and Δtbl to 0.1. This produces the table shown on the right, from which we see that $17.2 < x < 17.3$. Now set tblStart to 17.2 and Δtbl to 0.01, which reveals that x is between 17.2 and 17.21. This process can be continued to achieve any desired degree of accuracy.

Finally, the screen on the right shows the effect of setting Independent to ASK. You enter an x value into the first column, and the corresponding y values will be computed.

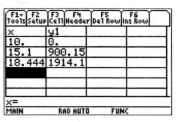

Section 1.7 Example 1 (page 147)	Solving a Linear Inequality

Section 1.7 Example 2 (page 148)	Solving a Linear Inequality

The `solve` feature (described on page 132) will solve inequalities as well as equations. (⟨2nd⟩⟨.⟩ types >; ⟨♦⟩⟨0⟩ types ≤; these symbols are also found in the MATH:Test menu.) While this is much faster, students should recognize that there are some benefits to doing problems like this by hand (the "hard" way)—specifically, working through the steps shown in the text gives one insight into what is going on, while using `solve` lends little to one's understanding of inequalities.

See also the discussion of Examples 5 through 9 (below) for another way to visualize the solutions to inequalities.

Section 1.7 Example 3 (page 149)	Solving a Three-Part Inequality

The `solve` feature will only handle one inequality at a time, so we must solve the two pieces separately (as shown) and then (optionally) join them with "and" (found in the MATH:Test menu). The final output shown is equivalent to $-\frac{7}{3} < x < 5$.

Section 1.7 Example 5 (page 150)	Solving a Quadratic Inequality

Section 1.7 Example 6 (page 151)	Solving a Quadratic Inequality

Section 1.7 Example 8 (page 154)	Solving a Rational Inequality

Section 1.7 Example 9 (page 155)	Solving a Rational Inequality

As the screen on the right shows, `solve` fails to give useful results for inequalities like these.

However, the TI-89's `when` function can be useful in visualizing solutions (as a way to check one's algebra). In the screen on the right, y1 was entered as `when(x^2-x-12<0,1,0)`, which means that y1 equals 1 whenever x satisfies this inequality.

In this window, we see that y1 is equals to 1 between -3 and 4, supporting the answer found in Example 5. Note that this picture does *not* help one determine what happens when $x = -3$ or $x = 4$; those two points must be checked separately.

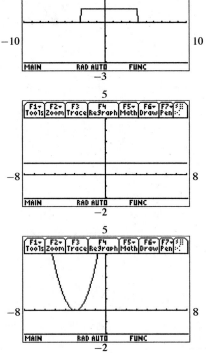

Extension: Can the calculator be used to solve the inequality $x^2 + 6x + 9 > 0$? Yes—if it is used carefully. Shown is the graph of the expression y1=when(x^2+6x+9>0,1,0). This suggests that the inequality is true for all x; that is, the solution set is $(-\infty, \infty)$.

This conclusion is **not correct**: The graph of y2=x^2+6x+9 touches the x-axis at $x = -3$, which means that this must be excluded from the solution set, since "> 0" means the graph must be above (not on) the x-axis. The correct solution set is $(-\infty, -3) \cup (-3, \infty)$.

This example should serve as a warning: Sometimes, the TI-89 will mislead you. When possible, try to confirm the calculator's answers in some way.

Section 1.8   Example 1   (page 161)   Solving Absolute Value Equations

The solve function described on page 132 of this manual can be used for these equations, too. Recall that abs(is found in the MATH:Number menu ([2nd] [5][1]).

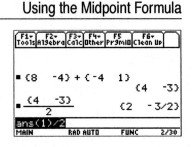

Section 2.1   Example 5   (page 186)   Using the Midpoint Formula

The TI-89 can do midpoint computations nicely by putting coordinates in a list—that is, using braces ([2nd][(] and [2nd][)]) instead of parentheses. When adding two lists, the calculator simply adds corresponding elements, so the two x-coordinates are added, as are the y-coordinates. Dividing by 2 completes the task. (Note that, although the list is displayed in the history area as "{8 -4}", it was entered as "{8,-4}".)

Section 2.1   Example 10   (page 190)   Graphing a Circle

The text suggests graphing y1=4+√(36-(x+3)^2) and y2=4-√(36-(x+3)^2). Here are three options to speed up entering these formulas:

- After typing the formula in y1, move the cursor to y2, press [ENTER], then press [2nd][STO▶] (RCL), then type "y1" and press [ENTER]. This will "recall" the formula of y1, placing it on the entry line for y2. Now edit this formula, changing the first "+" to a "−."

- After typing the formula in y1, define y2=8-y1(x). This produces the desired results, since $8 - y1 = 8 - (4 + \sqrt{36 - (x+3)^2}) = 8 - 4 - \sqrt{36 - (x+3)^2} = 4 - \sqrt{36 - (x+3)^2}$.

- Enter the single formula y1=4+{-1,1}√(36-(x+3)^2). (The curly braces { and } are 2nd (and 2nd), respectively). When a list (like {-1,1}) appears in a formula, it tells the TI-89 to graph this formula several times, using each value in the list.

The window chosen in the text is a square window (see Section 11 of the introduction of this chapter), so that the graph looks like a circle. (On a non-square window, the graph would look like an ellipse—that is, a distorted circle.) Note, however, that on the TI-89, this window is not square. Other square windows would also produce a "true" circle, but some will leave gaps similar to those circles shown in Sections 11 and 12 of the introduction (pages 126–127). Shown is the same circle on the square window produced by "squaring up" the standard window.

Section 2.2   Example 6   (page 205)   Using Function Notation

---

Section 2.2   Example 7   (page 205)   Using Function Notation

---

The TI-89 is quite good with function notation. In the screen shown, y1 has been defined as the function f from Example 6, and y2 as g from Example 7. It is then easy to compute $f(2)$ by entering y1(2), and (provided the variables a and q are undefined), we get the desired results from y1(q) and y2(a+1). The last entry shows that if a has a numerical value, the reported result is a number (rather than an expression). We can assure that all one-letter variables are undefined by pressing 2nd F1 1.

Section 2.3   Example 3   (page 215)   Graphing a Vertical Line

---

The text notes that such a line is not a function; therefore, it cannot be graphed by entering the equation on the Y= screen. However, the TI-89 does provide a fairly straightforward method of graphing vertical lines using the LineVert command.

From the home screen, type the LineVert command one letter at a time (upper/lower case is ignored), or using the function catalog (see page 122), then type the x-coordinate of the line. For example, LineVert -3 ENTER would draw the line $x = -3$ on the current window.

Alternatively, the vertical line can be drawn "interactively" using the GRAPH:Pen:Vertical command. This allows the user to move the cursor (and the vertical line) to the desired position using the ◁ and ▷ keys. Pressing ENTER places the line at that location, then allows more lines to be drawn. (Press ESC to finish drawing vertical lines.) Note that since, on the standard window, $x = -3$ does not correspond to a column of pixels on the screen (see page 126), the vertical line is actually located at $x \approx -3.038$, but the appearance on the screen is the same as if it were at $x = -3$. The process is illustrated below.

|2nd||F2||6| (move cursor) |ENTER| Make more lines, or |ESC|

Section 2.4   Example 5   (page 230)   Finding Equations of Parallel and Perpendicular Lines

In the discussion following this example (on page 231), the text notes that the lines from part (b) do not appear to be perpendicular unless they are plotted on a square window. See Section 11 of the introduction of this chapter (page 126) for more information about square windows.

Section 2.4   Example 6   (page 232)   Finding an Equation of a Line That Models Data

Section 2.4   Example 7   (page 233)   Finding a Linear Equation That Models Data

Aside from the methods described in these two examples, the text refers to the technique of linear regression on page 235. Figure 48 illustrates the steps on a TI-83; here is a more detailed description of the process on a TI-89 (using the data of Example 7).

Given a set of data pairs (x, y), the TI-89 can produce a scatter diagram and can find various formulas (including linear and quadratic, as well as more complex formulas) that approximate the relationship between x and y. These formulas are called "regression formulas."

The first step in determining the regression formula is to enter the data into the TI-89. This is done by pressing |APPS||6||3| (Data/Matrix Editor), then entering a name for the "data variable" (which will contain all of the numbers for the regression). Alternatively, use an existing data variable, if there is one.

In the spreadsheet-like screen that appears, enter the year values into the first column (c1) and the percentage of women into the second column (c2). If re-using an existing data variable, old data can be cleared out using Tools:Clear Editor, Utils:Delete, or Utils:Clear Column.

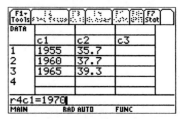

To find the line of best fit, press |F5| (Calc). For Calculation Type, choose LinReg, and set x and y as c1 and c2, respectively.

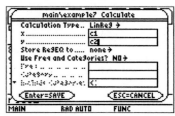

Pressing ENTER displays the results of the LinReg (shown on the right). These numbers agree (after rounding) with those in the text.

Section 2.4   Example 8   (page 235)   Solving an Equation with a Graphing Calculator

The text illustrates a graphical process for solving the equation $-2x - 4(2 - x) = 3x + 4$; in this discussion, we will show two graphical methods for solving the equation $\frac{1}{2}x - 6 = \frac{3}{4}x - 9$. (The answer is $x = 12$.)

The first method is the **intersection** method. To begin, set up the TI-89 to graph the left side of the equation as y1, and the right side as y2. **Note:** Entering the fractions in parentheses—e.g., y1=(1/2)x-6—ensures no mistakes with order of operations. This is not crucial for the TI-89, but is a good practice because some other models give priority to implied multiplication. See section 8 of the introduction, page 123.

We are looking for an x value that will make the left and right sides of this equation equal to each other, which corresponds to the x-coordinate of the point of intersection of these two graphs.

Next, select a viewing window which shows the point of intersection; we use $[-15, 15] \times [-10, 10]$ for this example. The TI-89 can automatically locate this point using the GRAPH:Math:Intersection feature. Use ⊙, ⊙ and ENTER to specify which two functions to use (in this case, the only two being displayed). The TI-89 then prompts for lower and upper bounds (numbers that are, respectively, less than and greater than the location of the intersection). After pressing ENTER, the TI-89 will try to find an intersection of the two graphs. The screens below illustrate these steps.

From the graph screen: F5 5   ENTER (choose y1)   ENTER (choose y2)

Move cursor ENTER   Move cursor ENTER   The intersection is found.

The x-coordinate of this point of intersection is calculated to 14 digits of accuracy, so if the solution were some less "convenient" number (say, $\sqrt{3}$ or $1/\pi$), we would have an answer that would be accurate enough for nearly any computation.

Note: An approximation for the point of intersection can be found simply by moving the TRACE cursor as near the intersection as possible. The amount of error can be minimized by "zooming in" on the graph. This is the only method available for graphing calculators such as the TI-81.

The second graphical approach is to use the x-**intercept method**, which seeks the x-coordinate of the point where a graph crosses the x-axis. Specifically, we want to know where the graph of y1-y2 crosses the x-axis, where y1 and y2 are as defined above. This is because the equation $\frac{1}{2}x - 6 = \frac{3}{4}x - 9$ can only be true when $\frac{1}{2}x - 6 - \left(\frac{3}{4}x - 9\right) = 0$. (This is the approach illustrated in the text for Example 8.)

To find this x-intercept, begin by defining y3=y1(x)-y2(x) on the Y= screen. We could do this by re-typing the formulas entered for y1 and y2, but having typed those formulas once, it is more efficient to do this as shown on the right. Note that y1 and y2 have been "de-selected" so that they will not be graphed (see section 12 of the introduction, page 127).

We must first select a viewing window which shows the x-intercept; we again use $[-15, 15] \times [-10, 10]$. The TI-89 can automatically locate this point with the GRAPH:Math:Zero feature. The TI-89 prompts for lower and upper bounds (numbers that are, respectively, less than and greater than the zero), then attempts to locate the zero between the given bounds. (Provided there is only one zero between the bounds, and the function is "well-behaved"—meaning it has some nice properties like continuity—the calculator will find it.) The screens below illustrate these steps.

(move cursor) ENTER   (move cursor) ENTER   Here is the result.

Section 2.5   Example 2   (page 246)   Graphing Piecewise-Defined Functions

The text shows how to enter piecewise-defined functions on the TI-83; for a TI-89, the appropriate way to enter the function in Example 2(a) is shown on the right. Note the difference between how the function is entered and how it is displayed; in particular, the display is similar to how the function appears in print. (Use ◆ 0 to type "≤".) The use of Dot graphing style is not crucial to the graphing process, as long as one remembers that vertical line segments connecting the "pieces" of the graph (in this case, at $x = 2$) are not really part of the graph.

Extension: A more complicated piecewise-defined functions, such as

$$f(x) = \begin{cases} 4 - x^2 & \text{if } x < -1 \\ 2 + x & \text{if } -1 \le x \le 4 \\ -2 & \text{if } x > 4 \end{cases}$$

is entered as

```
when(x<-1,4-x^2,when(x≤4,2+x,-2))
```

which the TI-89 displays as shown on the right. This tells the TI-89 to compute y1 as follows: (a) If $x < -1$, use the expression $4 - x^2$. (b) Otherwise (if $x \ge -1$), if $x \le 4$, use $2 + x$. (c) Otherwise, use -2.

Section 2.5   Example 3   (page 247)   Graphing a Greatest Integer Function

We wish to graph the step function $y = [\![\frac{1}{2}x + 1]\!]$. On the TI-89, the greatest integer function is called `floor` or `int`; the former is found in the MATH:Number menu (2nd 5 1 6), while the latter is in the CATALOG (or either can be typed one letter at a time). Thus, either y1 or y2 (as shown on the right) will produce this graph.

Section 2.6   Example 1   (page 253)   Stretching or Shrinking a Graph

---

Section 2.6   Example 2   (page 254)   Reflecting a Graph Across an Axis

---

Section 2.6   Example 6   (page 259)   Translating a Graph Vertically

---

Section 2.6   Example 7   (page 260)   Translating a Graph Horizontally

See page 128 for information on setting the thickness of a graph. Note that the symbol next to Y2 in the screen shown in the text indicates that the graph should be thick.

It is possible to distinguish between the two graphs without having them drawn using different styles. When two or more graphs are drawn, the TRACE feature can be used to determine which graphs correspond to which formulas: By pressing ⊕ and ⊖, the trace cursor jumps from one graph to another, and the upper right corner displays the number of the current formula. On the right, the trace cursor is on graph 2—that is, the graph of $g(x) = 2|x|$.

Section 2.7   Example 5   (page 272)   Evaluating Composite Functions

The expressions shown in the calculator screens on page 273 will also work on the TI-89's home screen. The command ▶Frac ("to fraction") is not necessary (nor is it available) on a TI-89; provided it is set to either EXACT or AUTO mode, results will be displayed as exact fractions.

Section 2.7   Example 6   (page 273)   Finding Composite Functions

The screen on the right illustrates how the TI-89 can perform these compositions (provided the variable xhas no numerical value assigned to it). This screen shows the functions f and g being defined on the home screen; we could also define y1 and y2 on the Y= screen.

Section 3.1   Example 1   (page 295)   Graphing Quadratic Functions

Section 3.1   Example 2   (page 297)   Graphing a Parabola by Completing the Square

Section 3.1   Example 3   (page 298)   Graphing a Parabola by Completing the Square

The TI-89 can automatically locate extreme values ("hills" and "valleys") in a graph using the Minimum and Maximum options in the GRAPH:Math menu (F5 from the graph screen). We illustrate this procedure for the function in Example 1(c).

Enter the function in y1, and graph in a window that shows the extreme value. Since the coefficient of x^2 is negative, this is a parabola that opens down, and the extreme point is a maximum value. Press F5 4, then use the arrow keys and ENTER to define lower and upper bounds, as was done previously with the Math:Zero and Math:Intersection commands—see the discussion on page 139 of this manual.

Depending on the window and the specified bounds, the x value may be off a bit from the exact answer, as is the case here. A limitation of the technology is that the calculating algorithms are programmed to stop within a certain degree of accuracy. It is important for the user to recognize this limitation and suspect slight errors when calculations are this close to integer values.

Section 3.1   Example 6   (page 302)   Modeling the Number of Hospital Outpatient Visits

See page 138 for information about using the TI-89 for regression computations.

Section 3.2   Example 3   (page 317)   Deciding whether a Number is a Zero

The TI-89's "function notation" evaluation method (page 137 of this manual) can also be used to check for zeros: In the screen on the right, y1, y2, and y3 have been defined (respectively) as the functions in (a), (b), and (c).

Section 3.3   Example 6   (page 327)   Finding All Zeros of a Polynomial Given One Zero

---

Section 3.4   Example 7   (page 340)   Approximating Real Zeros of a Polynomial Function

The TI-89's algebraic manipulation capabilities make problems like this very simple. The factor(and cFactor(commands are found in the Algebra menu (F2 2 on the home screen).

Section 3.5   Example 2   (page 352)   Graphing a Rational Function

Note that this function is entered as y1=2/(1+x), **not** y1=2/1+x. (The TI-89's "pretty print" display makes this sort of mistake unlikely.)

The issue of incorrectly drawn asymptotes is also addressed in Section 12 of the introduction to this chapter (page 127). Changing the window to xmin $= -5$ and xmax $= 3$ (or any choice of xmin and xmax which has -1 halfway between them) eliminates this vertical line because it forces the TI-89 to attempt to evaluate the function at $x = -1$. Since f is not defined at -1, it cannot plot a point there, and as a result, it does not attempt to connect the dots across the "break" in the graph.

Section 4.1   Example 7   (page 396)   Finding the Inverse of a Function with a Restricted Domain

Note that Figure 10 shows a square viewing window (see page 126); the mirror-image property of the inverse function would not be as clear on a non-square window. Note also that although this window is square on a TI-83, it is not quite square on a TI-89.

Section 4.2   Example 11   (page 412)   Using Data to Model Exponential Growth

See page 138 for information about using the TI-89 for regression computations.

Section 4.4   Example 1   (page 433)   Finding pH

The natural logarithm function (ln) is 2nd X. For the common (base-10) logarithm, use the CATALOG or type log one letter at a time.

For (a), the text shows -log(2.5*10^(-4)). The TI-89 does not have a "10^" function, but 1 0 ^ produces the same results. This could also be entered as shown on the first line of the screen on the right, since "E" (produced with EE) and "*10^" are nearly equivalent. The two are not completely interchangeable, however; in particular, in part (b), 10^(-7.1) **cannot** be replaced with E-7.1, because "E" is only valid when followed by an *integer*. That is, E-7 produces the same result as 10^-7, but E-7.1 is interpreted as (1E-7)*0.1.

Section 4.5   Example 8   (page 448)   Modeling Coal Consumption in the U.S.

The modeling function given in the text was found using a regression procedure (LnReg, or logarithmic regression) similar to that described on page 138.

Section 5.1   Example 2   (page 476)   Calculating with Degrees, Minutes, and Seconds

---

Section 5.1   Example 3   (page 476)   Converting between Decimal Degrees
                                                            and Degrees, Minutes, and Seconds

---

When working with angles measured in degrees, it is a good idea to select Degree mode (see section 9 of the introduction, page 123). In fact, when in Radian mode, the TI-89 automatically converts angles entered in degrees to radians, which can be confusing. (Radian measure is discussed in Chapter 6.)

In Degree mode, the conversion to decimal degrees is fairly simple: Enter the angle using [2nd][I], [2nd][=], and [2nd][1] for the degrees, minutes, and seconds symbols. The only potential snag is that, depending on the [MODE] settings, the TI-89 might attempt to display an exact (fractional) representation of the conversion, rather than a decimal (as in the first entry shown in the history area on the right). This can be overcome by either entering one of the quantities (degrees, minutes, or seconds) with a decimal point, or by entering the expression with [♦][ENTER] instead of just [ENTER]. (This produced the second output in the history area.) The third entry makes use of the ▸DMS operator, which causes an angle to be displayed in degrees, minutes, and seconds, rather than as a decimal.

If the TI-89 is left in Radian mode, a little more work is needed. The MATH:Angle menu ([2nd][5][2]) is shown on the right. It includes the degrees symbol, and the ▸DMS operator (mentioned above). Not visible in this menu is option 9: ▸DD (convert to decimal degrees).

When in Radian mode, simply entering 74°8'14" causes the calculator to first convert interpret this as degrees (and fractions of degrees), then to convert this angle into radians. The top line in the history area shows this (not-too-helpful) result. Appending the ▸DD conversion command to this forces the TI-89 to forego the conversion to radians. The second output arose from pressing [♦][ENTER].

When converting from decimal degrees to DMS while the calculator is in Radian mode, be sure to enter the angle with the degree symbol ([2nd][I]); otherwise, the TI-89 assumes that the given angle is in radians, so that it converts radians to degrees before splitting the result into degrees, minutes, and seconds. Note that some rounding error was introduced in the process, causing the seconds portion of the result to be slightly different from 1.2.

Section 5.2   Example 4   (page 484)   Finding Function Values of Quadrantal Angles

The alternative to putting the calculator in Degree mode is to use the degree symbol ([2nd][I]) following each angle measure; e.g., enter sin(90°) rather than just sin(90).

Unlike the TI-83 (used for the screens in the text), the TI-89 reports "undef" (undefined) when asked to compute tan 90°. Since the cotangent, secant, and cosecant functions are the reciprocals of the tangent, cosine, and sine, they can be entered as (e.g.) 1/sin(90). (This is illustrated in Figure 21 on page 485 of the text.) This reports the correct value (0) for cot 90°, even though tan 90° is undefined, and also correctly reports that sec 90° is undefined.

One might guess that the other three trigonometric functions are accessed with [•] followed by [Y], [Z], or [T] (which produce, e.g., sin⁻¹). This is **not** what these functions do; in this case, the exponent −1 does not mean "reciprocal," but instead indicates that these are inverse functions (which are discussed in Sections 5.3 and 7.5 of the text). The text comments on this distinction at th bottom of page 485.

Section 5.3   Example 6   (page 500)   Finding Function Values with a Calculator

The screen on the right shows how computations like the secant in part (b) and the cotangent in (c) can be entered on a single line. These computations were done in Degree mode; in Radian mode, the first computation is done correctly, but the second requires the degrees symbol ([2nd][I]) after the angle measure.

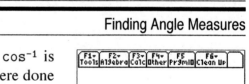

Section 5.3   Example 7   (page 500)   Using an Inverse Trigonometric Function to Find an Angle

Section 5.3   Example 8   (page 501)   Finding Angle Measures

The sin⁻¹ ("inverse sine," or "arcsine") function is [•][Y], while cos⁻¹ is [•][Z]. The computations shown in Figures 34 and 36 in the text were done in Degree mode; the screen on the right shows the result for Example 7 when done in Radian mode. Note that in the second entry, an attempt was made to get the TI-89 to report the result in degrees (by placing the degree symbol at the end of the entry), but this does not have the desired result.

Section 5.4   Example 1   (page 510)   Solving a Right Triangle Given an Angle and a Side

Section 5.4   Example 2   (page 511)   Solving a Right Triangle Given Two Sides

For problems like these, the ans(1) variable can be used to avoid loss of accuracy from rounding off intermediate results. Shown are computations for Example 1; when [ENTER] is pressed, the TI-89 confirms the measure of angle B given in the text. (Be sure the TI-89 is in Degree mode. Also, recall that the arcsine (or inverse sine) function is [2nd][SIN] —*not* [SIN][2nd][EE].)

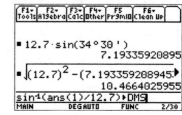

Section 5.4   Example 7   (page 514)   Solving a Problem Involving Angles of Elevation

The TI-89 can automatically locate the intersection of two graphs using the GRAPH:Math:Intersection feature. This was previously illustrated on page 139, but we repeat the description here: With the two functions graphed, press F5 and choose option 5 (Intersection). Use ⊙, ⊙ and ENTER to specify which two functions to use (in this case, the only two being displayed). The TI-89 then prompts for lower and upper bounds (numbers that are, respectively, less than and greater than the location of the intersection). After pressing ENTER, the TI-89 will try to find an intersection of the two graphs. The screens below illustrate these steps.

From the graph screen: F5 5   ENTER (choose y1)   ENTER (choose y2)

Move cursor ENTER   Move cursor ENTER   The intersection is found.

Section 6.1   Example 1   (page 535)   Converting Degrees to Radians

The number π is available as 2nd ^, and the degree symbol is 2nd I. With the calculator in Radian mode (see page 123), entering $45°$ causes the TI-89 to automatically convert to radians. The screen on the right shows the two ways of performing the conversion: Letting the TI-89 do the work by using the degrees symbol, or simply multiplying by $\pi/180$.

An alternative to using the degree symbol is to store $\pi/180$ in the calculator variable d (see page 123). Then typing, for example, 45d ENTER will multiply 45 by $\pi/180$. This approach will work regardless of whether the calculator is in Degree or Radian mode. (A value stored in a variable will remain there until it is replaced by a new value, or the variable is deleted or cleared.)

Section 6.1   Example 2   (page 535)   Converting Radians to Degrees

With the TI-89 in Degree mode (see page 123), the radian symbol (a super-scripted r), produced with 2nd 5 2 2, will automatically change a radian angle measurement to degrees.

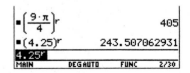

Alternatively, with the value $180/\pi$ stored in the calculator variable r (see page 123), typing $(9\pi/4)r$ ENTER will convert from radians to degrees regardless of whether the calculator is in Degree or Radian mode. (The same result can be achieved by *dividing by* the calculator variable d as defined in the previous example.)

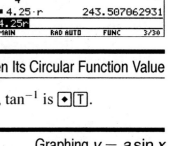

Section 6.2   Example 4   (page 549)   Finding a Number Given Its Circular Function Value

The arccosine (or inverse cosine) function is •Z — *not* COS^(-)1. Likewise, $\tan^{-1}$ is •T.

Section 6.3   Example 1   (page 559)   Graphing $y = a\sin x$

Note that the TI-89 must be in Radian mode in order to produce the desired graph. See page 128 for information on setting the thickness of a graph.

The graphs in the text are shown in the "trig viewing window," described on the top of page 558. The TI-89's default trig window (selected with •F27) is slightly wider than that shown in the text; it shows x between about -3.3π to 3.3π. (If the TI-89 is in Degree mode, xmin and xmax will be ±592.5 instead of $\pm3.3\pi$.) The graph below is shown using the text's trig window, rather than the TI-89's.

It is possible to distinguish between the two graphs without having them drawn using different styles by using the TRACE feature. On the right, the trace cursor is on graph 2—that is, the graph of $y_2 = \sin x$. This approach is discussed on page 141 of this manual.

Section 6.3   Example 8   (page 566)   Modeling Temperature with a Sine Function

The "sine regression" illustrated at the end of this example is a built-in feature of the TI-89, found in the Calc menu (F5) of the data editor. See page 138 for information about using the TI-89 for regression computations.

Section 6.4   Example 1   (page 578)   Graphing $y = a\sec bx$

Section 6.4   Example 2   (page 579)   Graphing $y = a\csc(x - d)$

See section 12 of the introduction (page 127) for information about graphing functions in the Dot graph style. A reminder: $\sin^{-1}$ (•Y) is *not* the cosecant function.

Section 7.1   Example 3   (page 609)   Rewriting an Expression in Terms of Sine and Cosine

The TI-89 automatically attempts to rewrite many trigonometric expressions in terms of sine and cosine, as the screen here shows. (This will only work correctly if x has not been assigned a numerical value.)

As an alternative to graphing these two functions, the TI-89's table feature (see page 134 of this manual) can be used: If the y values are the same for a reasonably large sample of x values, one can be fairly sure (though not certain) that the two expressions are equal. To make this approach more reliable, be sure to choose x values that are not, for example, all multiples of π.

Section 7.2	Example 1	(page 614)	Verifying an Identity (Working with One Side)
Section 7.2	Example 2	(page 614)	Verifying an Identity (Working with One Side)
Section 7.2	Example 3	(page 615)	Verifying an Identity (Working with One Side)
Section 7.2	Example 4	(page 615)	Verifying an Identity (Working with One Side)
Section 7.2	Example 5	(page 616)	Verifying an Identity (Working with Both Sides)

The TI-89 can do some simplification of this type, provided that all trig functions are entered in terms of the sine, cosine, and tangent functions. The screen on the right shows confirmation of the identities in Examples 1 and 4. For the first, the left side of the equation was entered, and the the output is equivalent to the right side. The second uses the TI-89's tCollect function, found in the MATH:Algebra:Trig menu ([2nd][5][9][9]). This can be used to simplify some trigonometric expressions; note that it reports that the difference between the left and right sides simplifies to 0.

The TI-89's methods of expansion do not always give the same results as those shown in these examples. Here is the output for the left side of the equation in Example 5 (which agrees with the expression found in the text). However, the TI-89 does not simplify the right side to the same expression. (With tCollect, though, it does confirm that the difference between the left and right sides is 0.)

Section 7.3	Example 1	(page 622)	Finding Exact Cosine Function Values
Section 7.3	Example 4	(page 626)	Finding Exact Sine and Tangent Function Values

The TI-89 can graphically and numerically support exact value computations such as $\cos 15° = \frac{\sqrt{6}+\sqrt{2}}{4}$. Starting with a graph of y1=cos(x), the TI-89 makes it possible to trace to any real number value for x between xmin and xmax, using the GRAPH:Trace feature or the GRAPH:Math:Value command. Simply type

a number or expression (like $1/\pi$ or $\sqrt{(2)}$), then press [ENTER]; the cursor then jumps to that x-coordinate, and shows a decimal approximation of y.

Alternatively, a table of values like those shown here can be used to find the value of cos 15°.

From the home screen, we see agreement to 12 decimal places for the values of yc (which contains the *y* coordinate from the GRAPH:Trace operation), cos 15°, and $\frac{\sqrt{6}+\sqrt{3}}{4}$. (Decimal points were placed in the second and third entries to get a decimal result.)

While this graphical confirmation might be more useful for other situations, it is actually unnecessary in this case, because the TI-89 knows how to use many of these identities to find exact values! Assuming that the Exact/Approx mode setting is AUTO or EXACT, the TI-89 computes the exact value of cos(15°), although it reports that exact value in a slightly different form from that given in the text.

Note that Example 8 in Section 7.4 (page 639) shows that cos 15° can also be written as $\frac{\sqrt{2+\sqrt{3}}}{2}$.

Section 7.4	Example 2	(page 634)	Verifying a Double-Angle Identity
Section 7.4	Example 3	(page 635)	Simplifying Expressions Using Double-Angle Identities
Section 7.4	Example 4	(page 635)	Deriving a Multiple-Angle Identity
Section 7.4	Example 6	(page 637)	Using a Product-to-Sum Identity
Section 7.4	Example 7	(page 637)	Using a Sum-to-Product Identity
Section 7.4	Example 8	(page 639)	Using a Half-Angle Identity to Find an Exact Value
Section 7.4	Example 9	(page 639)	Using a Half-Angle Identity to Find an Exact Value

The TI-89's tExpand function—in the MATH:Algebra:Trig menu—is more-or-less the opposite of tCollect; here we see it's expansion of the two sides of the equation in Example 2.

Note: According to the TI-89 manual, "for best results, tExpand() should be used in Radian mode." In fact, tExpand seems to do *nothing* when the TI-89 is in Degree mode.

tCollect works for some of these expressions, as well; here are it's results for Example 3.

Note, however, that there are often many equivalent ways to re-write a trigonometric expression. For Example 4, tExpand(sin(3x)) does not give the same answer as the text.

Similarly, the TI-89's version of $\tan 22.5°$ for Example 9 is not easily recognizable as equivalent to the text's $\sqrt{2} - 1$.

Section 7.5   Example 1   (page 646)   Finding Inverse Sine Values

Section 7.5   Example 2   (page 646)   Finding Inverse Cosine Values

Of course, it is not necessary to graph $y = \sin^{-1} x$ to find these values; one can simply enter, e.g., sin⁻¹ (1/2). Angles are given in radians or degrees, depending on the TI-89's mode setting.

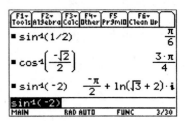

Note that if the TI-89's Complex Format is RECTANGULAR or POLAR, it does *not* give an error for the input sin⁻¹ (-2), but instead gives a complex result. (A Non-real result error occurs if Complex Format is set to REAL.) This is technically a correct result, but is not appropriate for the problems in this text.

Section 7.5   Example 4   (page 651)   Finding Inverse Function Values with a Calculator

Note that the answer given for (b), $109.499054°$, overrepresents the accuracy of that value. A typical rule for doing computations involving decimal values (like -0.3541) is to report only as many digits in the result as were present in the original number—in this case, four. This means the reported answer should be "about $109.5°$," and in fact, any angle θ between about $109.496°$ and $109.501°$ has a cotangent which rounds to -0.3541.

Section 7.5   Example 7   (page 653)   Writing Function Values in Terms of u

The TI-89 handles both of these expressions quite nicely, although it does not rationalize the denominator for (a), and only changes the second expression if the tExpand command is used.

Section 7.6   Example 9   (page 663)   Describing a Musical Tone from a Graph

Section 7.6   Example 10   (page 664)   Analyzing Pressures of Upper Harmonics

Note that the calculator screens shown in Figures 27–30 illustrate the importance of choosing a "good" viewing window. If we choose the wrong vertical scale (`ymin` and `ymax`), we might not be able to see the graph at all—it might be squashed against the x-axis. If we make the window too wide—that is, if `xmax` minus `xmin` is too large—we might see the "wrong" picture, like the one on the right (for Example 10): We see some suggestion of periodic behavior, but those sections of the graph that appear to be one full cycle actually consist of several cycles crammed together. The calculator cannot display sufficient detail to show the 44 full periods that fall between 0 and 0.1.

This observation—that a periodic function, viewed at fixed intervals, can appear to be a *different* periodic function—is the same effect that causes wagon wheels to appear to run backwards in old movies.

Section 8.3   Example 1   (page 716)   Finding Magnitude and Direction Angle

Section 8.3   Example 2   (page 716)   Finding Horizontal and Vertical Components

The TI-89 recognizes vectors entered in either of two formats:

   [*horizontal component* , *vertical component*] —rectangular format, or

   [*magnitude* , ∠ *direction angle*] —polar format.

(The square brackets are [2nd][,] and [2nd][÷], and "∠" is [2nd][EE].) Regardless of how the vector is entered, the TI-89 displays it according to the Vector Format mode setting (see page 123); specifically, it displays the vector in component form in RECTANGULAR mode, and in magnitude/direction form for either of the other two modes. (There are, however, commands to override how the vector is displayed.)

   Commands for manipulating vectors are buried several levels deep in the MATH:Matrix:Vector ops menu— [2nd][5][4][alpha][4].

For Example 1, the vector **u** $= \langle 3, -2 \rangle$ is entered on the TI-89 as [3,-2]. To convert to magnitude/direction form, either put the TI-89 in CYLINDRICAL or SPHERICAL mode, or use the ▸Polar command (either from the menu referred to above, or selected from the [CATALOG]), as the screen on the right illustrates. The second entry shows the decimal approximation of the magnitude and direction. (With the TI-89 in Degree mode, the angle returned is in degrees.)

For Example 2, one can find both the horizontal and vertical components at once, as the screen on the right shows. These computations were done with the TI-89 in Degree mode, so it was not necessary to include the degree symbol on the angle. Additionally, the TI-89 was in RECTANGULAR vector display mode; if it had not been, the ▸Rect command (found in the MATH:Matrix:Vector ops menu) could be used to force conversion to rectangular format. Note that the vector is *entered* with a comma before the ∠ symbol, but *displayed* (in the history area) without the comma.

Alternatively, the TI-89 has R▶Pr, R▶Pθ, P▶Rx, and P▶Ry conversion functions, found in the MATH:Angle menu (2nd 5 2) as options 3 through 6. As shown in text Figures 26 and 28, these can be used to convert between the vector formats. "R" and "P" stand for "rectangular" and "polar" coordinates. Rectangular coordinates are the familiar x and y values. Polar coordinates, described in Section 8.7 of the text, are r (which corresponds to the magnitude of a vector) and θ (the direction angle).

Finally, observe that the conversion for Example 2 could be done by typing 25cos(41.7) and 25sin(41.7); which approach to use is a matter of personal preference.

Section 8.3   Example 3   (page 717)   Writing Vectors in the Form $\langle a, b \rangle$

Note how easily these conversions are done in the TI-89's polar vector format. (The TI-89 was in Degree mode.)

Section 8.3   Example 5   (page 718)   Performing Vector Operations

Section 8.3   Example 6   (page 719)   Finding the Dot Product

Using the TI-89's vector notation, the vectors can be stored in calculator variables (see page 123) which can then be used to do the desired operations. Shown are the commands to compute 5(c): $4\mathbf{u} - 3\mathbf{v}$, and 6(a): $\langle 2, 3 \rangle \cdot \langle 4, -1 \rangle$. The dotP function is in the CATALOG or the MATH:Matrix:Vector ops menu—2nd 5 4 alpha 4 3.

Section 8.5   Example 2   (page 734)   Converting from Trigonometric Form to Rectangular Form

With the TI-89 set to Complex format:RECTANGULAR (see page 124), or by adding the ▶Rect command to the end of the computation, the conversion to the format $a + bi$ is done automatically when a complex number is entered. Complex numbers given in trigonometric format (like those in this example) can be entered much more conveniently using either of the other two complex formats: $r \cdot e^{i\theta}$ or $(r \angle \theta)$. The entries on the right illustrate this. These computations were done in Radian mode; note the degrees symbol.

This conversion can also be done using the real and imag functions in the MATH:Complex menu, or the P▶Rx and P▶Ry conversion functions from the MATH:Angle menu. These approaches are not illustrated here, but are analogous to those shown for vector conversion above.

Section 8.5   Example 3   (page 734)   Converting from Rectangular Form to Trigonometric Form

The abs and angle commands, found in the TI-89's MATH:Complex menu (2nd 5 5), can be used to compute the modulus r and the argument θ (respectively). On the screen on the right, note that what is displayed as "$|-\sqrt{3}+\iota|$" was entered as "abs(-√(3)+ι)." These functions are shown on page 737 of the text.

Another approach is to use R▸Pr and R▸Pθ from the MATH:Angle menu. To do this, enter the complex number $a + bi$ as an ordered pair (a, b), as is illustrated in the screen on the right.

More convenient is the TI-89's ▸Polar command, found in the CATALOG or in the MATH:Matrix:Vector ops menu. This gives both the magnitude and angle at the same time, although the format in which this is displayed depends on whether the TI-89 is in Radian or Degree mode. In Radian mode (the first entry in the history area on the right), the result is displayed in the format $r \cdot e^{i\theta}$—hence, $r = 2$ and $\theta = 5\pi/6$. When in Degree mode (the second and third entries on the right), the result is displayed as $(r\angle\theta)$—so $r = 2$ (as before), $\theta = 150°$ for (a), and $r = 3, \theta = -90°$ for (b). Note that $-90°$ is coterminal with $270°$, given in the text.

Furthermore, with the calculator's Complex format setting as POLAR (see page 124), the conversion can be done all at once, without the ▸Polar command. (As with the ▸Polar command, the format of the output depends on whether the TI-89 is in Radian or Degree mode.)

Section 8.5   Example 4   (page 735)   Converting Between Trigonometric and Rectangular Forms
Using Calculator Approximations

Aside from entering the expression in (a) as it is shown in the text (using the cos and sin functions), one can use the TI-89's polar format $(r \angle \theta)$, but be sure to either put the TI-89 in the correct mode (Degree or Radian) or use the degrees or radians symbol from the MATH:Angle menu. Both computations on the right were done in Radian mode, and the first result is incorrect.

Section 8.6   Example 1   (page 743)   Finding a Power of a Complex Number

While the TI-89 could be used to perform the various steps illustrated in the text (conversion to trigonometric form, etc.), note that it will compute the exact value of $(1 + i\sqrt{3})^8$ directly.

Section 8.6   Example 4   (page 746)   Solving an Equation by Finding Complex Roots

The TI-89's cSolve (complex solve) function can find all complex roots of a polynomial equation. The computation on the right was done in Degree and POLAR complex display mode.

Section 8.7	Example 3	(page 751)	Examining Polar and Rectangular Equations of Lines and Circles

Section 8.7	Example 4	(page 753)	Graphing a Polar Equation (Cardioid)

Section 8.7	Example 5	(page 753)	Graphing a Polar Equation (Rose)

Section 8.7	Example 6	(page 754)	Graphing a Polar Equation (Lemniscate)

To produce these polar graphs, the TI-89 should be set to Degree and Polar modes (see the screen on the right). In this mode, the Y= screen is really the "r=" screen; the TI-89 allows entry of up to 99 polar equations (r as a function of θ). One could also use Radian mode, adjusting the values of θmin, θmax, and θstep accordingly (e.g., use 0, 2π, and $\pi/30$ instead of 0, 360, and 5).

For the cardioid, rose, and lemniscate, the window settings shown in the text show these graphs on "square" windows (see section 11 of the introduction, page 126), so one can see how their proportions compare to those of a circle. Note, however, that on the TI-89, these window are not square; the Zoom:ZoomSqr option can be used to adjust the window dimensions to make it square.

Press ⬦F1 and set r1 to the desired expression (use ⬦⌃ to type θ).

For the cardioid, the value of θstep does not need to be 5, although that choice works well for this graph. Too large a choice of θstep produces a graph with lots of sharp "corners," like the one shown on the right (drawn with θstep=30). Setting θstep too small, on the other hand, produces a smooth graph, but it is drawn very slowly. Sometimes it may be necessary to try different values of θstep to choose a good one.

The lemniscate can be drawn by setting θmin=0 and θmax=180, or θmin=-45 and θmax=45. In fact, with θ ranging from -45 to 225, the graph of r1=∫(cos(2θ)) (alone) will produce the entire lemniscate. (θstep should be about 5.)

The rose can be produced by setting θmin=0 and θmax=360, or using any $360°$-range of θ values (with θstep about 5).

Section 8.7	Example 7	(page 755)	Graphing a Polar Equation (Spiral of Archimedes)

To produce this graph on the viewing window shown in the text, the TI-89 must be in Radian mode. (In Degree mode, it produces the same shape, but magnified by a factor of $180/\pi$ — meaning that the viewing window needs to be larger by that same factor.)

Section 8.8   Example 1   (page 761)   Graphing a Plane Curve Defined Parametrically

Place the TI-89 in Parametric mode, as the screen on the right shows. In this mode, ◆F1 allows entry of up to 99 pairs of parametric equations (*x* and *y* as functions of *t*). The TI-89 will graph any pair of equations for which at least one of *x* and *y* is selected (has a check mark next to it).

The value of `tstep` does not need to be 0.05, although that choice works well for this graph. Too large a choice of `tstep` produces a less-smooth graph, like the one shown on the right (drawn with `tStep=1`). Setting `tstep` too small may produce a smooth graph, but it might be drawn very slowly. Sometimes it may be necessary to try different values of `tstep` to choose a good one.

Section 8.8   Example 3   (page 762)   Graphing a Plane Curve Defined Parametrically

This curve can be graphed in Degree mode with `tmin=0` and `tmax=360`, or in Radian mode with `tmax=2`π. In order to see the proportions of this ellipse, it might be good to graph it on a square window. This can be done most easily with the Zoom:ZoomSqr option. On a TI-89, initially with the window settings shown in the text, this would result in the window $[-8.3, 8.3] \times [-4, 4]$.

Section 8.8   Example 5   (page 763)   Graphing a Cycloid

The TI-89 *must* be in Radian mode in order to produce this graph.

Section 8.8   Example 6   (page 764)   Simulating Motion with Parametric Equations

Section 8.8   Example 8   (page 765)   Analyzing the Path of a Projectile

Parametric mode is particularly nice for analyzing motion, because one can picture the motion by watching the calculator create the graph, or by using TRACE (◆F3F3) and watching the motion of the trace cursor. (When tracing in parametric mode, the ⓞ and ⓠ keys increase and decrease the value of *t*, and the trace cursor shows the location (x, y) at time *t*.) Figure 80 illustrates tracing on the projectile path in Example 8. Note that the value of *t* changes by ±`tstep` each time ⓞ or ⓠ is pressed, so obviously the choice of `tstep` affects which points can be traced.

Section 9.1   Example 8   (page 792)   Using Curve Fitting to Find an Equation Through Three Points

Note that the equation found in this example by algebraic methods can also be found very quickly on the TI-89 by performing a quadratic regression (QuadReg—see page 138) on the three given points. These agree with the coefficients found in the text.

Section 9.2   Example 1   (page 802)   Using the Gauss-Jordan Method

---

Section 9.2   Example 2   (page 804)   Using the Gauss-Jordan Method

---

Before describing these operations, a few words about entering matrices into the TI-89. The matrices shown in the calculator screens in the text have the names "[A]" and "[B]." On the TI-82 and TI-83, all matrices have names of the form [*letter*]; on the TI-89, matrices can have any variable name. (In fact, variable names *cannot* include the bracket characters on the TI-89.) One way to set the values in a matrix is by "storing" the contents on the home screen; an example is shown on the right. (Note the difference between how this is *entered* and how it is *displayed* in the history area.) The square brackets are 2nd , and 2nd ÷.

Alternatively, press APPS 6 (Data/Matrix editor) and either create a new matrix, or open an existing one. If creating a new matrix, you will be prompted for a name and the size of the matrix, as the screen on the right illustrates.

The matrix editor resembles a spreadsheet. Individual values of the matrix can be entered, or the matrix can be resized or sorted using the Util options (2nd F1). Press 2nd ESC (QUIT) when finished.

Here are the formats for the matrix row-operation commands (2nd 5 4 alpha ×), along with examples of their effect on the matrix $\mathtt{mat} = \begin{bmatrix} 1 & 4 & 7 \\ 2 & 5 & 8 \\ 3 & 6 & 9 \end{bmatrix}$:

- rowSwap(*matrix*,*A*,*B*) produces a new matrix that has row *A* and row *B* swapped.

  Input: rowSwap(mat,1,2)   Output: $\begin{bmatrix} 2 & 5 & 8 \\ 1 & 4 & 7 \\ 3 & 6 & 9 \end{bmatrix}$

- rowAdd(*matrix*,*A*,*B*) produces a new matrix with row *A* added to row *B*.

  Input: rowAdd(mat,1,2)   Output: $\begin{bmatrix} 1 & 4 & 7 \\ 3 & 9 & 15 \\ 3 & 6 & 9 \end{bmatrix}$

- mRow(*number*,*matrix*,*A*) produces a new matrix with row *A* multiplied by *number*.

  Input: mRow(-4,mat,1)   Output: $\begin{bmatrix} -4 & -16 & -28 \\ 2 & 5 & 8 \\ 3 & 6 & 9 \end{bmatrix}$

- mRowAdd(*number*,*matrix*,*A*,*B*) produces a new matrix with row *A* multiplied by *number* and added to row *B* (row *A* is unchanged).

  Input: mRowAdd(2,mat,1,3)   Output: $\begin{bmatrix} 1 & 4 & 7 \\ 2 & 5 & 8 \\ 5 & 14 & 23 \end{bmatrix}$

Keep in mind that these row operations leave the matrix mat untouched. To perform a sequence of row operations, each result must either be stored in a matrix, or use the result variable ans(1) as the matrix. For example, with mat equal to the augmented matrix for the system given in this example, the command shown on the right takes that augmented matrix and multiplies the first row by 1/2 (the appropriate first step in the Gauss-Jordan method), displaying the resulting matrix on the screen—but mat is exactly as it was before. Note the use of ans(1) in the three screens below, which complete the steps of the Gauss-Jordan method.

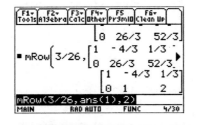

As a shortcut, the TI-89's rref(command ([2nd][5][4][4]) will do all the necessary row operations at once, making these individual steps seem tedious. However, doing the whole process step-by-step can be helpful in understanding how it works.

Section 9.3   Example 1   (page 813)   Evaluating a 2×2 Determinant

Section 9.3   Example 3   (page 816)   Evaluating a 3×3 Determinant

The determinant of any square matrix is easy to find with a TI-89. (At least, it is easy for the user; the calculator is doing all the work!) Simply choose the command det(from the MATH:Matrix menu ([2nd][5][4][2]), then type the matrix or the name of matrix variable. Note that trying to find the determinant of a non-square matrix (for example, a 3×4 matrix) results in a Dimension error.

Section 9.4   Example 1   (page 825)   Finding a Partial Fraction Decomposition

The TI-89's expand(command (found in the Algebra menu, [F2][3]) automates the task of expanding a rational expression into partial fractions.

Section 9.5   Example 2   (page 832)   Solving a Nonlinear System by Elimination

See the discussion of Example 10 from Section 2.1 on page 136 of this manual for tips on entering formulas like these.

The TI-89's `solve` function can handle system like this: Enter

    solve(x^2+y^2=4 and 2x^2-y^2=8,{x,y})

and the result is

    x=2 and y=0 or x=-2 and y=0

Section 9.6   Example 1   (page 843)   Graphing a Linear Inequality

With the TI-89, there are two ways to shade above or below a function. The simpler way is to use the Above and Below graph styles (see page 128), which mean "draw the graph of this function and shade the region above/below it." This style produces the graph shown below on the right. Note that the TI-89 is not capable of showing the detail that the line is "dashed."

The other way to shade is the Shade command, accessed in the [CATALOG]. The format is

        Shade *lower*,*upper*,*min x*,*max x*,*pattern*,*resolution*

Here *lower* and *upper* are the functions between which the TI-89 will draw the shading (above *lower* and below *upper*). The last four options can be omitted. *min x* and *max x* specify the starting and ending *x* values for the shading. If omitted, the TI-89 uses `xmin` and `xmax`.

The last two options specify how the shading should look. *pattern* determines the direction of the shading: 1 (vertical—the default), 2 (horizontal), 3 (negative-slope $45°$—that is, upper left to lower right), or 4 (positive-slope $45°$—that is, lower left to upper right). *resolution* is an integer from 1 to 10 which specifies how dense the shading should be (1 = shade every column of pixels, 2 = shade every other column, 3 = shade every third column, etc.). If omitted, the TI-89 shades every other column; i.e., it uses *resolution* = 2.

To produce the graph shown above, the appropriate command (typed on the home screen) would be something like

        Shade -(1/4)x+1,10.

The use of 10 for the *upper* function simply tells the TI-89 to shade up as high as necessary; this could be replaced by any number greater than 4 (the value of `ymax` for the viewing window shown). Also, if the function y1 had previously been defined as `-(1/4)x+1`, this command could be typed as `Shade y1(x),10`.

One more useful piece of information: Suppose one makes a mistake in typing the Shade command (e.g., switching *upper* and *lower*, or using the wrong value of *resolution*), resulting in the wrong shading. The screen on the right, for example, arose from typing Shade -(1/4)x+1,1. In order to achieve the desired results, the mistake must first be erased by pressing F4 (Regraph) or 2nd F1 1 (Draw:ClrDraw). Then return to the home screen, correct the mistake in the Shade command, and try again.

Section 9.6   Example 2   (page 844)   Graphing Systems of Inequalities

The easiest way to produce (essentially) the same graph as that shown in the text is to use the "shade above/below" graph style (see page 128). The screen on the right (above) shows the style for y2 being set to Above; the style for y1 is also Above. The results are shown on the graph below. When more than one function is graphed with shading, the TI-89 rotates through the four shading patterns (see the previous example); that is, it graphs the first with vertical shading, the second with horizontal, and so on. All shading is done with a resolution of 2 (every other pixel).

The Shade command (see the previous example) can be used to produce this from the home screen. If y1=(6-x)/2 and y2=x^2/2, the commands at right produce the graph shown above.

A nicer picture can be created, with a little more work, by making the observation that if y is greater than both $x^2/2$ and $(6-x)/2$, then for any x, y must be greater than the larger of these two expressions. The TI-89 provides a convenient way to find the larger of two numbers with the max(function, located in the MATH:List menu (2nd 5 3). Then max(y1(x),y2(x)) will return the larger of y1 and y2, and the Y= screen entries shown on the right (above) will produce the graph shown below it. (Note that y1 and y2 have been set to graph as solid curves, while y3 has the Above style.) The home-screen command Shade max(y1(x),y2(x)),11 would produce similar results.

Extension: The table below shows how (using graph styles or home-screen commands) to shade regions that arise from variations on the inequalities in this example, assuming that y1=(6-x)/2 and y2=x^2/2. (The results of these commands are not shown here.)

For the system...	or equivalently...	the command would be...
$x < 6 - 2y$ $x^2 < 2y$	$y < (6 - x)/2$ $y > x^2/2$	shade below y1 and above y2, or enter `Shade y2(x),y1(x)`
$x > 6 - 2y$ $x^2 > 2y$	$y > (6 - x)/2$ $y < x^2/2$	shade above y1 and below y2, or enter `Shade y1(x),y2(x)`
$x < 6 - 2y$ $x^2 > 2y$	$y < (6 - x)/2$ $y < x^2/2$	shade below y1 and below y2, or enter `Shade -10,min(y1(x),y2(x))`

Section 9.7   Example 2   (page 854)   Adding Matrices

Section 9.7   Example 3   (page 855)   Subtracting Matrices

Section 9.7   Example 4   (page 856)   Multiplying Matrices by Scalars

---

Section 9.7   Example 6   (page 859)   Multiplying Matrices

See page 156 for information about matrices on the TI-89.

Section 9.8   Example 1   (page 868)   Verifying the Identity Property of I_3

On the TI-89, the function to produce identity matrices is `identity(`, located in the MATH:Matrix menu (2nd 5 4). The screen on the right shows the 3×3 identity matrix.

Section 9.8   Example 2   (page 870)   Finding the Inverse of a 3×3 Matrix

---

Section 9.8   Example 3   (page 872)   Identifying a Matrix with No Inverse

---

The TI-89 will quickly find the inverse of a square matrix (if it exists) by simply raising that matrix to the power −1 (that is, type the matrix, followed by ^ (-) 1). An example is shown. Attempting this with a non-square matrix results in a `Dimension` error. A `Singular matrix` error occurs when we try to find the inverse of this matrix. ("Singular" means noninvertible.)

Section 10.1	Example 1	(page 893)	Graphing a Parabola with Horizontal Axis
Section 10.1	Example 2	(page 894)	Graphing a Parabola with Horizontal Axis
Section 10.2	Example 1	(page 904)	Graphing Ellipses Centered at the Origin
Section 10.3	Example 1	(page 914)	Using Asymptotes to Graph a Hyperbola

See the discussion of Example 10 from Section 2.1 on page 136 of this manual for tips on entering formulas like these.

When entering these formulas, make sure to use enough parentheses, so that operations are performed in the correct order; e.g., for Example 2 of Section 10.1, the formula in y1 should look like this:

> y1=-1.5+√((x-.5)/2)

(The TI-89's "pretty print" display should make it easy to notice a mistake in order of operations.)

Also, when looking at a calculator graph like the one shown in Figure 18 (page 595), keep in mind that the apparent gap between this graph and the x-axis is not really there; it is a flaw that arises from the calculator's method of plotting functions (see discussion on page 128 of this manual).

Section 11.1   Example 3   (page 939)   Modeling Insect Population Growth

One way to produce this sequence (and similar recursively defined sequences) is with the ans(1) variable, as shown on the right. After pressing [1][ENTER], then typing the next line and pressing [ENTER], we simply press [ENTER] over and over to generate successive terms in the sequence. Each time, ans(1) is replaced by the previous result.

Figure 4 of the text shows a table of values. A similar table can be created by putting the TI-89 into Sequence mode, and making the definitions shown on the right. (This screen is the Y= screen, accessed with [♦][F1].) The plot in Figure 5(b) was also created in this way; see the discussion of Example 7 from Section 11.3 (below) for details.

Section 11.1   Example 4   (page 941)   Using Summation Notation

---

Section 11.2   Example 9   (page 953)   Using Summation Notation

The seq(command can be found in the MATH:List menu ([2nd][5][3]). Given a formula a_n for the nth term in a sequence, the command

    seq(*formula*, *variable*, *start*, *end*, *step*)

produces the list $\{a_{start}, a_{start+step}, \ldots, a_{end}\}$. If *step* is omitted, a value of 1 is assumed. The size of the resulting list is limited by available memory.

Note that *variable* can be any letter (or letters)—K and I are used in the text, but x, y, z, or t would be more convenient (since they can be typed with a single key).

The sum(command is also found in the MATH:List menu ([2nd][5][3]). sum can be applied to any list—either to a list variable, or directly to a list created with the seq(command. Evaluating summations on the TI-89 requires first generating the sequence as a list, then summing the list. The summation in Example 4 can be performed as shown on the right, using the ans(1) storage variable.

Alternatively, the sum(and seq(commands can be combined on a single line. The screen on the right uses this approach to find the answer for Example 9(a).

Section 11.3   Example 7   (page 960)   Summing the Terms of an Infinite Geometric Series

The plot shown in the text can be produced in at least two ways. The first method involves putting the TI-89 in Sequence mode, then entering the formula for S_n on the u1= line of the Y= screen, as on the right. Also, it is not necessary to specify the value of ui1 (the initial term in the sequence); this is only needed for recursively-defined sequences.

Next, press [♦][F2] and make the settings shown on the right. The viewing window is as shown in the text (xmin = 0, xmax = 6, ymin = 0, ymax = 2). Pressing [♦][F3] should produce a plot like that shown in the text. (If it does not, press [♦][F1][2nd][F2] and check that Axes is set to TIME.)

The second method begins by storing lists in two variables (we have used L1 and L2) as shown on the right. Note that this approach is less appealing for recursively defined sequences.

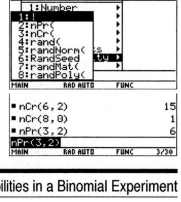

Next press ◆[F1]⊙[ENTER] and make the settings for a statistics plot as shown on the right. Finally, set up the viewing window, and check that nothing else will be plotted; that is, go to the Y= screen and make sure that the only Plot1 has a check mark next to it. Pressing ◆[F3] should produce a plot like that shown in the text.

Note: When finished with a statistics plot like this one, it is a good idea to turn it off so that the TI-89 will not attempt to display it the next time ◆[F3] (GRAPH) is pushed. This can be done from the Y= screen using [F4] to un-check the plot, or by pressing [F5][5] (All:Data Plots Off).

Section 11.4   Example 1   (page 971)   Evaluating Binomial Coefficients

---

Section 11.6   Example 4   (page 984)   Using the Permutations Formula

---

The nCr(and nPr(functions and the factorial operator "!" are found in the MATH:Probability menu ([2nd][5][7]). Note, though, that "!" is much more easily typed as ◆[÷]—this is one of those "hidden" key combinations that is revealed by ◆[EE]. The TI-89's format for nCr and nPr is different from the TI-83's (shown in the text); instead, enter these functions as shown on the right.

Section 11.7   Example 6   (page 999)   Finding Probabilities in a Binomial Experiment

The TI-89 does not have statistical distribution functions like binompdf. The computations shown in this example must be done by manually entering the entire binomial probability formula (or by obtaining a program to automate such computations.) Note that if the TI-89 is in AUTO or EXACT mode, the results can be more detailed than is useful.